Eberl/Puma
Innovative Minds

Innovative Minds

A Look Inside Siemens' Idea Machine

by Ulrich Eberl and Joerg Puma

Publicis Corporate Publishing

Bibliographic information published by Die Deutsche Nationalbibliothek
Die Deutsche Nationalbibliothek lists this publication in the Deutsche
Nationalbibliografie; detailed bibliographic data is available in the Internet
at http://dnb.d-nb.de.

Illustrations used in the book:
DONG Energy/Winther airphoto (page 114 right), akg-images (pages 249, 253), Prof. Dr. Wolfgang Ziegler/Dr. Joerg Puma (page 251), Bridgeman Art Library (page 254), Krones AG (page 256, lower picture).
Copyright for all other illustrations: Siemens AG.

This book was carefully produced. Nevertheless, authors and publisher do not warrant the information contained therein to be free of errors. Neither the authors nor the publisher can assume any liability or legal responsibility for omissions or errors. Terms reproduced in this book may be registered trademarks, the use of which by third parties for their own purposes may violate the rights of the owners of those trademarks.

www.publicis-erlangen.de/books

Contact for authors: gerhard.seitfudem@publicis-erlangen.de

ISBN 978-3-89578-299-2

Editor: Siemens Aktiengesellschaft, Berlin and Munich
Publisher: Publicis Corporate Publishing, Erlangen
© 2007 by Publicis KommunikationsAgentur GmbH, GWA, Erlangen

This publication and all parts thereof are protected by copyright. All rights reserved. Any use of it outside the strict provisions of the copyright law without the consent of the publisher is forbidden and will incur penalties. This applies particularly to reproduction, translation, microfilming or other processing, and to storage or processing in electronic systems. It also applies to the use of extracts from the text.

Printed in Germany

The Courage to Do Something New

One thing that editorials, talk shows, political speeches, and even advertising campaigns have in common is a preoccupation with the term "innovation." Indeed, references to innovation are so frequent and inflated that the word is at risk of becoming meaningless. Nevertheless, it is clear that a broad spectrum of the population has realized how important innovations are for the success of companies and economies. According to its original definition, as formulated by Joseph Alois Schumpeter, an innovation is a "creative restructuring." More precisely, it is the commercially successful market application of an invention or other new idea. To put it simply, if research is the process of transforming money into knowledge, innovation is the process of transforming knowledge into money.

Many management books describe the ideal way to generate innovations – by using the right strategies, tools and processes, for example. But reality is almost always more complicated, and the roads to innovation are more complex than management theories admit. Hardly anything has been published about how innovations are born, the character traits that make up a typical innovator, and what he or she has to do in order to overcome all sorts of obstacles. This book aims to close that gap by offering portraits of 30 inventors and innovators. Together with their teams – and in some cases with external partners – they have created some of the most successful innovations of recent years. Their achievements range from piezoinjector technology for automobiles to new computer and magnetic resonance tomographs, from the halogen lamp to industrial automation, and from the gas sensor for building technology to the gas turbine for power generation. Of course, not all of these developments have been instant successes; some are only now being implemented, while others have faced almost insurmountable obstacles. These portraits also show that alongside new products, innovations often involve the optimization of processes or the development of new business models.

Over and over, we've been asked who is responsible for successful – and unsuccessful – innovations at Siemens. As with most things, the story is more complicated than one might expect. Innovators are by no means only researchers and developers; their ranks include specialists in marketing, production and sales, as well as strategists and managers, all of whom play a role in propelling an idea from its inception to market success. For those interested in generating their own innovations, this book will prove to be a veritable treasure trove of new approaches from successful innovators, which we hope will inspire you too to strike out in new directions! Seek out the partners you need to reach your goal. And if you're a manager, create an environment that will attract, promote and challenge outstanding innovators. After all, a culture of innovation is the fertile ground in which tomorrow's innovations will bear rich fruit. Have the courage to do something new – and enjoy the journey! Knowing that you've helped to shape our future will make all your efforts worthwhile.

Munich, April 2007
Ulrich Eberl and Joerg Puma

Contents

Innovators as Entrepreneurs

Hermann Requardt
It's All About People *12*

Klaus Wucherer
Helping to Shape Tomorrow's World *15*

Managers on Innovation *19*

Visionary Personalities

Piezo Injection – Keeping Faith with an Idea *22*
Paradigm Shift – The Electronic Wedge Brake *30*
Sensors in the Wall *38*
Digital Bloodhounds *45*
Merging Data Streams *52*
New Momentum for Trains *58*
The Colors of Success *64*

The Path Is the Goal

Factory of the Future *74*
Revolution According to Plan – Whole-body MR Tomography *81*
Reactive Power Counts Too – New Solutions in
    Power Transmission *90*
All Ears for Customers *97*
Analysis Instead of Spontaneity – Innovation Steps for
    Gas Turbines *104*
Harnessing the Wind *112*

Siemens and the World

The Future of Manufacturing Execution Systems	123
I-WLAN – From University Research to a Global Product	129
Biolab on a Chip	136
Recipe for Success from China	143
Simplicity as a Principle – Telephoning via Cable Networks	150
An Ocean of Energy	156

Innovation Is More Than Technology

Machines for People	166
The Power to Keep Ideas Alive	174
Software for a Global Player	179
Financing by Saving	185
Body Codes	191
The Yin and Yang of Innovation	199

From Idea to Business Success

From "Local Hero" to Number One in Automation	210
The Universal Language for Medical Systems	217
The Man Who Helped the U.S. Postal Service to Save Hundreds of Millions of Dollars	226
Ups and Downs in the Communication Age	232
The Triumph of the Halogen Lamp	239

A Final Picture ... 247
The Authors ... 255

Innovators as Entrepreneurs

Breaking out of the Ivory Tower

It's All About People

Hermann Requardt

A company that invests more than €5 billion annually in research and development, operates 150 R&D centers all over the world, employs almost 50,000 researchers and developers, owns more than 62,000 patents and comes up with around 45 inventions every working day is undoubtedly a unique idea workshop. With such a track record, it's not surprising that Siemens has long regarded itself as a global network of innovation. But R&D investments alone don't inevitably lead to business success, nor is every invention automatically an innovation. "Ideas are of little value in themselves. The value of an invention is in its practical application," said Werner von Siemens – anticipating today's definition of the word "innovation." Innovations are inventions translated into marketable products. These can be technological innovations, new production processes, unconventional business models, gradual improvements, or revolutionary breakthroughs.

In this sense as well, company founder Werner von Siemens was far more than just a brilliant inventor. He protected his ideas with patents and turned them into successful commercial products, developed simple production processes and knew how to motivate his employees and fire his customers' imagination. He was one of the first people to work across international borders, and he had the courage to take calculated risks. In short, he was an innovator par excellence. A company's success is based on people like him. That's truer today than ever before, because global competition is being won by brilliant thinkers rather than factory smokestacks.

There are plenty of management books that analyze innovation processes and strategies – but few that use authentic biographies of innovators to investigate the different ways that innovations are actually generated, the hurdles these innovators had to face and how they finally overcame them. This book fills that gap. It looks behind the scenes and introduces some of the people who are helping Siemens continue its tradition of successful innovations.

Having been responsible for developments such as piezo technology, halogen lighting and intuitive user interfaces, these innovators have revolutionized entire sectors, introduced new production processes, tapped new markets and generated billions of euros in sales. With 30 selected portraits, this book takes a look into the idea workshop of a global corporation. And by the way, the term "workshop" should be taken literally. Innovation is often hard work – or, as Thomas Alva Edison concisely put it, it's "One percent inspiration and 99 percent perspiration."

One thing becomes very clear as we look at these portraits: Innovators are generally people who think outside the box. They prefer unconventional methods and approaches. They can be irritating, and they don't fit into pigeonholes. They break with traditions and generally observed rules. They counter the classic argument "That won't work" with "Let's just try it one more time." Mistakes are permitted, provided they're the basis of a learning experience. Expertise, the ability to work within a team, broad vision, problem-solving, and open communication are the virtues of today's innovators.

Above all, the innovator is a committed entrepreneur of his or her own ideas. The most brilliant insight lacks practical value if it has no potential customers. Even though it's often difficult or even impossible to precisely assess the market value of an idea in its early phases, the innovator's top priority must be to translate an idea into competitive products. Professional project management, clear and convincing business plans, precise cost calculations, an attractive midterm return on investment, targeted market and customer analyses, and a well thought-out business model are vital to commercial success.

The innovator needs to take a holistic approach. He or she must keep technology trends in mind, but nonetheless be able to break the currently valid rules of the game – dealing critically with accepted traditions and daring to strike out in new directions. "The longer a system has been

Prof. Dr. Hermann Requardt, 51, is a member of the Corporate Executive Committee of Siemens AG and the head of Corporate Technology, the central research department at Siemens. After completing his studies in physics and philosophy at the Darmstadt University of Technology and Johann Wolfgang Goethe University in Frankfurt and receiving a doctorate in biophysics, he worked at the Institute of Aerospace Medicine at the German Aerospace Center. In 1984 he joined the Medical Solutions Group of Siemens AG, where he was responsible for projects in the Magnetic Resonance (MR) division. He was appointed head of the division in 1995. From 2001 to 2006, as a member of the Executive Management of the Medical Solutions Group, he was responsible for several areas, including technological development. Prof. Requardt holds a number of patents in the area of coil technology for MR devices.

on the market, the greater the probability that it can be replaced," says Bernd Gombert, whose electronic wedge brake stands a good chance of revolutionizing the entire brake market. Innovators must not only know their markets and customers inside and out, but must also be prepared to create entirely new markets. After all, innovations not only fulfill existing needs – sometimes they create new ones.

In 2004 and 2005, innovators at Siemens won the German Federal President's Future Prize – the country's highest honor for innovations. Siemens innovators were also awarded the Innovation Prize of the German Economy in 2005 and the Global Energy International Prize, a kind of Nobel Prize for the energy technology sector, which is endowed with $1,000,000. In this book, you'll meet the fascinating people behind these innovations, as well as many of the other outstanding inventors that Siemens has been honoring for more than a decade with its "Inventor of the Year" award. In addition, you'll be hearing from innovators who have successfully transformed a languishing factory into one of the company's most profitable production plants, conquered the global market with innovations generated at the regional level, and attracted new customers by means of imaginative business models.

Innovators of this caliber can thrive only in stimulating surroundings, where different influences come together and where the trajectories of top universities, research institutes, start-ups, major industries, and customers intersect. There are no sure-fire recipes or concepts leading inevitably to success – but there are methods for avoiding errors, limiting risks, optimizing processes and creating a culture that fosters innovation. The famous development of the Post-it sticker at 3M was the result of unplanned activity – but it was possible only in the kind of relaxed and communicative atmosphere that promotes such innovations. "If you put fences around people, you get sheep," said William McKnight, the general manager of 3M, then still in his 20s, at the beginning of the 20th century. Innovators must have room to develop. "Find the best – for the best ones win." That's the magic formula for companies operating in the global league of top innovations. As this book impressively demonstrates, it's all about people.

Helping to Shape Tomorrow's World

Klaus Wucherer

Business success is the goal of every company. That means generating constant growth and remaining profitable in the long term. For 160 years, the key to Siemens' sustained success has been innovation – in other words, the ability to transform new ideas in a focused way into business success. Analyses reveal that there is a clear connection between the technological position of a business area, its market position, its earnings and the extent to which it can safeguard jobs and even expand its workforce. In general, businesses that combine an outstanding technological position – in other words, a high level of innovative power – with a strong global market position (Number 1 or 2) also post excellent earnings and provide secure jobs.

Today, global markets, competing companies and the general economic context are all changing at a rate that has seldom been experienced before. Companies that intend to stay in the vanguard of progress must constantly evolve, quickly adapting their processes and products to changing circumstances. At the same time, they need to know how to deal with long-term issues such as disruptive technologies that can transform entire sectors, and the systematic creation of teams of experts. A clear vision of the future development of technologies and markets is a key prerequisite for companies that intend to actively shape long-term developments. With this holistic approach to future planning in mind, Siemens developed its unique "Pictures of the Future" process.

New technologies are only one aspect of innovation. They can launch trends and have a massive impact on markets. But business success is dependent on a lot more. In particular, it requires well-founded sector expertise that combines technological know-how with an awareness of market demands. That's the only way technological potential can be translated into solutions with high customer value and lasting market success – in all of Siemens' areas of operation, from industrial automation to building technology, from steel production to complete airports, from the healthcare sector to ensuring a supply of safe drinking water, and from power plants to transportation technology. Our company's in-depth understanding of these sectors is the factor that enables us to think ahead for the benefit of our customers, anticipate future demands, and generate successful innovations.

Consequently, a systematic focus on customer value and top quality is one of the most important ways to ensure our innovations' market success. This book presents a broad spectrum of examples, from new drive systems for rail vehicles to industrial automation, from wind turbines to biometric security solutions, from postal automation to energy savings contracting, and from easy-to-use CT scanners to the reliable use of WLANs for industrial applications. For all of these innovations, our developers first asked themselves the question: What will bring our customers a crucial amount of added value?

Prof. Dr.-Ing. Klaus Wucherer, 62, is a member of the Corporate Executive Committee of Siemens AG. His fields of responsibility include the Groups Automation and Drives, Industrial Solutions and Services, and Transportation Systems, as well as the top+ Business Excellence program. After completing his studies with degrees in electrical and mechanical engineering, Wucherer joined Siemens AG in 1970. In his various positions at the company, he promoted projects such as the development of industrial automation (Simatic) and headed an engineering department in Brazil. In 1996 he was appointed to the Group Executive Management of the Automation Group, and since 1999 has been a member of the Managing Board of Siemens AG. Prof. Wucherer is an honorary professor at the Technical University of Chemnitz (mechanical engineering) and the Technical College of Osnabrück (electrical engineering and computer science), a visiting professor at the universities of Nanjing and Shandong in China, and Vice President of the Association of Electrical, Electronic and Information Technologies (VDE).

The special feature of this book is that it does not present dry theories, but instead gives innovations a human face by focusing on the people who generate them. It connects the innovations with the individual histories of the people behind them. What makes this book unique is its combination of concrete and up-to-the-minute examples of practical innovations with the innovative personalities who created them in the course of very different careers and using very different approaches.

Thanks to their authenticity, each of these innovation portraits offers a series of lessons – for all those who would like to generate their own innovations, as well as for readers in the areas of marketing, production, sales, strategy and corporate management who are responsible for successfully bringing researchers' and developers' ideas to market. In short, everyone who wants to find out what makes innovators tick should read these portraits!

After all, if a company intends to be successful through its innovations, it must cultivate a culture of innovation. It must find ways to gain the loyalty of inventors and innovators and give them sufficient leeway to do their work, while at the same time guiding them so that their innovations become part of the company's overall strategy. And it must do so in a worldwide and networked manner – whether its innovators work in Erlangen, Shanghai, Bangalore, St. Petersburg or Princeton.

This isn't always easy, because it's often the most innovative employees who like to shake up conventions or existing structures. In such cases, top management must support these employees, clear away potential obstacles and promote understanding for new ways of doing things. Many projects that break new technological ground go through difficult phases, making it crucial for management to have faith in innovators' capabilities. Many new ideas first need a protected niche where they can develop before they can assert themselves in the rough-and-tumble of the marketplace.

In addition, it's necessary to set clear, long-term goals, systematically work on their implementation, and provide the best processes and methods available. In this regard, Siemens, as a global corporate company, offers its innovators a broad range of supportive tools. These include innovation radar, innovation benchmarking – a systematic comparison with world-class competitors – the development of sector-wide platforms, synergies, multiple-impact technologies, the global exchange of best practices, and holistic future planning and strategic visioning methods.

In its 160-year history, Siemens has generated key innovations that have shaped the world. In my view, the innovators portrayed in this book and their projects show that we can expect to continue along this path in the future. Thanks to the extraordinary personal commitment of its innovators, Siemens will certainly also be shaping the world of tomorrow.

Managers on Innovation

It's break time at a management conference at the Siemens Global Leadership Center in Feldafing, Germany on the shores of Lake Starnberg, south of Munich. Managers stream out of the conference room and head toward the refreshments. Accompanied by the sound of clinking plates and glasses, people begin to fall into casual conversations. At one of the tables, Christian, a division head, raises his glass and proposes a toast: "To our new Leadership Center!" "Yes, the conversion has been a great success," chimes in Stacey, a dynamic young American. "The building looks more modern and more elegant somehow. It has a more global feel but concentrates on the essentials at the same time." Everyone nods. Meanwhile, Walter, a plant director from Erlangen, is gazing thoughtfully at a bust of Werner von Siemens that's standing on a plinth in the foyer. "With all the changes we're going through right now, I sometimes wonder if we'd be able to employ him today."

The others look quizzical, so Walter continues: "There's no doubt that the founder of our company was a great visionary. Just think of all his inventions — from the pointer telegraph to the dynamo. But would his way of creating innovations still work today? We live in a world of quarterly reports, portfolio restructuring, risk management and cost-cutting. Might Werner von Siemens be seen as an unconventional thinker and perhaps even a nuisance?" Key account manager Bao Jun nods. "As a major corporation, we have highly complex processes and a huge responsibility to retain jobs," he says. "It's easier for a startup like the one Werner von Siemens founded to take risks and try out new approaches."

The contemplative silence at the table is broken by John, who comes over to join in. "I hope you don't mind me butting in," he says. "I'm a corporate consultant, and I think that visionaries and unconventional thinkers are just as important today as they were 160 years ago. And there are more of them at your company than you seem to think. I've just been doing some interviews about cultures of innovation with various people who fall into that category, and I was really impressed. It seems that some people would do basically anything to promote their ideas, even if nobody else believes in them. And often, their innovations win through in the end. I'd be happy to tell you about them, if you like."

"That sounds really interesting," says Matthias, the sixth in the group. "Why don't we meet by the fireplace in the recreation room this evening? I'd like to hear those stories when we have more time."

Visionary Personalities

Pioneers and Unconventional Thinkers,
Breakthrough Innovations

That evening, the fire is already crackling as Christian, Stacey, Walter, Bao Jun and Matthias join John, who is sitting at a round table in the recreation room and enjoying a glass of red wine. "John, you promised to tell us an exciting story about innovative visionaries," says Christian with a smile. John nods and says, "I think we'd all agree that we are living in a very fast-paced era. Well, the person I'd like to talk about worked for 20 years on an idea before finally achieving the breakthrough." Seeing the dubious looks on his friends' faces, he continues, "The man in question was interested in piezo injection. His project involved faster and more precise injection valves for automobile engines that significantly reduce both fuel consumption and emissions. Today it's a field that posts billions of euros in sales and in which thousands of people work. The original idea was born back in 1980. However, it required the combined force of a stubborn man from Westphalia and his many supporters before the idea could go into mass production 20 years later..."

Piezo Injection – Keeping Faith with an Idea

The inconspicuous ceramic lamina is thinner than a postage stamp, and it crumbles if you don't hold it carefully between your fingers. Yet within it slumbers tremendous power that can be brought to life with just a small amount of electric current – courtesy of the piezo effect. "If I apply an electric field to a piezoelectric ceramic element, the element expands within fractions of a second," says Prof. Hans Meixner, who headed the Sensor & Actuator Systems technical center at Siemens Corporate Technology in Munich until the fall of 2004. "Theoretically, this force could even lift an elephant off the ground." Meixner took advantage of this effect and, together with his team, developed a revolutionary injection valve for diesel and gasoline engines. Today, almost every automaker in the world is investing in this technology, which is helping to spur the renaissance of the diesel engine and has created approximately 10,000 jobs at Siemens VDO and its competitor Robert Bosch GmbH alone.

However, the path from there to here was not a straight one: Around 20 years elapsed between the initial idea and its premiere on the world market, which was marked by the beginning of series production at Siemens VDO in September 2000. "The important thing is to be convinced that your technology will one day bear fruit – maybe not today or tomorrow, but perhaps the day after tomorrow," says Meixner, who, together with colleagues from Siemens VDO and Bosch, received the German Future Prize at the end of 2005 in recognition of his development. The prize is sponsored by the German President and is endowed with €250,000. Keeping your eye on the ball is therefore the most important recipe offered by Meixner – an enthusiastic tennis player – when it comes to developing an innovation to market maturity. And the advice is relevant even if the time doesn't seem ripe for industrializing the idea. "It all started in 1980," says Meixner. "At that time we had a wealth of ideas on how the piezo effect could be utilized. Since then we've implemented many of them, including the Siemens inhaler for medical applications or the knock sensor you'll find in around 40 million vehicle engines today." The initial spark for piezo injection systems came from the automaker Mercedes. Meixner recalls: "Our colleagues from Mercedes approached us and asked if we would like to develop a piezo injection technology for them, so we got to work."

Prof. Dr. Hans Meixner's most important innovation demonstrates how much patience is sometimes required before a vision can become reality. In this particular case, around 20 years elapsed between the initial idea of using piezo ceramics for injection valves in automobile engines and the beginning of mass production. But the inventor's stubbornness and the quality of his ideas ultimately paid off. Almost all automakers worldwide plan to use this technology in the future. Today, Siemens and Bosch already employ around 10,000 people in this area. Together with two other innovators, Hans Meixner was honored for his achievement with the German Future Prize in 2005.

Success in the Laboratory

It took only a few months to build an initial laboratory model. "The preconditions were good. We already had a lot of experience with piezo technology and fantastic laboratories. Besides, the materials development department was nearby, so our colleagues could supply us quickly with the ceramic laminae we needed." According to the calculations of the Siemens developers, applying an electric current to the ceramic would make it expand at lightning speed, move the injection needle and thus spray the fuel into the cylinder much more precisely than was previously possible. However, in the engine trials the first piezo injector couldn't deliver what it had promised in theory – the forces and reaction speeds were much lower than the developers had expected.

It took Meixner only a few hours to find out where the problem lay. "We had glued the ceramic laminae together with a two-component adhesive. But these layers of adhesive behaved like the disks in your spinal cord: They dampened the speed and the force of the reaction."

After realizing this, the researchers developed a cuboid made of hundreds of ultrathin piezo ceramic strips separated from one another by electrodes. That was how they dealt with the problematic fact that large voltages are needed in order to make any noteworthy deformations in larger piezo components. By contrast, 160 volts are sufficient to trigger the piezo effect in an individual lamina that is only 0.08 mm thick. The vital trick is therefore to stack hundreds of these laminae together and connect them electrically in parallel. That enabled the improved prototype to show exactly what it was capable of.

"That was a milestone," Meixner exults. "We were finally able to implement in the lab everything the theory had predicted. That's the basic prerequisite of every innovation."

Environmental Friendliness That Was Ahead of its Time

However, it was a long time before this revolutionary technology was applied in practice. The customer, Mercedes, was impressed by its potential to make engines cleaner and more fuel-efficient, but ended the project nonetheless. The main reasons for this step were the high costs for valves using piezo technology and, above all, the mood of the 1980s. "This technology was simply ahead of its time," says Meixner in retrospect. "Neither environmental awareness nor emissions regulations were considered as important in those days as they are today. Besides, at that time people weren't paying so much attention to gasoline prices – 20 years ago a liter of gasoline cost less than the equivalent of €0.60."

We have Meixner's native Westphalian stubbornness – and various automakers – to thank for the fact that piezo technology was not laid to rest then and there. "In 1986, BMW engineers asked us if we were interested in developing something entirely new for automotive technology. In response, we organized a three-day retreat with BMW and discussed various ideas," he recalls. "The result was the PEP Engine project, whose acronym stands for 'more power, more efficiency, but less pollution.' It was clear to us that we were witnessing a new opportunity for piezo injector technology." In order to demonstrate the advantages of the new technology in terms of fuel consumption and low pollutant emissions, Meixner's team built the injectors into a gasoline engine, which they then accelerated to 1,000 and 4,000 rpm. "The result was groundbreaking: With our injection system we could boost engine performance and considerably reduce nitrogen oxide emissions while at the same time lowering fuel consumption by up to six percent," says Meixner. "Partly as a result of our success, Siemens invested even larger amounts in automotive technology. Today we can reduce pollutant emissions by up to 30 percent with the help of quick-acting piezo valves, which – unlike the previously used solenoid valves – make multiple targeted injections possible during a single cylinder stroke. Fuel consumption can also be reduced by up to 30 percent, and engine performance can be boosted by approximately five percent. Besides, the engine noise becomes much quieter."

 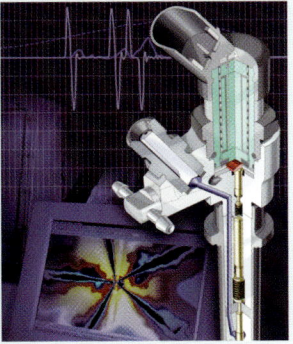

Speedy ceramic. When subjected to an electrical voltage, the stack of thin piezo ceramic laminae (green area in the image at right) expands far enough to open the fuel injector valve – in fractions of a thousandth of a second. This happens with a speed and precision that significantly reduces fuel consumption and emissions.

Today, when Meixner, 67, looks back over the years, one lesson stands out from all the rest: "A technology can't be brought to maturity before the time is ripe. In addition, researchers need colleagues in the

Groups who not only realize this fact but are also prepared to provide sufficient funding. After all, it takes lots of money and courage to replace competing solutions that have been around for a long time with new technologies. That's partly because established solutions tend to be less expensive." Back in the mid-1990s, the Group board members at Siemens Automotive decided that it would be premature to introduce piezo injectors in gasoline engines. They decided instead to first make the technology marketable for use with diesels – thereby setting the stage for the current boom in diesel car sales. Their decision was primarily influenced by the French automotive industry, which was pro-diesel. However, it was ultimately the personal contact between Edward Krubasik, a member of Siemens' Corporate Executive Committee, and the Peugeot family that proved decisive in ensuring the "diesel piezo's" success. Robert Peugeot, the head of technology, actually visited Hans Meixner. "We showed him our lab facilities and engine testing rigs," remembers Meixner. "I think he was very impressed." In 2000 the French company became the first automaker to use Siemens injector nozzles in series-produced vehicles.

Mass Production and Systems Expertise

"There's no doubt that mastering mass production is an essential part of successful innovation," says Meixner. "In our labs we can produce maybe 100 piezo stacks monthly – all of them built by hand. But quality improvement – and reduced costs – can't really be achieved until the series production stage." To help things along here, Meixner arranged a meeting with the head of development at the Siemens plant for ceramic components in Deutschlandsberg in the late 1980s. Inspired by a new, monolithic production process that the plant was using to make multi-layered ceramic condensers, Meixner suggested that the very same process could be used to build piezo stacks – an idea that marked the start of series production. Today, only the Epcos company, which emerged in 1999 from a joint venture between Siemens and Matsushita Components, and recently Kyocera, a Japanese company, are using monolithic production to build piezo stacks. Epcos also supplies the stacks that Bosch uses for its piezo valves.

The piezo stack alone cannot guarantee market success, however. System expertise is also required. After all, the customer is buying the complete system, not just injectors. In addition to the fuel injectors, the system includes sensors, software and sophisticated electronics. That's why Siemens VDO is striving to optimize the entire system. Meanwhile, the use of piezo technology in diesel injection systems has proved so successful that Siemens VDO began the series production of injectors for gasoline engines in late 2006 – about 26 years after the birth of the original idea.

Meixner had the stamina to stay the distance on the long road from the idea to the product. He was helped here by his ability to slowly but surely establish a first-class reputation among potential sponsors. However, his team's expertise was only one of the keys to his success. "It's also important to always be open and straightforward," he says. "You should never conceal problems from your supervisors, regardless of whether they are technical or human. It's also crucial to integrate supervisors, contracting parties and customers at an early stage. They have to be not only convinced but also enthusiastic. In short, they must share a fascination for the new technology."

Experiments for Board Members and Customers

One approach proved to be particularly useful when it came to easing tensions and clearing hurdles. "I remember a discussion about alternatives to the expensive piezo stacks," says Meixner. "We were looking at magnetostrictive materials. They're less brittle and just as fast, but they behave like flint. And that turned out to be a big problem. Should gasoline run out of the engine as a result of a crash, they produce showers of sparks. And that could have caused a massive explosion." Some board members, however, had fewer doubts about the material than the Siemens scientist. But he stuck to his guns and personally arranged an appropriate experiment for the then Siemens Automotive Systems boss, Dr. Franz Wressnigg. "It was a real sparkler!" laughs Meixner, when he thinks back. "And that was the end of the magnetostrictive materials."

Meixner also clears bigger hurdles in the same way. "About four years ago the EU's lead-free directive came into force – after our injectors had already gone into series production," he says. "The EU criticized our piezo stacks, whose ceramic contains a lead zirconate titanate." The main worry was that lead could be released into the environment when old engine blocks were melted down. "The best way to ease concerns is to demonstrate the validity of the counterargument. So we invited the EU specialists, scientists and representatives of the automobile industry to a few experiments." The demonstration reassured the guests, who were able to see at first hand that the lead didn't endanger the environment, despite the high temperatures in the smelting furnaces. "Afterwards, things quieted down and everybody was happy," says Meixner.

A father of two daughters, he has other avid interests besides his work. When he's not busy with his family, he's a keen sportsman. "I'm a Bavarian Club Tournament player and I like both downhill and cross-country skiing," he says. "Sport has always helped me to maintain a good level of physical and mental fitness, which in turn helps me do my job well."

A professor of physics and engineering, Meixner also sets great store by the work of his younger scientific colleagues – which isn't surprising, given that students wrote an important part of the piezo success story. "Our young graduate and postgraduate students have helped us get through some difficult times," says Meixner. "Young university students are not only relatively inexpensive but also bring lots of commitment and new ideas. We couldn't have managed our development work without our students." Some of the former postgraduate students and coworkers

Lessons learned	Hans Meixner's advice for innovators
• As an innovator, you have to consistently stick to your idea and remain true to your course. You shouldn't change direction from day to day.	• Never hide problems from your supervisor, regardless of whether the problems are technical or human. Always actively promote cooperation at an early stage.
• Success needs a great deal more than just having a good idea and carrying out an experiment to show that it works in principle.	• Hardware developers in particular must not be too short-term in their thinking. They need to maintain a certain consistency and steadfastness from day to day – after all, not every idea can be realized quickly.
• You have to believe in your own idea – even if the technology to accomplish it will not be available today or tomorrow, but only the day after tomorrow. You also need supervisors who see things your way.	• It's important to understand the technology and the physics of the idea. The next step is to be able to verify it experimentally and to determine the effect on the overall system.
• You have to involve supervisors and colleagues at an early stage and address all problems openly.	• Interdisciplinary thinking is a decisive factor in success. Simply staying within your field can quickly lead to a dead end.
• You need to put the right team together and offer its members a perspective. Teamwork is decisive if the idea is really to be brought to sufficient maturity for production and a subsequent market launch.	• You should always let the team participate in success.

such as "Siemens Inventors of the Year" Dr. Andreas Kappel, Dr. Bernhard Gottlieb and Dr. Maximilian Fleischer have themselves become successful innovators (see also "Digital Bloodhounds"). Meixner, who retains an office at Corporate Technology despite having retired, also feels a certain satisfaction when his former students contact their old professor for advice. "Let people participate, get them interested – that's one of the keys to success," he emphasizes. Most members of the board were aware that Meixner was always on the track of a new discovery. "Prof. Weyrich, the head of CT, often held meetings in Perlach," says Meixner. "When the time came for the participants to stretch their legs, they often came by and asked me if I had anything new to show them. And believe me," says the passionate physicist with a twinkle in his eye, "I always had something exciting up my sleeve."

"Wow," says Christian slowly and turns his gaze from the rustling fire towards his colleagues, "That's really impressive. I wouldn't have thought that anyone still had the strength of purpose to persist with an idea for 20 years. When I think about how short the innovation cycles for many electronic devices are, or the quarterly financial statements the stock market companies have to make..." Stacey laughs: "Yes, persistence really was crucial – as were plenty of good ideas. It's surprising how much a piezo valve like this involves: materials research, electronics, software." "And don't forget the systems expertise and the need to develop the cheapest possible mass production methods," adds Walter, the plant director.

"The way Hans Meixner went about things reminds me of old-time inventors like Thomas Alva Edison and George Westinghouse with their many series of experiments and their famous demonstrations," says Stacey. " Not to mention the 'eureka' effect for customers and managers," says Bao Jun laughing. John grins: "An experiment like the shower of sparks from the magnetostrictive materials says a thousand times more than the best Powerpoint presentation. By the way, Professor Meixner also named another important factor when it comes to being a successful innovator – always being honest with supervisors and customers. It's vitally important for the innovator's credibility that he or she is absolutely authentic and has a convincing personality." Everyone nods in agreement. "Incidentally, talking of personalities, I know another innovator from the automotive sector who is also very charismatic..."

"Come on, John! Don't keep us in suspense. Tell us your story!" prompts Matthias.

Paradigm Shift –
The Electronic Wedge Brake

Who is Bernd Gombert? Depending on whom you ask, you'll get different answers to that question. Entrepreneurs know him as a brilliant technician, a real all-rounder among inventors. Researchers and developers regard him as an entrepreneur. And how does he describe himself? Gombert, 46, says he's neither one nor the other – instead, he's a talented all-rounder. He's not the best technician, salesman, bookkeeper or manager, but is nevertheless good at all these activities – like a decathlon runner. And that's exactly how he feels when he's trying to create a commercially successful application for one of his pioneering inventions. This practical focus, he says, is what really makes a good innovator. "It's not the invention alone that makes the innovation," he says. "It's the idea's business success." In this regard, he feels an affinity with one of his idols, Rudolf Diesel, whose brilliant new engine concept was ignored by commercial markets for many years until it finally achieved success. That's why Gombert is particularly proud of one of his rewards: the golden Rudolf Diesel Medal of the German Institute for Inventions in Munich, which he received in November 2006 in the "Honors Hall" of the Deutsche Museum. In contrast to the Nobel Prize, which primarily honors scientific achievement, the Rudolf Diesel Medal also pays tribute to the entrepreneurial achievement connected with the inventions – in other words, the inventions' commercial relevance. Just one month later, in December 2006, Gombert was named a "Top Innovator" of Siemens AG – the company's recently introduced distinction for its best innovators.

Bernd Gombert founded several successful companies when he was still a young man. A gifted technician, he holds approximately 150 patents and enjoys breaking out of habitual thought patterns. Two years ago he changed careers when he was appointed technical manager of the Body & Chassis Electronics Group at Siemens VDO Automotive in Regensburg, Germany.

An Entrepreneur Launches SpaceMouse

After completing an apprenticeship in precision engineering in Marburg, Germany, Gombert studied mechanical engineering and precision mechanics in Gießen and also completed a course of General Studies in Munich. In 1986 he began work as a research assistant at the German Aerospace Center (DLR) in Oberpfaffenhofen near Munich. There, he not only developed the first robot arm for space flights, which was later used in the D2 mission, but also invented a force-torque sensor for robot control. However, DLR decided not to further develop the sensor. It was at this point that the young engineer showed his mettle. Gombert still remembers a morning coffee break with colleagues who laughed at him when he announced his intention to set up his own company for marketing the force-torque sensor that would ultimately become the SpaceMouse. Today this company has 150 employees and is the world's leading producer of 3D input devices. In fact, few designers who work with computer-aided design programs for three-dimensional drawing and drafting can get by without the SpaceMouse. This device enables them to intuitively move virtual objects around in three-dimensional space – in the same way they would use a joystick on two-dimensional surfaces.

In 2001 Gombert's company, Spacecontrol GmbH, was bought up by Logitech – and he became a rich man. Other people in his place would have spent there money on a villa and a few expensive cars – but not Gombert. He reinvested all of the profits from the sale – "all of them," he emphasizes. Except for the house where he lives with his wife and two children, he also invested all of his private assets in his next company, eStop GmbH, with which he intends to do nothing less than revolutionize the entire field of brake technology. He claims that his invention, the electronic wedge brake, will not only replace traditional braking systems, including ABS and ESP, but surpass them in effectiveness. Gombert is already being celebrated for this initiative. At the Hanover Fair in April 2004 before an elite audience of leading entrepreneurs, he was the first-ever recipient of the Hermes Award, the Oscar of German industry, for his wedge brake. Gombert has received no less than 40 of his 150 patents for the electronic wedge brake.

Inspiration from Horse-Drawn Carriages

Using wedge actuation to brake wheels is nothing new. Drivers of horse-drawn carriages did it in the old days. They simply thrust a wedge between the wooden wheel and the wheel well. The rotation of the wheel pulled the wedge in tight and blocked the wheel from further motion until the carriage stopped. It's a very effective braking method, but the abrupt blocking makes it undesirable for automobiles. That's why brakes are still being pressed or pulled today by powerful hydraulic or pneumatic systems. Brake designers have long considered the wedge an uncontrollable deceleration method, and no engineer was willing to tackle the challenge of improving it. But it's exactly challenges like this that fascinate Gombert and spur him on to rethink the whole issue from the ground up. A lover of paradigm change and success against all odds, he lives by the motto that "the longer a system has been on the market, the greater the probability that it can be replaced." That's how he came to reconsider the idea of the wedge.

Gombert's electronic wedge brake (EWB) consists of a wedge-shaped brake pad moving along a series of rollers. During braking, the brake pad is pulled into the space between the brake caliper and the brake lining by the brake disc itself. The brake pad is stopped electronically at a level of brake pressure that is defined via the brake pedal. The brake pad, which is in a kind of equilibrium state between push and pull, is controlled by small electric motors – and that's the innovative feature. This millisecond-fast control of the brake requires 97 percent less energy than conventional brakes. In addition, at a speed of 100 kilometers an hour

A revolutionary brake. Thanks to the electronic wedge brake, vehicles will be able to brake faster and more safely in the future – without hydraulics. The system can easily handle three consecutive emergency stops from a speed of 210 kilometers per hour – although such extreme forces cause the brake disc to glow (left).

it shortens the braking distance by two meters compared to present-day braking processes, even on very slippery surfaces. What's more, because of its significantly higher efficiency the wedge brake can be smaller and lighter. There is also no longer any need for brake pipes, brake boosters or brake fluid reservoirs, which frees up a volume of around 22 liters in the engine compartment, giving vehicle designers added scope.

The antilock braking system (ABS) that is almost ubiquitous today and the less common electronic stability program (ESP) will be replaced by the software integrated into the EWB system. It takes between 140 and 170 milliseconds for a conventional ABS to generate full braking power. The EWB, on the other hand, needs only around 100 milliseconds. Gombert believes that the shorter reaction time will be especially advantageous on uneven or icy roads. The innovative braking system is now being extensively tested and is expected to be ready for mass production around 2010.

As a robotics and mechatronics engineer at DLR, Gombert knew very well that a system can simultaneously push and pull – in other words, that it can not only push in a wedge but also pull it out again before it locks. But before he appeared on the scene, this knowledge had never been applied in the traditional field of mechanical engineering known as braking hydraulics. There's a lamentable lack of synergies in this area, according to Gombert. "We have to learn how to think outside the box in many more disciplines," he says. His wedge brake is an outstanding example of such interdisciplinary thinking. Here, computer control combines with sensor technology, drive technology and mechanical engineering to create a completely new product that will have far-reaching consequences for automotive technology.

A Taste for Billion-Dollar Markets

The electric brake is an important step along the way to a completely electric power train, in which the steering is controlled electronically rather than hydraulically. "As far as tomorrow's automotive technology is concerned, the master of the electric power train will also be the master of the platform strategy," declares Gombert, adding that this platform strategy will point the way to wholly automated driving. The more that the human factor is removed from the driving process, the safer road traffic will become, he says, adding that he is "personally committed to this opinion," knowing very well that he is again becoming controversial. But that doesn't discourage him, because determination is one of his personal strengths.

This quality must have been noticed by Heinrich von Pierer, former Siemens CEO and afterwards speaker of the company's supervisory board. Pierer was sitting in the first row when Gombert received the Hermes Award from then German Chancellor Gerhard Schröder. Not untypically, Gombert asked if he could deviate from the evening's protocol and speak a few words. His brief talk, which reflected his no-nonsense approach, so impressed Pierer that he ultimately hired Gombert to work at Siemens. In his search for a business partner for his electronic wedge brake, Gombert had previously appealed to 170 venture capital companies and all of the major brake manufacturers. He finally succeeded in convincing the top management at Siemens VDO that his invention had tremendous potential.

If the wedge brake works – something Bernd Gombert has never doubted – a billion-dollar market will open up for Siemens, not only in the automotive sector but also in other fields. That's because in addition to transforming automobile brakes, wedge technology will have a major impact of drive systems in a variety of areas, ranging from rail travel to elevators and conveyor belt technology. Gombert's vision is that "in the future, it will be possible to brake everything that is driven by a power system with a wedge brake in a controlled and efficient manner." One example would be new braking systems for high-speed trains, which are currently equipped with extremely maintenance-intensive and therefore expensive braking systems. Gombert also has an eye on the field of automation technology, which employs all sorts of motors. As a Siemens VDO manager, he enjoys envisioning the fundamental ways in which his technology could change devices such as automotive safety belts. Today, a twisting torsion bar absorbs the energy when a passenger is being held back by a safety belt during an accident. Up to now, most experts believed that nothing could absorb energy as quickly as a torsion bar. It was exactly the kind of belief Gombert loves to question. After all, this mechanical system doesn't distinguish between light and heavy bodies, so the shock energy sustained by the rib cage is always the same. The same amount of pressure is exerted on the ribcage of a 12-year-old girl weighing 30 kilograms as on that of a man weighing 100 kilograms – causing proportionately more injury.

"There's got to be a better way," says Gombert – and, thanks to the wedge brake, there is. His somewhat modified wedge brake can not only regulate the amount of force according to the individual passenger's weight – it also reacts significantly faster than a torsion bar. Whether the passenger is a little girl or a heavy adult man, in the event of a crash all the passengers are braked evenly over the extension length of their safety belts and cushioned by their airbags. Electronics instead of mechanics

– that's another of those paradigm shifts that Gombert is enthusiastic about. He even took a long and hard look at another well-established technology: the electric motor. Why, he wondered, does it still consist of copper wire and iron sheeting, as it did a century ago? These materials encourage recurring problems, such as internal short circuits.

Posed with this question, his development team inevitably came up with another paradigm shift. Their idea is a motor that doesn't need windings, uses 80% less electrical energy but develops ten times as much torque as a conventional motor. "This is going to turn Siemens upside down," predicts Gombert, who is already working on a trademark protection strategy to protect his new invention on the market – "but, as ever, I won't do anything without my team," he adds.

Rebel Talent Scout and Motivator

Gombert's team of 100 developers, which he has gathered together in the former Werner plant in Regensburg, is his greatest treasure. The envy of many, his team underlines the claim that "a good leader will always attract good people." Gombert says that finding the right people is a difficult job, but it's one he's good at – and the effort is worthwhile. He has patiently built up many development teams and has never delegated the job to anyone else. In fact, this is one of the secrets of his success. He merely smiles when he thinks of the project management processes large companies often use – with their large-scale meetings and workshops – in the hope of achieving quick results. "It's people, particularly talented individuals and their ideas, that move developments forward, not processes," he says, adding that Siemens has such innovators. However, he believes that they have to be scouted out individually rather than marshaled in large numbers through management processes.

It seems that even when it comes to team building, Gombert is a rebel, an entrepreneur and an inventor who does not fit into any predefined category. And that's why he's so valuable, not only for Siemens but also for society as a whole, which, as Gombert puts it, "demands innovations but is wary of change." That's also why he is often invited to give presentations. People are curious about his new, unconventional ideas. A charismatic talker, he's able to inspire many of his listeners, because he avoids abstract theories and talks instead authentically about the ups and downs of being an inventor. He's particularly keen to get young people and college students interested in technology: "You have to talk to them and encourage them," he says. "Have confidence in yourself and get the job done" is the message he puts across in his inimitable way to his young audiences – and they thank him for it. Who knows? Maybe one of them will turn out to be the next Bernd Gombert.

Lessons learned	Bernd Gombert's advice for innovators
• The greatest innovators are not eccentric specialists but all-rounders who can present their own ideas effectively. In addition to good ideas, innovators need enormous determination, persuasiveness and a talent for selling their ideas. • The most successful innovators stand out because of their ability to make their ideas pay off commercially. • Creative work depends to a large extent on the leeway provided by supervisors. • Flat hierarchies allow employees to develop their own ideas, because there's less regulation. • Innovation needs the support of top management, since without it the innovation flower can't bloom. These new flowers always start to grow in a niche before they seed themselves elsewhere – and while they are in the niche they need care, protection and good fertilizer.	• You are your own best motivator – money doesn't even come close. • You have to seek out good employees. They'll guarantee your success. • Successes are accompanied by failures. So don't lose heart – follow your passion. • Success is inevitable if you really want it. • It's important to be steadfast in following your own goals, but be careful not to rush into ill-considered ventures.

"He's a real all-rounder," says Stacey admiringly after John has finished his report. "I'd love to be on one of Gombert's teams," murmurs Matthias as he puts another piece of wood into the fire. Somewhat more loudly, he asks the group, "Isn't that a prime example of what people call transformational leadership – the kind that sets an example of how to run a successful innovation process?"

"You're right," says John. "Bernd Gombert has charisma. He inspires his employees by conjuring up visions instead of just prescribing targets; he challenges old ways of thinking, stimulates new ideas and promotes discussions – and the culture of open debate that's so important for nurturing innovations. It's a textbook case of transformational management behavior."

Matthias nods. "People like him are the ones who really move us forward. He says that 'the longer a system has been on the market, the greater is the probability that it can be replaced.' However, most people don't think that way." "He's really someone who thinks outside the box and loves to throw everything into question," says Walter. "This attitude certainly often makes established colleagues feel uncomfortable, but if a manager has the courage to support people like that, they can change the world."

"Come on, you know you're exaggerating just a bit," laughs John. "Experience tells us that not all the ideas of unconventional thinkers end up changing the world. But there's something in what you say: If visionaries of this kind meet up with like-minded top managers who have faith in them, they can do great things." "Especially if they're as smart as Gombert and insist on hand-picking their team members," adds Bao Jun. "After all, in most cases it's people and their ideas that push a development forward – not processes, as he rightly observes."

"But isn't this kind of trust between managers and innovators only the ideal case?" Matthias asks the group. "After all, researchers and developers are very far removed from management decisions..." John breaks in: "But the more basic the innovation is, the more important is this contact between innovative thinkers and management. In most cases, there are certain milestones in the innovation process where the management has to decide whether to continue or cancel a project. Here, facts from the development process and talks with major customers are just as crucial as the trust between innovators and management. However, the usual decision criteria, such as detailed business plans, are often not very helpful when it comes to groundbreaking innovative projects – so such a project can easily get bogged down by delays or wrong decisions."

Walter agrees: "I think I know a good example of how an innovator with the right management support can be successful – or, alternatively, be a trend scout without management support and do a lot of work with no significant results." "Tell us more," says someone. Walter begins: "I'm thinking of a truly global innovator who has made a long journey in more ways than one – going from Calcutta via Bangladesh to Canada and the USA, and from nuclear technology to microsystems for use in building automation applications..."

Sensors in the Wall

When Osman Ahmed thinks back on his life, he describes it as a journey made by someone who wanted to do something new – and who wanted to decide for himself what to do. Yet his very first project, when he started working as an applications engineer in 1988 at Landis & Gyr Powers, near Chicago, was like a carefully planned show-jumping event. "The goal was clear, and the way to get there was largely described," remembers Ahmed, a mechanical engineer. His job was to develop airflow control applications for critical environments, such as laboratories where research is carried out on viruses. His company was not yet active in this market, which offered a lucrative opportunity as compared to conventional climate control systems in traditional office buildings, and competition was heating up.

The solution Ahmed finally developed was not only superior to the competitors' products in several technical aspects; it also provided great energy savings to customers. The trick was to have the air flow run up to full capacity only when people were actually working, enabling the system to drastically reduce its full-load operating time and thus also its electricity consumption. "The customers were delighted – and often such control systems for critical environments served as a first step toward selling other systems for less critical areas," Ahmed says. "Customers like to do one-stop shopping for their entire building automation systems and services." Within a few years, Landis & Gyr Powers became the market leader in the specialized segment for critical environment control systems.

This was a crucial successful experience for Ahmed. However, even prior to joining Landis & Gyr Powers he knew that one has to adapt in order to achieve success. For example, he quit a

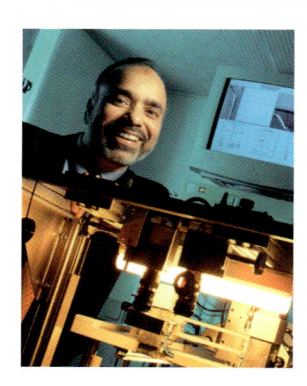

Life is an adjustment, according to **Osman Ahmed, PhD**, who also says this applies to his own personal story. Born in Calcutta, he grew up in Bangladesh and has enjoyed success in Canada and the U.S. Ahmed also views innovations as adjustments made in accordance with customers' needs. His ideas on microelectromechanical systems could revolutionize building engineering systems in the future.

Ph.D. program in nuclear engineering in the early 1980s when he realized that the chances of getting a good job in that area were quite slim, as he could already see that no new nuclear power plants would be built in the U.S. over the medium term. His experience with his first development project showed him – as he puts it – that it's not the technology itself that makes an innovation into a successful product, but the ability to tailor that innovation to meet the needs of the market.

Years later, when he developed adaptive control systems with his team, he was motivated to find a solution that would require minimum or no user intervention for keeping environmental conditions in a building stable. This would make the systems more or less autonomous, thus eliminating the high labor costs that result from periodic manual tuning of the control loop in buildings around the world.

Technology Scout on a Lonely Mission

"But unfortunately, following my first great success, I was headed for the low point of my career," says Ahmed. Within a few years, he was given new responsibility to act as a technology scout in the U.S. to find exciting new innovations, develop them further, and make them usable for the new company in the form of new products and solutions. However, the management team in the technology department failed to successfully commercialize some of the great ideas Ahmed and others on the technology development team had to offer. The researchers didn't have enough contact with product and business line managers, who were regularly in touch with the customers. This was the biggest mistake, admits Ahmed today when he looks back on that time. "Nobody knew what anybody else was doing. In the end we had a lot of patents and inventions – but no product. We never related what we were doing to our customers, and we didn't know how to make money with what we had."

He is reminded of that time whenever he drives from his present workplace in Buffalo Grove to nearby Chicago. From the highway, the 344-meter Hancock Center stands out prominently on the skyline. If you stand in front of it on a warm day and look up at the one hundred floors, you can see the air shimmering in front of the building. The black aluminum of the external cladding heats up during the day and the air-conditioning system has to work at full load to keep temperatures bearable inside the tower. The system uses ice made with cheaper electricity during the night, which then melts in the basement during the day while air flows over it that is then pumped into the offices. Ahmed and his team worked on a solution that predicts the air-conditioning requirement for the Hancock Center a full day ahead, because every kilo of extra ice produced would drive up costs unnecessarily.

"We thought that a system based on artificial intelligence would be able to estimate the right quantity of ice more efficiently and precisely," says Ahmed. They continued with their research, ending up with a working system that management at the Hancock Center actually liked – but they didn't buy it, and the team failed to find any other customers who were prepared to order it. "We were blinded by technical enthusiasm and literally forgot to carry out a market analysis," Ahmed recalls. "I was determined that this wouldn't happen to me again." The technology scout team was ultimately disbanded due to lack of commercial success. But Ahmed continued to search for an innovation that would make a big impact.

Vision as a Driving Force

When Ahmed found out in 1998 that Siemens was planning to acquire his employer – the Swiss-American company Landis & Staefa – he was thrilled, because he had already discovered an exciting area of work that could only result in marketable products with the help of resources from a major corporation. The technology known as micro-electromechanical systems (MEMS) is based on the special properties of silicon. This material, out of which computer chips are made, can also be used in sensors – for measuring pressure, for example, or, with certain sensing layers, for detecting gases.

Ahmed heard about this technology for the first time in 1997, and was immediately enthusiastic. It has been part of his life ever since. The thing he enjoys most about his job – being able to develop technologies into marketable applications – allowed him to pursue a vision that ultimately motivated not only his peers, but also the Marketing department and the Group Managing Board at Siemens Building Technologies. It was clear that MEMS technology could truly revolutionize building engineering services. Until that point, every single sensor had had to be individually wired up, at great expense. But in the future, it would be possible to put hundreds of small MEMS sensors in the most inaccessible places, and they could even be made so tiny that they might one day disappear into the paint on a wall.

"Instead of just recording and reporting the temperature, as they do today, the sensors of the future, which we are developing, will be able to do a lot more," says Ahmed. "They'll be able to feel how strong a draft of air is, measure the percentage of carbon dioxide in the air, the inten-

MEMS on fingertips: The tiny micro-electromechanical systems could be used in the future as versatile sensors. In addition to monitoring buildings, they could immediately process the data collected and wirelessly forward it to a control system.

sity of light, and even the volume of sound – such as the noise made by construction workers in the next room." And that's not all: Integrated circuits on the same silicon chips will be able to process data and communicate the results by radio to other chips. "What we'll then see will be a decentralized, self-regulating control system that will also cut costs in two ways," says Ahmed. "First of all, customers will understand exactly how their buildings are consuming energy, and will then use this knowledge to develop energy-saving strategies. Secondly, wireless technology will make expensive wiring unnecessary, which will significantly reduce product costs for Siemens."

The development phase of MEMS commercialization began in the fall of 2006; the first product with some of the features should be on the market this fall or winter. Meanwhile, more and more potential customers have heard about the solution and contacted Buffalo Grove directly. Siemens headquarters also appreciates the inventiveness of Ahmed and his team, and the prospects they offer for a paradigm shift in building systems engineering. As a result of the patents related to microsystems that he registered, Ahmed was named Siemens Inventor of the Year in 2004.

At the awards ceremony, Ahmed had the privilege of talking to then Siemens Supervisory Board Chairman Dr. Heinrich von Pierer and other top managers. He says he was very impressed by the open atmosphere at the event. Ahmed feels that communication is perhaps one of the most important – but also one of the most overlooked – qualities an innovation manager needs to have. He attributes his skills in this area to his father's guidance and mentoring. Ahmed's father was a trade diplomat in Pakistan's foreign ministry who taught Ahmed a lot about communication. "My father always taught me to be honest, open, polite and positive," he says, adding that the best advice his father ever gave him was that "life is an adjustment."

The Best of Many Worlds

Ahmed, 50, has been married for 23 years and has two sons. His life story really has been a journey of adjustment. Ten years before he was born, the India that gained independence was divided into predominantly Muslim Pakistan and today's India. Born near Calcutta, Ahmed – himself a Muslim – experienced how the new states became more and more estranged and finally enemies. His father had meanwhile become a Pakistani diplomat and for many years could not visit his family, which had emigrated to Bangladesh. It was there that Ahmed earned a bachelor's degree in mechanical engineering at the renowned Bangladesh University of Engineering and Technology (BUET) in Dhaka, the country's capital. In fact, he attended the same university where the noted structural engineer Dr. F.R. Khan, who designed Chicago's Hancock Center, got his engineering degree. Ahmed later obtained a master's degree in the same field in Canada in 1983. The United States then became his "adoptive mother," as he puts it. This is where he settled and got the opportunity to develop his skills, including those he honed through his work for Siemens many years later.

He now wishes to pass on this wealth of experience to his team of junior development engineers at Siemens Building Technologies. "Development work is only fun in conditions of freedom and independence," he says. "However, it has to be a controlled freedom, one that doesn't degenerate into personal technology indulgence, but is instead clearly oriented toward customers' desires. Siemens innovation managers could help us achieve this in the future." Ahmed is firmly convinced that only close cooperation between developers, product managers and business developers can achieve the joint objective of finding innovative solutions that are successful on the market.

He realizes, however, that it isn't always easy for freedom-loving people to also love a freedom that is structured and disciplined. He admits that "I was always lucky in that I could set my own limits for my activities,

Lessons learned

- **Share knowledge.**
  The more experts from your working environment you get on board, the more input you will receive. You won't contribute much added value if you keep all your knowledge to yourself and regard it as your personal property. As the old saying goes, "Knowledge is the only asset that increases when you share it with others."

- **Be a good listener.**
  Don't immediately discard crazy ideas or suggestions, because later on you might recognize the great ideas that are sometimes concealed within them. And anyone who has the courage to express an apparently idiotic idea has proved that he or she is at least an independent thinker.

- **Show respect.**
  If you act superior, especially when managing a team, you won't be able to rely on the full support of your co-workers. The key is to have mutual respect and trust.

- **Be a team player.**
  Everything that has been ascribed to me – including the inventor award I received – is based on teamwork and is actually the success of my team. I'm really only there to help my team achieve the best possible results.

- **Lead with vision.**
  People don't want to hear about technology, they want to know how innovations can improve their lives. So if your job is to develop and market technology, you have to be a good storyteller. That's the only way to motivate your team over the long term.

Osman Ahmed's advice for innovators

- Innovation must be closely linked with corporate business strategy. It should be geared more toward management's actions than its statements.

- A culture of openness also means being open to mistakes. If you learn from your mistakes, you've done something right. If you fear to receive criticism and punishment for your mistakes, you become intellectually immobile – and that's fatal for innovation departments. You can only learn from mistakes if they become transparent.

- Young development engineers should always get to know the history of their company, and that's especially true for a company like Siemens, which has been successful for nearly 160 years. The past often holds the key to why we do things a certain way today and how we should do things in the future.

- Always try to take a long-term view. This applies not only to new technologies but also to possibilities for cooperation and product marketing. The Internet and other cultural technologies in the global village give us opportunities we should not neglect.

- Follow your passions, even if others at first think you're crazy. This may sometimes lead you into the wilderness, so to speak, but occasionally you'll come back from there with precious discoveries.

because my immediate supervisors trusted my judgment and market focus." While clearly structured innovation processes can be helpful and necessary for companies like Siemens, paradigm shifts – or disruptive change – can perhaps only occur when a special talent utilizes an open environment – and maybe even ignores certain rules at the right time. Osman Ahmed is such a talented individual, and in a few years' time his tiny silicon chips should be able to do everything that is now done by devices and controllers that are much bigger and bulkier.

"It's a story from everyday life," Stacey says. "This inventor had his share of ups and downs." "That's right," says Walter. "And in the process he gained important insights. Never forget the customers and the markets, be a good listener and team player, lead with vision, live a culture of openness and mutual respect... this is where he benefits from his experiences with different cultures and with people from around the world, including Muslims, Hindus and Westerners." "And don't forget his mantra: It isn't technology alone that makes an innovation successful; it's skillful adaptation to the needs of the market," adds Bao Jun.

"Innovation is adaptation," says Christian in agreement. "That's an interesting aspect – and a quite logical one: Find out where the markets are heading, what the customers' real needs are and develop the best innovations to meet those needs." "You make it sound so easy," says John with a laugh. "In the end, it's a kind of game in which the ball is passed around among inventors, marketing and sales experts, production experts and so on. If communication breaks down, the process will most likely fail. For managers it's most important to determine the strengths and weaknesses of an idea, assess its chances and risks, recognize its potential, be supportive of leading-edge thinkers and, now and again, try new things – even when there's no way to know exactly what the outcome will be. By the way, that reminds me of a student of Professor Meixner who's developing things that are similar to Osman Ahmed's innovations – sensors at the microchip level." "Really? Tell us more."

Digital Bloodhounds

Dr. Maximilian Fleischer is only 45 years old, but based purely on the number of patents he's registered, it would be easy to assume he's well into his retirement years. Fleischer joined Siemens' central research unit – Corporate Technology (CT) in Munich, Germany – in 1992. Since then he has registered 150 inventions and had an equally impressive number of articles published in specialized journals. That's ten times per year, a track record that makes him one of a select few. "I just like to try out new things," Fleischer says. Then, realizing this is far too modest an explanation to account for his productivity, he quickly adds: "Well, OK, I guess you could say I'm a hard worker." Without a doubt, his abundant creativity and imagination also play a part. Still, he has realized many of his patents by taking the results of basic research and pushing them just a bit further. "You really have to ask yourself 'How could this be used to do something better? What have others overlooked?'" It's this process that often yields new applications.

One of Fleischer's inventions makes him seem like Gulliver among the Lilliputians. The "little people" in this instance are miniature chemical sensors used to detect the presence of various substances, such as toxic gases, industrial pollutants and stale air in conference rooms. The tiny high-tech units measure only a few square millimeters, about the size of the chocolate flakes in a mug of café latte. And that's not all: The microchip sensors feature a simple design that makes them inexpensive. Some of the sensors from Fleischer's lab are being used in place of complex instruments that used to cost thousands of euros. In 2003, Siemens honored Fleischer with the "Inventor of the Year" award, which is presented by the company to its most productive and creative researchers. The jury had high praise for "the broad spectrum

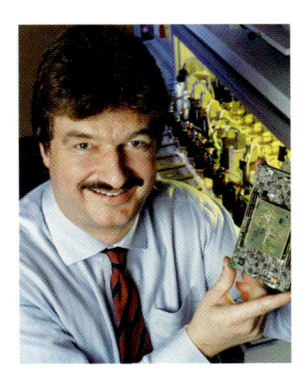

With 150 invention applications, **Dr. Maximilian Fleischer** is one of the top inventors at Siemens. His special focus is microchips that serve as gas sensors. The potential areas of application for such chips range from building systems and automotive technology to mobile sensors for a higher quality of life.

of applications for his inventions." The first of Fleischer's sensors have been in commercial use for several years now, including sensitive microchips that monitor combustion in the small gas-fired boilers found in many homes. Others haven't undergone practical testing yet. Tiny alcohol sensors for car drivers will soon be launched on the market, and there are also medium-term plans to introduce measuring probes that recognize asthma and other illnesses by their smell.

Everyday Needs Instead of Ivory Towers

A characteristic feature of Fleischer's work is the fact that he has followed his own personal vision. "There are a lot of people who try doggedly to optimize their approach and wind up frustrated in the end," he says. "That's where you've got to be flexible and just try something new." And that's what he's been doing, right from the start. After graduating from high school, Fleischer began studying physics in 1981 at the Munich University of Technology. "Back then, though, there were so many people there espousing abstract, idealistic notions. That was all a bit too lofty and unrealistic for me." He wanted a career in industry, "where the work is focused on real-life concerns." One of his professors suggested that Fleischer should apply to study under a former doctoral student of his own – Hans Meixner, who has since gone on to become a Siemens researcher and expert specializing in innovative applications of piezoceramics (see also "Piezo Injection – Keeping Faith with an Idea").

Fleischer was accepted and began his thesis studies under Meixner – doing practical research far removed from the theorist's ivory tower. He began work on the further development of a piezo motor – a small drive unit made of types of ceramic that deform mechanically when a voltage is applied. At the time, such motors could turn in only one direction. Fleischer's assignment was to develop a motor that could reverse its rotation, which is essential for many applications. "My colleagues had been working for a very long time on the problem, without success," he recalls. "As a graduate student, I had the freedom to try something new – and I was able to develop a piezo motor that could turn in two directions." The little motor was a sensation, and in the end Fleischer's thesis project yielded his first two patents and five published papers. That made a big impression: When he graduated, Siemens offered him a permanent position – at a time of bleak employment prospects for physicists.

But Fleischer turned the job down. He wanted to get his doctorate, so working freelance was the best option. He had concluded that all the interesting piezoceramic research had been done, and he was looking for something new. Meixner suggested a project that would later have a formative influence on Fleischer's research: developing a fast oxygen sensor. In order to optimize the oxygen sensor for use in automotive engines, Fleischer tested new materials – including the ceramic gallium oxide. As it turned out, however, the material wasn't very sensitive to oxygen – but Fleischer did notice something odd about one of the measurement curves: The substance was highly sensitive to carbon monoxide (CO). At that point, nobody had any inkling of this. Fleischer showed his findings to Meixner, who was very impressed. Fleischer had not only discovered a new method for detecting toxic CO exhaust, he had also found the basis for his first chemical sensor.

"Of course, it wasn't yet a full-fledged innovation," Fleischer says. "An innovation is an idea that actually becomes a product. You've really got to have patience. In our industry, it can easily take ten years to go from the initial idea to actually manufacturing a product. Anyone who claims that you can turn something entirely new into a marketable product in two years is badly mistaken." It took ten years for the gallium oxide sensor to be fully developed, and it's been in series production for three years. The Vaillant company equips small furnace systems with the sensor, which measures the CO in the system's exhaust gas. With these measurement values, the furnace can electronically optimize its gas combustion, and do so far better than was previously the case. Vaillant has already sold about 30,000 of these new heating systems, with sales of millions of euros. The sensor only costs between €20 and €30, but it generates tremendous added value. Studies conducted by Intechno Consulting in 2004 estimate that by 2010 the global market for gas sensor systems will be worth roughly €2.9 billion a year.

Alcohol-, Asthma- and Drowsiness Sensor

The gallium oxide sensor was also worth a lot to Maximilian Fleischer. His dissertation had taken on a twofold scope, with the first part focusing on the oxygen sensor and the second on the CO sensor. "At the time my advisor asked me if the second part was necessary," says Fleischer. "I replied that it was the most important part." After Fleischer received his doctoral degree, Siemens immediately hired him for a permanent position. He's still doing gallium oxide research and finding new applications. The keys to his success include frequent discussions with users and colleagues from the Siemens Groups and participation in international conferences. But it often still takes time to get results. Take the alcohol sensor, for example. In a project involving Siemens VDO, production of a gallium oxide sensor for the Swedish automotive industry is scheduled to begin soon. The sensor will measure the alcohol volume in a driver's breath just as reliably, but far more cheaply, than the instruments currently used by police departments. It has yet to be decided how the concept will be implemented. "We're thinking of a small add-on device in the car that detects alcohol volumes that violate the legal limit and sends an electronic signal to automatically lock the ignition," Fleischer says. Such alcohol tests are mandatory in Sweden and the U.S., and they'll soon be introduced throughout the European Union.

But gallium oxide isn't the only possible approach, and Fleischer and the four members of his team have long since developed other concepts. One of them involves field-effect transistors (FET). Here, unlike the case with gallium oxide, the substances to be detected don't "dock" onto the sensor's outer surface, whose electrical resistance is changed as a result. In FET sensors, the gas flows through a "tunnel" between a special molecule-capture layer and the FET structure. The advantage is that many different materials can be used for the FET sensor's special layer, greatly expanding the range of applications. Gallium oxide, however, reacts with only a few substances.

A few years ago Fleischer applied for a patent for a FET-based carbon dioxide sensor for use in automotive climate-control systems. The sensor is to play an important role in future vehicle air-conditioning systems

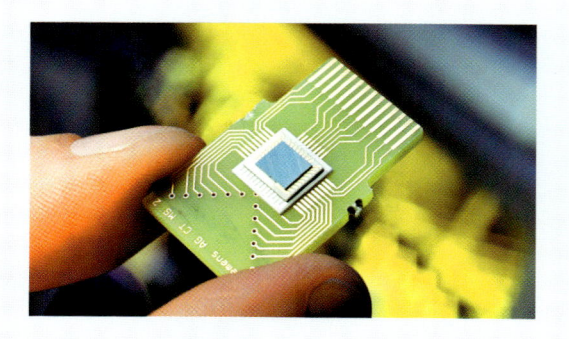

Carbon dioxide sensor. Field-effect transistors like this one help to detect CO_2 in the air. They're suitable for applications ranging from conference room ventilation systems to vehicle air-conditioning systems, which use CO_2 as a refrigerant. However, a CO_2 leak here could prove fatal, as the gas causes fatigue.

that run on carbon dioxide (CO_2) instead of ozone-damaging chlorinated hydrocarbons. Should such an air conditioning system leak, the sensor will prevent CO_2 from accumulating in the vehicle's interior and thus ensure that drivers didn't become fatigued, or even fall unconscious. The sensor could also be used to automatically ventilate working and living areas. For example, having detected stale air by measuring the CO_2 level in the office, the sensor could automatically activate a ventilation system. Conventional CO_2 sensors rely on optical detection, and thus use equipment that is much more expensive than Fleischer's uncomplicated chip structure. FET sensors, such as those used to detect nitric oxide, are also well-suited for detecting certain illnesses. When an asthmatic is about to suffer an attack, the nitric oxide level in his or her breath increases. The sensor could provide an early warning of such a situation.

Fleischer's key contribution was to take the FET principle out of the universities and use it in a number of different applications. He enjoys collaborating with universities and other companies, and frequently travels to conferences – more for the opportunity to talk with colleagues than to hear the presentations. "The knowledge sharing that occurs throughout the scientific community is essential for my work," Fleischer says, happy that his employer shares this view. "Other companies want you to be much more circumspect – publishing 150 papers would be out of the question there." Fleischer enjoys his freedom at CT so much that he "can't conceive working elsewhere."

Success Breeds Freedom, Freedom Breeds Success

Fleischer has deep roots in Munich. He was born in the city and went to the local university, so he's right at home here. When talking, his Munich accent is often punctuated by a hearty laugh. He's a big, powerful man – and when he becomes so engrossed in work that he forgets to eat, he'll go to a restaurant in the evening and order "something for his sweet tooth," like a Bavarian fruit-filled pastry with a dollop of ice cream. And he knows how to unwind. Even though he's had some of his best ideas while relaxing, maybe over a glass of wine, he generally forgets about work in his free time. In terms of his career, he's particularly grateful to one man: his former boss Hans Meixner. "He gave me lots of freedom to try out my ideas and realize their potential. Many other supervisors might have reined me in."

Although he's modest, Fleischer knows that the creative freedom he enjoys is largely due his own success. "An innovator has to earn this freedom through concrete achievements. That earns trust, which in turn gives you the freedom to try another new idea." The decision-makers in management trust Fleischer implicitly. And then there's his trademark saying – "If it doesn't work, I'll eat my hat." So far, he's lived up to this claim: His hat is still hanging on its hook.

He claims never to have encountered an insurmountable obstacle during the course of his career. Nevertheless, it's not as if he has carte blanche: "Just like at the university, or at any company, you've got to apply for funding and hope that your request will be approved." Even now, he's got to convince management of the potential gains of each new idea. After all, you can't create a product without certain resources. The sensors for gas-fired boilers weren't approved. Fleischer offered the CO sensor several times to Siemens colleagues in the various Groups. "There's no demand," was always the response. "For a developer, that's the end of the road in an industrial company. If a product unit isn't interested in an invention, it won't become a product." In some cases, though, external players show an interest. Vaillant heard about the sensors, for example, which are now being manufactured by a partner company licensed by Siemens. "They're having great success with it," says Fleischer.

Even after 15 years in the lab, Fleischer says he still wants to remain a researcher. Needless to say, he's had many offers to work elsewhere. He has rejected offers to teach at universities despite having now finished his postdoctoral research. Even when a major company wanted him to

Lessons learned

- You first have to earn the trust of others before you can expect to be given the freedom to do what you think is best.
- New approaches often lead to finding better solutions more quickly. It's important to be open to the new and the unexpected.
- Innovations take time.
- Applying for grants and funding isn't fun, but it's part of a researcher's everyday responsibilities – not only at universities, but also in industry.
- Even the best ideas are worthless if no one is interested in them.

Maximilian Fleischer's advice for innovators

- Be conscientious and hard-working.
- Have patience.
- Take part in discussions with other experts whenever possible.
- Give dependable employees lots of freedom to explore their ideas.
- It's OK to be a little stubborn when it comes to realizing your own ideas.

become its director of research, he turned the offer down. "It would have been a pure management job. I could have had a bunch of people at my beck and call, but in the end I would simply have been managing the research of others." Fleischer is content with his "fairly modest" working group: "We have opportunities to do great work." At the same time, he tries to give his team the freedom that he himself so highly values. "Maybe they have too much freedom," he says and laughs. "My colleagues used to listen to me, but that was a long time ago."

"He's the perfect personification of an inventor," says Matthias. "Imagine, 150 inventions registered in 15 years – amazing! He must be one of the very best at Siemens." "And there are few of his caliber at any company," John adds. "What really surprised me is that Fleischer also had 150 articles and papers published in scientific journals. He works almost like a researcher at a university."

"That's exactly the secret of his success, if I've understood it correctly," Christian chimes in. "He goes to lots of conferences, talks with other researchers and seeks out collaborations. He then works hard to push the basic results just a little bit further – and finds applications that no one else thinks of." "And he's also not at all blinkered, like many researchers at universities who can't see beyond their own specialist areas," John remarks. "Fleischer's different; he's very flexible. If something doesn't work, then he simply tries something new – that seems to be one of his strengths."

"I see," murmurs Stacey. "Be very creative while at the same time concentrating on possible applications – and not only in one direction, but looking for applications in very different areas. The last time I was at Siemens Corporate Research in Princeton, I met a researcher like Fleischer." "We're all ears. Let's hear it," says John. "Sure. This isn't about materials, though. It's about software and a researcher who succeeds in finding and using synergies between medical applications and, for example, automotive technology…"

Merging Data Streams

A road runs right through the middle of Dorin Comaniciu's office. At first you don't see it. But when Comaniciu walks in, gently shuts the door behind him and begins outlining his work, the road starts to take shape. It's a road where ideas run on parallel paths like lanes, but where all the lanes travel together toward a common destination.

The commonality of the ideas is not immediately obvious, though. The ideas run the gamut of applications, from new ways of interpreting the contours of a beating heart or fetal head to technologies for automatically keeping cars at a safe distance from one another, or giving tomorrow's doctors a way of visualizing genetic data in the context of structural molecular information.

Dorin Comaniciu, PhD, is head of the Integrated Data Systems Department at Siemens Corporate Research in Princeton, New Jersey, and is responsible for coordinating Siemens' activities in biomedical informatics. Ultimately, his work boils down to teaching machines to see and interpret accurately – for a variety of applications.

As Comaniciu explains, his job is not only to keep the ideas humming along in their respective lanes – with new ones from himself and the 30-plus people in his department merging into the stream at regular intervals – but to ensure that no one loses sight of where they are going. "I encourage people to think," he says. "They have to keep the core question in mind – not just the immediate problems."

Data Democracy

And the "core question" is a very big one, because it ultimately concerns the use of machines to interpret and understand the real world. The road to that goal begins with what is arguably Comaniciu's most far-reaching patent – a mathematical invention called Robust Information Fusion, which boils down to a novel way of detecting and weeding out questionable information from any given data source. The result is a kind of data democracy in which bits and bytes from different sources can be merged seamlessly into a single stream of information. What's more, since Robust Information Fusion is generic, it applies with equal effectiveness to improving the quality of data delivered by, say, an automotive radar-based distance control system, a smart surveillance camera or an ultrasound transducer.

Robust Information Fusion is based on the principle that each measurement that a sensor produces comes with a level of uncertainty. Engineers and mathematicians had been wrestling with the question of how to statistically weigh uncertain information. But no one could come up with a system that could robustly deal with both the variability of data interactions – essentially how multiple sensors affect each other's output – and the thorny question of how to weigh "inliers" and "outliers" – bits of data that are statistically outside the normal parameters of a data set – until Comaniciu came up with his data fusion method. "What we have done," explains Comaniciu, "is to develop a statistical method that weighs the combination of different pieces of data to obtain an optimum result. This is the core of our discovery. Essentially, the output of each sensor can be characterized statistically."

Experts in the Algorithms

Comaniciu is using Robust Information Fusion to pave the way to the next logical step toward machine-based interpretation. "Once you have reliable data that can be fused, you can develop expert systems to evaluate it and draw conclusions from it," he says. The idea is called "database guidance," which, quite simply, boils down to translating the knowledge of experts into algorithms that can support human decision-making in areas as different from one another as medical diagnostics and driving a car. "A very realistic picture of the future," says Comaniciu, who earned a PhD in data compression in Romania before moving to the U.S. in 1996, "is that in a few years you'll be able to go to a general practitioner, have a body scan, and a full-color, anatomically clear image will come up on the screen, complete with values for each part of your anatomy and highlights on anything that may be of concern."

The first step down that road has already been taken. It's called "Auto EF" – a unique database-guided program based on a Comaniciu patent that can be used in the context of an ultrasound examination to automatically measure the heart's ejection fraction (EF) – the fraction of the total volume of blood in the heart chambers when the muscle is relaxed (diastole) that is pumped in a single beat. "Today," says Comaniciu, "this crucial measurement is either estimated or determined manually. An expert needs a couple of minutes to do it, but it takes the software two seconds to do the same thing."

Coming up with a breakthrough like Auto EF is no easy matter, though. "There were times when one or two months would go by without any progress," recalls Comaniciu. "But those are the times you keep your chin up and say, 'We are Siemens. We can do it!'" A big part of "doing it," he adds, is motivating his team: "You have to be innovative. You have to think out of the box. However, as a manager you have to learn to care for your people and to stimulate and enthuse them. To accomplish that, it's essential to be committed. Personally, I strongly believe that the technologies we've been developing can make a real difference in people's lives. This is not always obvious. But when you're in a children's hospital and you see those little kids, you become very motivated."

Perhaps the largest program Comaniciu is involved in is called Health-e-Child. As head of the science committee guiding this four-year effort, he envisions the development of a biomedical information platform that integrates data from genetic, clinical and epidemiological sources. The program focuses on pediatric heart diseases, inflammatory diseases and brain tumors. Following up on another one of his patents, Comaniciu's team is working on other programs that will accelerate key ultrasound tests in obstetrics in a similar fashion. They are also involved in longer-range projects to develop databases that will eventually support automated identification of colon cancer, prostate cancer and autism based on magnetic resonance scans.

Transforming Information into Knowledge

"Robust Information Fusion holds the promise of turning database-guided systems into a major, mainstream service supporting virtually every field of activity," says Comaniciu. "For instance, in the autism project it will be used to combine and interpret molecular information and neuronal information taken from MR scans."

According to Comaniciu, who is married – his wife is a professor of wireless communications – and has a five-year-old daughter, the market for database-guided systems is large and increasing. "Automatic, accurate data analysis has ramifications in all domains – from the merging of data from magnetic resonance and ultrasound with general patient records to the identification of surface anomalies on turbine blades in the power generation field and the merging of data from cameras, radar and other sensors in the automotive area in order to improve automatic driver assistance systems," he says.

Naturally, these fields are not going to go from zero to sixty overnight. Developing the database that allows a system such as Auto EF, for instance, to recognize the perimeter of a beating heart in real time from fuzzy ultrasound images is a significant challenge. To do so, top cardiologists must invest hours viewing images and annotating them with information regarding how they interpret them. With this in mind, Comaniciu's team, in collaboration with Siemens Corporate Technology, plans to establish a center of competence in Bangalore, India, to focus on developing software tools designed to simplify annotation in the field of database-guided medical diagnostics.

Formula for Ideas

Database diagnostics and breakthroughs in Robust Information Fusion are what Comaniciu refers to as "powerful science" – that is, science that can unleash new applications across the board. "Most of the time," he says, "innovation is defined as developing something new. But it is also possible to bring about fundamental scientific discoveries by combining existing solutions, and with enough of a push it is possible to bring them forward to the extent that they make a real difference across a spectrum of technologies." He adds, however, that one of the crucial elements in such success stories is communication. "First, you have to be able to convince management. Second, you have to be able to connect with your customers. Third, especially for a team like ours that has members in the U.S., Germany and India, you have to get the researchers to communicate with one another. They have to be able to do that in order to learn from the group experience and from mistakes."

How does powerful science get started? "Naturally, you first have to develop ideas to the point where they achieve critical mass, in order to get innovations moving," says Comaniciu. "In this case, some of the ideas came from my own background and some from our research. My own formula for developing ideas is quite simple. It involves understanding the current state-of-the-art and asking how we can go beyond it." He adds that his department has a core of very strong scientists "and we develop many ideas here that come from brainstorming and from a culture of innovation. We have several departments that have been developing complementary technologies and that interact synergistically. So we can combine the best from all the different areas."

Manager's Tightrope

But achieving top results isn't just a question of top science. Every new idea has to be sold. Every concept has to be proven. And every operating company that makes an investment in a new technology has to be convinced that its customers will want what it has to offer. Once money is committed to a project the real pressure begins. Deadlines are set and milestones have to be reached. "People come to me and say 'It's not possible,'" says Comaniciu, "And my response is: 'Try it again!'" Comaniciu, 42, who has had 13 patents granted and has more than 70 additional patent applications to his name, received Siemens' "Inventor of the Year" award in 2004. His motto is simple: "Never take no for an answer." In his opinion, a degree of stubbornness is essential to push forward anything new, and as a manager one has to walk a tightrope. "You have to have a plan and know how to stick to it. But you also have to brainstorm, leave room for creativity, have fun, and know how to convince your team that they're doing something that will help society," he says.

Dealing with the unexpected is one of Comaniciu's biggest challenges. He handles it by implementing what he calls a "paranoia pays" strategy. "You always have to consider the worst possible outcome. That's the only way to stay ahead of the game!" he says with a grin. All in all, it can be a long road from vision to polished product. But when all the lanes are heading toward a single far-sighted objective that holds the promise of transforming the relationship between data and knowledge, you might feel like driving day and night.

Lessons learned	Dorin Comaniciu's advice for innovators
• Push the limits.	• Think outside of the box.
• Never take no for an answer.	• If you develop systems for healthcare, visit a children's hospital and you will be motivated.
• Prepare for the worst.	
• Remember that innovation is never a straightforward process.	• Convince your team that they are doing something that will help society.
• Never forget that innovation is fun.	• Encourage scientists to talk with each other. That's one of the best ways for them to learn from mistakes.
	• When in doubt, remember one thing: We are Siemens. We can do it!

"Comaniciu is one of the true visionaries, the people who can inspire their teams and motivate them to work together toward a common goal," Stacey sums up. "And he too repeatedly stresses thinking outside the box and perseverance, which a visionary's got to have to succeed." "Right," says Christian, "but isn't 'Never take no for an answer' also a risky motto to live by? I know a few colleagues in my division who also take this approach. They have lots of ideas and aren't too concerned about what we in management have to say. If one of their ideas is rejected by my colleagues and me on our innovation committee, which allots funding for projects, they try to covertly continue work on the idea in the form of a 'submarine project'."

"Well, granted, it's important to be prudent with funding, but I also believe that an innovator can't simply throw in the towel at the first sign of an obstacle," adds Walter. "That's where I feel a good innovation process is helpful, one that makes it possible to continually review decisions," John says. "It's true that there can be very good reasons at any given point to stop a project and to cut off funding for it. But if new, pertinent information emerges, it should be possible to resume it at any time. Just consider the 'three-liter car.' Let's say it's being developed at a time when the market demands vehicles with three liters of displacement instead of three liters of fuel consumption. It wouldn't be a success. But if fuel becomes very expensive, and everyone's talking about sustainability and environmentally friendly cars, the project has to be revived."

"So 'Never take no for an answer' should motivate people to find good new arguments for projects?" asks Stacey. "Exactly," John replies. "And innovators often find such arguments by observing the market." "If a major customer says 'That's exactly what we need,' the organization will be won over. That's why innovators also should combine their ability to develop ideas with a certain degree of salesmanship." "That's exactly what Comaniciu means when he points out the importance of communication: motivating colleagues and employees, not losing sight of the goal and convincing management – that's what is crucial for success."

"I agree," says Walter. "In particular, I think emphasizing teamwork is one of the most important keys to success. Without a good team, it's nearly impossible to develop market-ready innovations these days. And that brings to mind a good example from an entirely different field – rail technology. It shows that when trying to move a visionary idea forward, it can even pay off to recruit a brilliant team leader from outside, even if he's never worked in the field in question..."

New Momentum for Trains

Friends sometimes just smile and shake their heads when he gets on his bike in the sweltering heat and pedals 200 kilometers across the Swabian Alb in eight hours. Or when he's struggling over mountain passes on the way up the Alps with his mountain bike. Dr. Lars Löwenstein calls this sort of relaxation "actively unwinding." It's his way of putting some distance between himself and his work, which he says also involves plenty of "drive." Löwenstein, 32, has been working at Siemens Transportation Services (TS) in Erlangen, Germany, for three years. During that time, he's been running "a project worth ten million euros, which makes it currently the most expensive R&D project at TS." The aim of the project is to build a unique drive system for trains.

The revolutionary concept is called "Syntegra," and a team that sometimes included as many as 80 members participated in the project. Löwenstein is the head of the team that got Syntegra up and running – from the first drafts on paper to the finished prototype. Syntegra was designed as an underfloor system. In such systems, all the drive machinery is installed under the vehicle floor and control cabinets in the cars are eliminated, leaving more room for passengers. In late September 2006 at the trade show InnoTrans, TS presented the invention – the innovative chassis concept which fully integrates gearless drive, bogie and braking technology – to the public for the first time.

And the premiere had a sensational impact. After all, Syntegra turns the established technology completely upside down. Conventional underfloor drives are all similar in design. A transmission conveys power to the wheel axles, which rest on one of the two bogies under the car. But in addition to being a source of

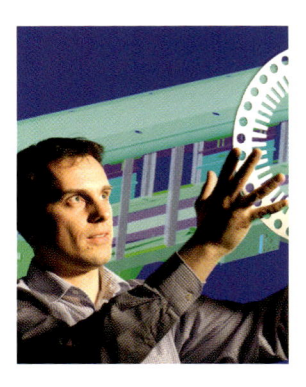

Before **Dr. Lars Löwenstein** came to Siemens, he developed innovative concepts for cars and aircraft; he didn't know a lot about trains. But the young electrical engineer was nevertheless entrusted with a major project: the development of a new drive system for trains. In only three years, he and his team succeeded in building a prototype vehicle with this new drive – the revolutionary "Syntegra" system.

unpleasant noise, the gears and couplings are subject to wear, require maintenance, and occasionally need to be replaced. But that's no longer the case, thanks to Syntegra. The cylindrical electric motor rests like a ring on a finger directly on the drive axle – the wheelset axle. There's no longer any wear and tear. The motor uses a permanent rotor magnetic field generated by permanent magnets, which are based on high-energy magnets that contain rare-earth materials and have recently become economical to use. Motors of this type are designed in such a way that they develop a large torque even at very low speeds. A transmission is unnecessary.

Optimizing Mechanical Parts and Electronics

The benefits – higher efficiency and lower energy consumption – are possible because the motor power is transmitted directly to the axle. The weight decreases as well. In the case of the prototype vehicle, it's reduced from the usual seven metric tons per bogie down to only five metric tons. A standard car with two bogies is thus four metric tons lighter, which also saves energy. But Syntegra is more than that; it's an exceptionally compact, light and efficient mechatronic system that for the first time fully integrates bogie, traction and braking technology. "In the past, these components were developed almost in isolation from one another, and each was optimized for itself," says Löwenstein, explaining the difference between the new technology and classic technology. "With Syntegra we have achieved an optimum system for the first time."

When Löwenstein came to Siemens in 2003, he was venturing into uncharted waters. Until then, the electrical engineer had been working as a scientist at the Institute of Electrical Machines at the RWTH Aachen, where he completed his doctoral thesis and worked on several cooperative projects with industry partners. The companies defined the objectives and contributed the funding, while Löwenstein took responsibility for the technical development. Their efforts resulted in a maglev (magnetic levitation) system for luggage transport, an electrical starter generator for cars – and even a variant for fighter planes. "But I didn't know a thing about trains," Löwenstein says. "I knew the difference between the front and the back, but that was about all." Impressed by his project experience, however, TS decided to entrust the pragmatic newcomer, who was then 29, with the project manager's job. Although his employees still answered to their own separate departments, Löwenstein was responsible for coordinating their work, distributing assignments and ultimately for realizing the Syntegra concept. For Löwenstein, Syntegra was "the most interesting project I could imagine" – and one with a budget larger than that of any undertaking he'd ever worked on.

By the time Löwenstein came on board, the funding had already been approved, costs had been estimated and a rough schedule had been worked out. He needed two months to familiarize himself with the subject and "find his feet." His first job was to create a detailed schedule and to formulate requirements – the "basic parameters." With the essential features of the Syntegra concept already clear, Löwenstein had to define how the plans on paper would be converted into a vehicle of steel. "In a train, for example, axle load is one such characteristic parameter," explains Löwenstein, referring to the load that each axle exerts on the track. A train has many parameters of this sort – and they first had to be established.

Even the technical departments assisting him were chosen by Löwenstein himself. At this point in the project, though, a team didn't yet exist – aside from the five most important developers. Löwenstein brought together the right employees from four different business units – specialists from the unit Vehicle Electrical Systems and Vehicle Mechanics in Erlangen, engine experts from Automation and Drives in Nuremberg, bogie developers from Siemens TS Austria in Graz and, finally, railcar body specialists from Krefeld and Vienna, Austria. "It wasn't easy," he adds. "After all, people have enough to do in their own units, and they can't be withdrawn just like that for a new project." At that point, the only certainty was that the Mass Transit division would support the work: The plan was to create a prototype of a subway vehicle based on the new Syntegra drive.

Purveyor of Ideas

Although the funding had been given the green light, Löwenstein initially had to win support in the company for his ideas. "That was one of the main tasks at the beginning," he recalls. One of his strengths, he says, is his ability to sell – to make a presentation. "I definitely wouldn't want to work at a car dealership, but when it comes to using information to win people over, that's something I do well," he says. Löwenstein quickly learned that you have to be communicative in a large company, and approach people on your own initiative. "Otherwise you and your project are steamrollered by big contracts involving tremendous numbers of production units." Another crucial aspect is winning over non-specialists. Business-oriented colleagues, in particular, sometimes don't see the sense or the necessity of a technical innovation.

At first there was nothing more than ideas on paper, so gaining support was initially difficult. "In a situation like that, you have to be able to get people excited about an idea. Nothing can be substantiated or verified. There's no reliable data on hand." Löwenstein succeeded in bringing Stadtwerke München on board as an external partner – a company that has the infrastructure and staff needed to test the prototype under everyday conditions. Soon, the first Syntegra vehicle will begin operating in trials on the tracks of the Bavarian capital.

The Syntegra idea is particularly appealing because of its elegance. The gearless approach is new, and so is the brake concept, which Löwenstein developed himself with help from a colleague. So far, the new brake has led to six patent applications. Trains generally have two independent braking systems – an electrical system and a mechanical system that intervenes if the first system fails. Like the transmission, the mechanical brake is a wearing part. It's also an assembly that TS has to buy in. From the beginning, TS planned to use the new drive as a brake, too. The magnets inside the motor are "permanently excited." In other words, they are permanent magnets instead of electromagnets. That makes them failsafe, and they can be used as a reliable electric brake. In an emergency, the drive brakes much like an eddy-current brake, eliminating the need for an additional mechanical backup brake.

Löwenstein's job proved to be the "classic project manager role" – coordinating various aspects and fitting them together. However, he also assumed responsibility for developing the alternative brake, which gave him an opportunity to do some "private tinkering." "Here, I was playing the role of the developer rather than the manager." As far as Löwenstein is concerned, that was the best part of the job. "I'm not someone who enjoys solving the one-hundredth mathematical integral. I'm a good mixture of a theoretician and a practical person. For me, it's important that the final result really works."

Thanks to the brake, Syntegra features three key advantages: The bogie is compact (nearly a meter shorter than conventional bogies), has no transmission and dispenses with a full-fledged mechanical brake. "That's a world first," says a confident Löwenstein. "To date, no one else has developed such a comprehensive solution." He estimates that the Syntegra system puts TS two to three years ahead of the competition. Löwenstein and his colleagues believe that Syntegra has what it takes to replace much of the established technology. Syntegra is suitable for not only subway trains but also for regional and high-speed trains, so the drive specialists expect a market volume in billions of euros. Together with the Trains division, Löwenstein is now developing the first regional train concepts. Syntegra is so versatile because the developers always had series production in mind. From the beginning, they designed the system in such a way that it can easily be modified for a variety of applications.

A Pragmatist's View of Perfection

Löwenstein says that he's good at structuring things and analyzing them. But he's obviously also a pragmatist. He spent innumerable hours in the shop hall with the prototype vehicle, gradually getting to know the system better and better. "Hands-on experience enables you to understand a lot of things much better than you can on paper," he says. Löwenstein knows that engineers will optimize many details of his innovation in the future. "You never reach 100 percent," he says. "You can't push an

Lessons learned	Lars Löwenstein's advice for innovators
• It's not a good idea to try to push an innovation to perfection. If you do, you miss the right time to launch it on the market. The first 80 percent of an invention comes quickly, and the next ten percent takes an equal amount of time. You can't ever reach 100 percent. An innovation can always be developed further.	• Contacts of all kinds are important if you want to get your idea established.
	• You should be communicative and show interest. You'll only be noticed if you actively seek contact.
• If someone says, "we've always done it like that," you should think things over carefully before following this advice. On the one hand, it may be based on valuable, longstanding experience; but it may also indicate a short-sighted attitude.	• A good presentation is the key to success. But it should always be adapted to the audience. If you bore non-specialists with technical jargon, you won't achieve anything.
	• A clear sketch often says more than 1,000 words.
• Similar tasks have similar solutions. To work out a problem, you should learn from other disciplines. Sometimes there's already a solution in another field that can be applied to your own work.	• You should listen to non-specialists, because naive questions from outsiders sometimes confront you with the heart of a problem. You might find yourself thinking: "We never looked at it that way."
• An idea that you have today is outdated in two to three years at most.	
• You should always be prepared to sell your idea once more – and enjoy doing it. Otherwise it can't be a success.	

innovation to perfection. You have to be able to let it go. If you keep on making improvements, sooner or later you miss the right time to put your invention on the market." Tackling things head on, making decisions, moving things forward – that's Löwenstein's way. Bureaucratic obstacles, such as complicated billing statements and time-consuming applications, often make him very frustrated.

But overall he's very content. The Group management supports the project, says Löwenstein, and Syntegra is held in high regard there. He also knows that you have to fight much harder to get funding for smaller projects. "I have great freedoms here that make the work easier – and enjoyable." Löwenstein, a native of the Sauerland region of Germany, and his wife live not far from Erlangen, where the couple feel at home. The city offers everything you need, he says, and neighboring Nuremberg also has a lot to offer. Löwenstein rides his bike 25 kilometers to work almost every day. But he doesn't consider that anything special. "I have a coworker who rides 35 kilometers to work each day – 35 there and 35 back," he says. Without a doubt, Löwenstein is impressed by this performance. Maybe because he knows better than anyone that being a top performer pays off.

"That's an extraordinary story of innovation," says Matthias. "A 29-year-old university researcher is hired right off the bat to supervise a ten-million-euro project, and to develop an innovation in a field he hadn't worked in before at all?" "Yes it is, isn't it?" replies Walter. "Maybe it was precisely his uncluttered view and fresh approach that brought the whole thing to a successful conclusion. Maybe someone who'd been part of the organization for a long time would have seen too many hurdles, which Löwenstein then cleared like a champion athlete."

Bao Jun smiles at Walter's sports metaphor. "Löwenstein's courage in taking on this challenge – and management's courage in entrusting it to him – are definitely admirable," he says. "And did you notice that he also stresses the importance of communication and the ability to 'sell' an idea – especially when it was time to put together a team of employees from entirely different departments and find a lead customer. What's more, he tackled this challenge with ideas that only existed on paper?" "Yes," agrees Walter, "the vision really has to inspire confidence – and the person who presents it has to exude charisma and strength." "And," adds Matthias, "the customer utility has to be clearly recognizable. I know another story about a Siemens researcher who succeeded in having his invention applied in very different fields – from face recognition to hearing aids and automotive technology..."

Christian looks at the clock. "It's late – but I think we have time for one more story," he says. "Let's hear it, Matthias!"

The Colors of Success

On the wall outside Frank Forster's lab in Munich hangs a poster of a young woman with horizontal colored bars projected across her face. It's an unusual image that inevitably invites questions. When answering them, Forster, 32, is plainly in his element. He tells the story of color-coded triangulation, a process used to scan 3D surfaces, which he developed as a young researcher at Siemens, and which would subsequently provide the cornerstone for a range of new products. For Forster, it was a dream come true – even if it took some time to get there. Forster had already tried out a number of different avenues after graduating from high school. He first started a chemistry program, only to give it up after a few weeks and change to a computer science program at the University of Würzburg, Germany, where he also did a couple of semesters of math. He then went to the U.S., where he gained an MSc. in New York and, at the height of the dotcom boom, took on a job at a renowned Internet consulting firm in San Francisco. This experience demonstrated the disadvantages of a purely academic career and persuaded him to focus instead on challenging practical problems whose solutions can be quickly translated into useful products.

In 2000, Forster joined Siemens Research as a doctoral student. His project was to develop a process to scan 3D surfaces accurately, quickly and cheaply in real time. This project was itself part of a Eu-

As a doctoral student, **Dr. Frank Forster** developed a process called color-coded triangulation, which is used to scan three-dimensional surfaces accurately, quickly and cheaply. This has turned out to be the basis for a variety of new products, ranging from a 3D face-recognition system to Siemens' iScan, which is used to precisely fit hearing aids.

ropean research project titled "High-Speed 3D and Colour Interface to the Real World." After investigating a range of approaches, he eventually settled on the well-known principle of structured illumination: Here, a pattern of light – for example, a strip pattern – is projected onto something, while at the same time a simple digital camera takes a picture of the object thus illuminated. If, for example, the object is a face, the forehead, cheekbones, nose and chin will deform the strip pattern, thereby creating an image unique to the person in question. An image processing algorithm then uses this deformation pattern to reconstruct the spatial structure of the object. The calculation of the three-dimensional form is made in accordance with the simple geometrical formulas of triangulation, which takes into account the distance between the projector and the camera, the angle of observation, and the position of each pixel. This method of structured illumination itself wasn't new – but the procedures that existed for it at the time were associated with practical disadvantages.

Forster therefore developed color-coded triangulation within a period of just a few years. The light pattern in this technique consists of several hundred parallel color strips, which can be generated with either visible or infrared light. The color strips here are precisely arranged either spatially or temporally according to a predefined rule. This enables the system to clearly and reliably register each individual strip and monitor its deformation. The process functions so well that the computer doesn't have problems later analyzing areas of discontinuity, such as the tip of a nose. Another advantage of the new procedure is that it's similarly precise as previous techniques – but much faster. For example, it requires only a single video image (i.e. a practically realtime recording) to determine the three-dimensional shape of a face with a measuring point precision of 0.3 millimeters. The new method is also less expensive, as the color strips can be generated using a simple color slide, and the calculation process is not particularly complex.

Facial Contours

A prototype 3D face-recognition system was soon ready for use (see Siemens' *Pictures of the Future* magazine, Spring 2003, www.siemens.com/pof). The timing was very appropriate, given that security concerns were in the global spotlight. This innovative new technology radically improves traditional recognition methods utilizing color or black-and-white images, as it takes the three-dimensional shape of the face into account. Unlike a photograph, the shape of a face is always the same, irrespective of lighting or head position. It is also extremely difficult to replicate. In order to exploit this technological advantage as swiftly as possible, Siemens Building Technologies, Corporate Technology and ViiSAGE Technology Inc. (now L-1 Identity Solutions), the global market leader in the field of personal identification, signed a cooperative agreement.

Soon, however, the method of color-coded triangulation was being applied in other fields. In fact, while applying for the EU project, managers at Siemens had already recognized the possibility of further synergies. It seemed clear that due to rapid advances in video technology for the consumer electronics sector 3D recognition was destined to become increasingly powerful and cheaper, and would thus provide the basis for many more products. Before long, the next application was on the way. In collaboration with Siemens Automation and Drives, Forster developed an automotive production line system that precisely scans the alignment of the vehicle chassis by means of a 3D image of the turning wheels. On this basis, assembly workers can then accurately adjust the toe-in and camber of the wheels. This low-cost system, which was introduced on the market in the fall of 2006, has a wide range of applications in the workshop and promises to generate a high business volume. Automakers like BMW, DaimlerChrysler and Porsche are already utilizing the solution. The third synergy application which Forster developed for Siemens Audiology Group involves hearing aids. Although the device in question is the smallest application for which the technology is used, it

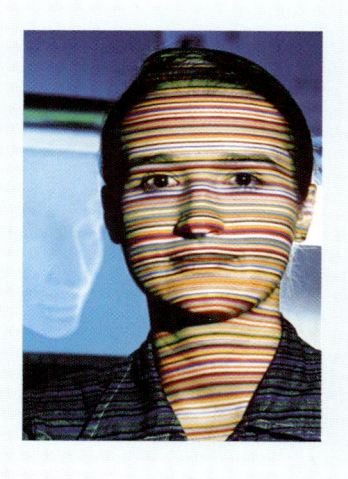

Enhanced security with biometric technology. Colored bars projected onto a person's face are deformed in line with facial contours. On this basis, it is possible to determine the precise 3D structure of a face, thus providing a fast and secure method of identification.

is also manufactured in the largest unit volumes. The unit in question is a handy 3D scanner that digitizes auditory canal imprints, such as those required for producing hearing aids that fit precisely in a person's ear. Here, the experts for hearing aid acoustics create a virtual 3D depiction of the imprint and send it via e-mail to the manufacturer. This procedure excludes the possibility of loss or damage to the auditory canal imprint – something that can occur if the imprint is sent via conventional mail. It also saves time and postal charges. Such a device is already being successfully marketed worldwide under the name Siemens iScan, and new products are now in the pipeline.

Recipe for Innovation

In Forster's case, the translation of the original idea into new products was made easier by the fact that the research topic was already prescribed in detail, which is unusual for a doctoral project. In fact, it had actually been broken down into concrete tasks with fixed deadlines – even though in Forster's opinion it's difficult to plan a research project. Having clearly defined milestones is certainly an incentive to work in a fast and focused way, he says, but innovations can only really be planned to a limited degree. In fact, according to Forster, it's an illusion to try and predict to within a few weeks when the best results will be produced. He also points out that very concrete parameters and tight deadlines are inevitably a hindrance to creativity. On the other hand, he readily concedes that an alternative approach is not really practicable in an industrial environment. There is no simple recipe for dealing with complex challenges of this nature, he says. The typical approach of the computer scientist is to break down a complex task into individual problems and then resolve them on a step-by-step basis: "This kind of systematic approach is often – though not always – applicable."

When it comes to translating research results into marketable products, Forster also points out the importance of being able to deal with the problems that inevitably arise. "With the right amount of patience and perseverance, these can almost always be resolved," he says. Here it's vital to recognize critical issues at an early stage, analyze them honestly and then tackle them head-on. On no account should this confrontation be put off. It's also important to try to deal with mistakes in a relaxed way: "They happen, and they're inevitable when you enter into uncharted territory." It's therefore wrong to be afraid of making mistakes, says Forster, since this only hinders the creative process. What is important, he adds, is to react quickly and to be frank with everyone involved. That's because everyone values an honest analysis of the situation and the accompanying risks, rather than an attempt to smooth over the problem. Forster admits that this can complicate dealings with managers, who always expect an immediate solution with a clearly defined timetable for every unexpected problem. Such a response is not always possible when breaking new ground. Here, the only solution is to ensure as close and resilient a relationship as possible between all those involved and to encourage intensive communication. No one should be allowed to lose sight of the common goal, says Forster: to develop a great and innovative product.

The Importance of Staying Power

Forster's aim was always to take products from the original idea to mass production – and he was given the chance to do just that, even if it proved to be a laborious process. For Forster, new research is always

Lessons learned	Frank Forster's advice for innovators
• Innovations cannot always be precisely planned; but setting milestones and timetables does help to structure a project. • Even minor details and seemingly banal issues can endanger an innovative product; they should therefore be dealt with quickly and rigorously. • Persuasiveness, persistence and immense staying power are required to drive new developments forward. • Mistakes and problems are inevitable with new developments; the crucial thing is therefore to identify critical problems as soon as possible, acknowledge them openly and deal with them rapidly. • The workplace has a strong influence on the innovation climate; Siemens Corporate Technology is a good example of a positive innovation climate.	• Try to identify long-term technological trends and ways of profiting from them. • Break down more complex tasks into individual projects, each of which will then seem much less daunting. • Establish close contact with customers and business partners in order to understand their problems and requirements; should problems occur at a later date, you will still be able to count on a good and resilient relationship. • Think positive, be optimistic and don't be disheartened by problems, which are inevitable with new developments. • Problems should be analyzed honestly and tackled head-on, not deferred.

a big adventure, involving lots of fun. "But as soon as you have to turn your piece of pioneering technology into an everyday product, the fun factor starts to wane," he says. Taking care of all the details and painstakingly solving even the smallest problems is just not as fascinating as developing new ideas. As a researcher in industry, you therefore need staying power. "You've also got to be prepared to deal with topics such as large-scale production and quality assurance," he says. If you're not, an innovative product can easily founder on a minor practical detail.

With iScan, for example, the leap from the lab stage to large-scale production was by no means easy, because the development team was confronted with a host of new details. For example, tolerances had to be fixed for all the accessory parts in order to ensure that the shipped 3D scanner always has the same quality. Likewise, help was required to set up a production line to manufacture many thousands of the devices. Despite being required to work on tasks that Forster, as a researcher, regarded as untypical, he never lost sight of his goal: seeing his own ideas turned into products that benefit customers around the world.

The fire in the hearth has already burned down to the last few glowing embers as Matthias concludes his story. "It's just fascinating how one good idea can have so many different areas of application," says John. "Automotive technology, hearing aids, security systems ... in principle, Siemens operates in all these fields." "But in the case of 3D face recognition, we opted to market the technology with an external partner," Christian interjects. "And why not, if this means rapid realization of a very promising product?"

"Quite right," says John. "You can't afford to think too narrowly. Just go for the best solution. Did you notice, by the way, that in addition to having a good initial idea, Frank Forster also said that working in a creative team and good communications were major factors of success? Over the years, the very best inventors, innovators and visionaries also develop a talent for not only producing ideas but also for selling them, forging partnerships and alliances, and working in a team. As Osman Ahmed said, you can't achieve very much single-handedly."

"Well, John, you've certainly convinced me," says Walter, returning to the point where the discussion started. "Werner von Siemens would still be able to push ahead with innovations in our company today and to find kindred spirits. But he was more than just a good inventor with a compelling vision; he was also very determined. In fact, without his determination to build up something step by step, our company wouldn't exist today. In my opinion, innovation is about more than just realizing new products. Innovative processes are every bit as important. And that means optimizing produc-

tion processes, for example, so that new products can be manufactured as cheaply, quickly and flexibly as possible and to a reliable quality level. One of my colleagues is really great at that sort of thing. How about taking a walk during tomorrow's lunch break and reviewing a few examples of this kind of innovation?"

"Great idea. Let's do it! Well, goodnight everyone ... I'm just going to sit up for a while and think about the sort of innovations I'd like to realize over the next few years," says Stacey with an uncharacteristically pensive look.

Space for your own thoughts

What innovations would you like to realize?

Who might help you to achieve your objective?

What arguments could you use to convince management, partners and customers that your ideas will benefit them?

The Path Is the Goal

Process Optimization, Analyses,
Continual Improvements

*T*he golden sunlight falls on the trees in front of the Global Leadership Center. A gentle breeze is blowing the red and yellow leaves along the path. It's one-thirty, and the five managers and the consultant gather at the entrance. "Great to see you all," says Walter. "Why don't we take advantage of this beautiful fall weather and take a walk around the lake?"

He continues, "While we're walking, I'd like to tell you a story about an aspect we didn't really talk about yesterday. We often hear about technical innovations and successful new products, but we're rarely told about process innovations. For established businesses, one of the ongoing sources of innovation is to keep asking questions. How can we do things better? What can we leave out? Can we eradicate time-consuming processes that don't actually benefit the customer very much? In aviation, for instance, the no-frills airlines are cheap and growing rapidly because they cut out processes and other aspects that customers aren't prepared to pay for. Or what about direct banks, which operate without any actual branches? Process innovations are evident everywhere you look. A colleague of mine runs a large production facility in Germany. His story proves that you don't have to outsource to low-wage countries in order to be successful; you can produce goods in Germany at a very competitive price, too."

Factory of the Future

Huge production halls, office buildings, a cafeteria and a surrounding fence – the Siemens Electronics Manufacturing Plant in Erlangen, Germany, looks much like any other large factory. Appearances can be deceptive, however. This is best exemplified by the large poster hanging above the entrance to Hall 42. Featuring the cover of Wirtschaftswoche business magazine from April 2004, the poster proclaims that this facility has received the "Best Factory 2004" award. A jury of specialists selected the plant as the best factory in Europe in 2004, citing the fact that its 1,100 employees work in a way that is often recommended by management books but seldom put into practice. Fractal factories, group work, flexible working-time accounts – "we've got it all here, and in most cases we were the first to implement these features," says plant manager Josef Röhrle. "Shut down" is a word Röhrle never uses. That's because it represents a step backwards. "We either continually develop further or completely reinvent ourselves," he says.

Röhrle, 57, worked his way up from the factory floor, learning on the job in a manner that few top managers today can match. After completing an apprenticeship as a precision mechanic – and acquiring a university entrance qualification along the way – he became an aircraft instrument mechanic in the German Armed Forces before moving to Siemens in 1973, where he developed software and hardware. Initially, he worked on control technologies for adjustment valves at power plants. Although Röhrle gained professional experience in this position, he felt it was not his calling – mainly because he saw himself as nothing more than a small cog in a big machine. What he really wanted was to be part of the big picture, with an opportunity to do something meaningful. This wasn't possible, however, until he moved to the automation sector, where he registered patents for many of his inventions during the almost 20 years he worked there as a developer. In addition, he served as director of the Hardware Center and eventually became manager of the manufacturing plant in Erlangen.

Innovation involves much more than developing new products. Optimizing production processes and working models can be just as important. **Josef Röhrle** successfully transformed a languishing production plant into a "Factory of the Year" and one of the Siemens Group's most profitable facilities.

His big break came in 1992. Back then the mechanical engineering industry was experiencing a major crisis. The Erlangen unit responsible for equipping machine tools was in the red, and it seemed that its Electronics Manufacturing Plant would have to be shut down. Röhrle fought to get a stay of execution, which enabled him to successfully implement his ideas. Today, the plant, which is part of the Motion Control Systems division at the Automation and Drives Group, posts sales of €570 million per year from the manufacture of numerical control and drive systems for machine tools, production machines and cranes. As one of the most profitable factories in the Siemens Group, it can be proud of its achievements. With a market share of more than 27 percent, the Motion Control Systems division is now the number one company in its business sector in Europe. In fact, it is competing head to head with its rival Fanuc to be number one in the world.

Intelligent Solutions instead of Hiring and Firing

These days, this type of success can normally be achieved only by transferring production to cheaper manufacturing locations abroad and by laying people off. That, at least, is the opinion of many managers Röhrle has met at industry seminars who boast about the job cuts they've implemented. Röhrle is unimpressed by their so-called achievements. "Hire and fire policies aren't particularly intelligent," he says, adding that no one gets fired at his plant, where the workforce is satisfied and the works council fully supports all the changes and innovations that are necessary in order to increase the facility's global competitiveness and thus safeguard jobs.

One of the instruments used here is an amazingly simple time distribution model. If there's a lot to do, everyone works a lot; if there's little to do, some of the employees stay home. Working-time accounts are allowed to fluctuate between minus 100 and plus 500 hours, with weekly working times ranging from 30 to 40 hours. The top priority here is the focus on customers, who ultimately determine when and how long employees work. If, for example, a customer has been told a component will be delivered on Friday, and it's not ready when Friday comes around, employees work on Saturday, even if that means they have to stay home on Monday. High quality, delivery reliability, just-in-time logistics and complete shipments, including invoices, are the reality in Erlangen – and not just empty promises.

Röhrle's success makes you wonder why everyone else hasn't long adopted his simple, successful approach. The answer is that many managers have – but with different results. The most important factor is the employees' attitudes, particularly with regard to their work: Röhrle only picks the best and most motivated applicants when he hires management staff, employing special selection methods and examining candidates' previous work experience and their degree theses. If someone with great talent applies for a job, Röhrle will hire him or her even if no position is currently available. "We're flexible here at Motion Control Systems," he says, though he also admits that in a large organization like Siemens bureaucracy can never be completely eliminated.

Thinking out of the Box

What does Röhrle regard as the most important trait a member of his staff should have? "He or she must be able to disagree with me." He doesn't like "yes people." But unfortunately, the business world is full of them. Often you have to conform in order to advance. "We need people who think outside the box and have unusual ideas and charisma," Röhrle says. He puts such people in teams according to the idea that the greater the differences in knowledge and personalities, the more suitable the team will be for the innovation process. Röhrle believes solutions are not generated primarily through research but instead through the sharing and communication of knowledge.

Individuals from different disciplines are not only more successful as a team; they also work much more quickly. In return, everyone – from managers to line workers – is given a high degree of personal responsibility and a say in decision-making. The goal is to have each employee submit at least five suggestions for improvements per year. Most of the ideas are implemented rapidly and contribute to productivity gains. Incidentally, on average the Siemens Group implements 1.1 suggestions per employee and year. That's nearly three times higher than the best level achieved by any other German company. The lion's share of the improvements and the resulting savings of €6 million to €8 million per year are realized using an extensive kit of methods used by interdisciplinary teams headed by a professionally trained moderator. The methods involved range from the "Ideamobile" to "2+2 Workshops" and "Six Sigma."

Röhrle – a father of two – also has plenty of ideas, the best of which come to him while he's riding his bicycle from home to the office, a distance of 35 kilometers. He does this almost every day because it clears his head. His trips by camel and Jeep through the Sahara and Negev deserts have had a similar effect, as have mountain climbing in Nepal and on Kilimanjaro, Africa's highest mountain.

Innovation Zigzagging

An idea by itself is not an innovation, says Röhrle, especially if its originator doesn't share it with others. Only after an idea has been transformed into a product – or in the case of the Electronics Manufacturing Plant, into a more efficient process – can it have a positive effect. Röhrle believes that an optimal innovation process in a factory like his should be a step-by-step procedure that doesn't just tolerate deviations but actually views them as productive.

In a similar vein, the shortest route to a mountain top is not always the fastest. The approach eventually taken depends on many factors. When it comes to the process of change at the Electronics Manufacturing Plant, a firm goal is always pursued. However, the only thing ever precisely defined is the very next step. The remainder of the journey is intentionally kept in a gray zone. In other words, the path is the goal. "If you don't give people freedom, you'll waste many ideas and miss the opportunity to achieve a much better result than you originally planned for," Röhrle says. The key is to gather experience as you move toward your goal and use the knowledge gained for the next step in the process.

Innovation proceeds in fits and starts. It's like a stairway with differently sized steps. The important thing is that each step is a step upwards. And a revolutionary step must always be followed by an evolutionary phase. Many people make the mistake of resting on their laurels after achieving a successful milestone, says Röhrle. But that's exactly when you have to look ahead, because if you stop getting better you've stopped being good. Röhrle therefore doesn't view innovation as a singular idea or a specific project; the process itself is the innovation. You have to be able to cope with failure and learn from it, because ultimately progress means standing up once more often than you fall down.

Röhrle also champions continuity – an attitude that doesn't necessarily contradict the idea of radical breaks in the innovation process such as those he has just described. "Changes only have a positive impact if they're designed for the long term." This is the key to the effectiveness of concepts such as the fractal factory – provided that they are applied correctly. Setting up autonomous teams – small factories within factories – is a good start, but you need to ensure that these teams will practice their individual responsibility correctly. You must be able to promote freedom and establish trust – in other words, let go and allow your staff to become entrepreneurs. If you can do this, cooperation will function well, even in crisis situations.

Support from the Managing Board

Like the ideal innovation process, Röhrle's career has also been marked by consistent upward movement. "I never had to fight for a new position – my superiors always had confidence in me," he says. In particular, Prof. Klaus Wucherer, the "automation pope" from Erlangen, had great faith in Röhrle. Wucherer, who is now a member of the Siemens Corporate Executive Committee, has always allowed Röhrle great freedom over the years. Perhaps this had something to do with Röhrle's ability to fire others with his enthusiasm – and the more innovative his ideas were, the more important this ability became. "You have to prepare the soil so that your seeds will sprout," says Röhrle. This works best when you share a good idea. And even if you already have a concept for a solution, you have to get your colleagues excited about the idea and not about the solution. Success doesn't mean having a good idea; it means being able to implement it – something that's best achieved when you have the support of many people. Employees must be part of the solution rather than part of the problem. This view is widespread at the Electronics Manufacturing Plant. The jury that handed out the Best Factory award especially praised the fact that employees are integrated into the problem-solving process. The Electronics Manufacturing Plant also won another multi-industry Best Factory benchmark competition in November 2006, making it the first plant in the world to win both competitions.

Röhrle has experienced at first hand the attitude that production plants are somehow less important than development and sales organizations. When he was transferred from development to production, many colleagues reacted as if he had been demoted. But he didn't feel that way. He says that Siemens still has a lot of people who understand how important production is as a core area of expertise, and that if you give it away, you'll have serious business problems at some point. Röhrle estimates that more than 80 percent of total manufacturing costs are today impacted by product design. However, whereas developers and production specialists used to waste time assigning blame, they now try to cooperate as much as possible. Moreover, anyone who gives up manufacturing will at some stage also lose control of development.

Other Siemens plants are now benefiting from Röhrle's knowledge and experience: In addition to frequently visiting plants throughout Siemens, he and his colleagues also make several trips a year to factories operated by other companies. Their mission here is to either learn from the best or pass on their own knowledge. Röhrle is convinced that the instruments and methods he has used successfully in production can also be applied in administration. "Order, tidiness, customer focus, continual performance measurements, continual improvement processes, lean processes and prevention of all types of waste – all these things can be taken for granted at our factory," he says. "Other Groups can learn from our experience."

Röhrle himself also continually discovers new role models that he seeks to learn from – for example, in the world of sports, where athletes are always looking for new techniques to improve their performances. Röhrle also looks up to Japanese companies, which have been the benchmark for optimal production processes since the 1990s. He says that while Siemens is equal to its Japanese counterparts in many areas, quality structures and continual improvement processes are more firmly anchored in Japanese corporate cultures. Röhrle is working hard to ensure "that alongside innovative products and processes, quality will become an unmistakable trademark at his plant." In honor of his achievements, Röhrle was presented with the newly introduced "Top Innovator" award from Siemens AG in December 2006.

Lessons learned	Josef Röhrle's advice for innovators
• Standing still is equivalent to stepping backwards. That's why you have to keep pushing forward on your own and not wait for market or management pressures to get you moving. • You don't need to constantly reinvent the wheel; other plants and businesses also have good ideas. A fair exchange of ideas benefits everyone. • Success doesn't mean having a good idea; it means being able to implement it – something best achieved when you have the support of many people. • You must give people freedom to act. If you don't, you'll end up wasting too many ideas and missing the opportunity to achieve a much better result than you originally planned for. • Requiring a high level of personal responsibility – for line workers as well – increases employee satisfaction and productivity. • A large company like Siemens must never relinquish its production expertise. Due to the close link between development and production, such a step would eventually result in the loss of development expertise as well.	• Lay the groundwork for new ideas and encourage extraordinary effort. • Surround yourself with people who think out of the box rather than those who say yes to everything, and set up creative teams. • Don't stigmatize employees as being part of the problem; make them part of the solution instead. • Knowledge shouldn't be abused as an instrument of power; you have to share it with others. • Everyone makes mistakes. That's why you should be tolerant of mistakes, learn from them and never repeat them.

Two joggers pass by at the shore of the lake just as Walter is finishing his story. One of the joggers is a lean, powerfully built middle-aged man; the other is a young, dynamic-looking woman with radiant eyes. Matthias grins after the two run by: "That's what I imagine Josef Röhrle's organization looks like – always on the move, not a gram of extra fat, and feeling fit and good about itself. It doesn't surprise me that he bikes 35 kilometers to work every day, has climbed Kilimanjaro and crossed deserts."

"I like that analogy, Matthias. Perhaps we should let athletes run our strategy projects in the future, instead of economists," Christian laughs. "The things Röhrle does correspond to the typical goals of many consulting projects," John says: "enhancing quality, increasing productivity and flexibility, and working continually on innovations. But sometimes implementation leaves something to be desired. For me, the key to his success is his credo that employees are part of the solution rather than part of the problem. He's popular among his employees because he doesn't opt for simple solutions like layoffs and transferring production to cheaper locations. They are given a great deal of personal responsibility and a say in decisions. In fact, as a hater of 'yes people,' he actually wants them to have the courage to disagree with him. He also puts together interdisciplinary teams. All of these things form the roots of a strong culture of innovation. If you punish people for mistakes, you end up with a rigid culture of error avoidance. But if the boss views failure as an unavoidable part of the process of change, there's no need to point fingers, and everyone can channel their energy into the next project."

"You're right, that's a lot more productive," says Matthias. "Definitely," says John. "Röhrle's right when he says that the process itself is the innovation. Other people often sit back and relax after a successful project – but not Röhrle. He's always finding new role models that he can learn from in order to get even better. We noticed that in one of the successful innovation projects we conducted, in which we discovered that the combination of the right methods and outstanding team spirit leads to success." "What exactly happened, John?" "OK, it had to do with Tim – who isn't a person, by the way. He – or it – is a revolutionary new technique for magnetic resonance tomography."

Revolution According to Plan – Whole-body MR Tomography

"Hi, Tim!" Robert Krieg must have been greeted with this remark hundreds of times. To some extent, it's his own fault. After all, he likes to wear an orange T-shirt that has "Tim" emblazoned on it. On occasions like this, he'll tell you that Tim isn't really his name but an acronym for a revolutionary technology that makes magnetic resonance imaging bet-

Dr. Robert Krieg is living proof that revolutionary inventions and sophisticated, precisely structured innovation processes aren't mutually incompatible. Thanks to his team's breakthrough in magnetic resonance tomography, Siemens was able to overtake General Electric as the world's number one in this area for the first time.

ter and faster. "Communication is enormously important in making an innovation successful," explains Krieg, who heads molecular magnetic resonance imaging at Siemens Medical Solutions (Med). Reversing this logic and judging by results in the marketplace alone, the MR scanners made by Siemens in Erlangen, Germany, must indeed be very innovative. Siemens has added enough percentage points to its market share, which was at that time below 30 percent, to overtake General Electric, the former market leader.

The main reason for these gains is Tim (Total imaging matrix) – the catchword that's become conspicuous on all sorts of related promotional materials (along with that orange color). This technology makes it possible to image a whole human body in less than a quarter of an hour, layer by layer, with a resolution of better than one millimeter. This is possible because up to 32 of the 102 selectable receiver coils can be used simultaneously to collect signals from the spinning nuclei of hydrogen atoms in the body. These signals can then be processed to visualize tumors and many other structures. This multi-receiver capability substantially shortens the exposure time and enables medical facilities to examine a greater number of patients.

Tim has revolutionized MR tomography. The process that allowed this technology to be envisioned, developed and marketed is also revolutionary. Nothing was left to chance. In fact, everything was done in accordance with a carefully worked-out master plan, making Tim a textbook example of innovation. "I'm a great fan of structured processes," admits Krieg. Now 42 and the father of three children, he studied theoretical physics at the University of Erlangen, then joined Siemens Med where he worked in several positions ranging from basic research to strategy and marketing before taking charge of the Tim project.

The Tim success story started in 2001. At that time, MR scanners of the prior model series were selling well, but it was clear – based on the usual five to seven-year product cycles – that a new model series had to be rolled out by 2004 at the latest. The strengths and weakness of the existing scanners were well known, as was the need to reduce costs by 30 percent. So what should the design of the new scanners look like? To help answer this question, an idea contest was launched among the development engineers. But in Krieg's view the results were quite disappointing. Typically, the proposals were limited to mere enhancements of existing systems – such as improving certain performance parameters – or to cost reductions in areas where savings had already been pinpointed. A great leap forward, particularly from a customer point of view, wasn't on offer.

Brainstorming at the Castle

The breakthrough came later in 2001 during a four-day workshop that brought together development engineers, customers and suppliers at Wernberg Castle near Amberg. Working intensively in teams, the participants networked ideas and discarded outdated concepts. Yet, as Krieg recalls: "On the second day, I still thought that nothing substantial was going to emerge." But the third day brought a breakthrough. It suddenly became clear how the cost of a signal channel could be reduced by two-thirds, and how this could make it possible to operate multiple channels simultaneously. Tim was born! Some people had originally considered the meeting's costs of around €15,000 to be money down the drain. However, the investment paid for itself many times over – a fact that was demonstrated by the rapid growth in market share that was soon to follow. Krieg isn't entirely sure what accounted for the breakthrough. Most likely it was a combination of several factors: The participants were able to put aside their daily business concerns, people who otherwise never met got to talk with each other, and the workshop brought together creative minds not only from within the company but also from the ranks of the suppliers.

The workshop also made a second vital decision. And according to Krieg, it was this decision that made the greatest difference: "We resolved to build nothing less than the world's best MR scanner." This might sound somewhat trite, because that's what every manufacturer wants to do. But this group of Siemens innovators was determined to back up their determination with a ground-breaking approach. Previously, the top priorities in planning a new MR scanner involved improvements to specific properties. For example, the aim might be "to build the MR scanner with the strongest magnetic field or with the fastest software." However, just as a more powerful engine and wider tires won't necessarily make a car better, mere technical attributes won't tell you whether an MR scanner will actually be the best tool for physicians and patients. Besides, the vision of building the world's best MR scanner is certainly more inspiring for the engineers involved than, say, "achieving a 30 percent cost reduction." At any rate, the new vision changed their focus from purely technical improvements to creating new benefits for the customers and the patients.

Ideas from Key Customers and Patients

After several refinements of the project plan, both the overarching goal and the underlying technology were given the go-ahead. In addition, the delivery date was scheduled for March 2004. But one open question remained unanswered: Was Tim really the best answer to the needs of physicians and patients? Tim might well be a technological milestone – but that on its own wouldn't persuade anyone to buy a machine which, with all its features, cost up to three million euros. An American marketing firm was therefore engaged to conduct a computer-aided survey of 300 customers. In addition, a series of workshops was held in conjunction with the Institute for Quality Management in Großbottwar (near Heilbronn) to learn the views and ideas of key customers in the US, Europe and Asia. Patients were also invited to express their opinions.

The resulting data were evaluated in a conjoint analysis designed to discern a kind of value system among those polled. This was done because it is usually difficult in such a survey to establish a clear-cut hierarchy of priorities. The requirements are typically interlinked in a much more complex tapestry. It's a little like selecting your next car. Ideally you might like a lot of engine power, but above a certain horsepower level, reason prevails and higher fuel economy becomes more important. Or, if your vehicle must accommodate three child seats, you might have to forget about the Porsche of your dreams. In the case of MR scanners, the relationship between the needs of the doctors and those of the patients are similarly complex and interdependent. Patients usually prefer a large bore size. However, such a feature might result in lower image quality. As well as confirming much that was already known, the results also revealed new information. For instance, although the limited bore size does tend to bother patients, it's the length of the tunnel that's most likely to make the experience very unpleasant. And when the patient is fitted with a head coil, which fits like a medieval helmet, the bore size no longer makes much of a difference.

A factor the engineers had previously underrated was the drumming noise generated by the gradient coils. Patients considered this to be at least as annoying as the limited bore size. Utilization management was also reassessed. This was partially examined by continuously analyzing scanners of selected customers – with their consent – using operational data that was transmitted automatically to Erlangen. In these studies, the engineers learned, for example, that doctors very rarely utilized the entire 50-centimeter field of view (FOV) and most often scanned smaller areas. But in the end, reducing the FOV – the horsepower of the new car – proved to be impractical. This was because most medical systems are ordered by purchasing agents – non-physicians – based on predefined capabilities. And since a 50-centimeter FOV has evolved into an industry standard, this specification has to be met by new models.

Whole-Body Scans in Minutes

In the next step of the development, requirements had to be converted into product attributes. Here too the team employed a tool that has since become widely used at various Siemens business units: Quality Function Deployment (QFD). This tool combines customer requirements and technical feasibilities within a matrix and assigns a calculated point score to potential product attributes. The results included the Magnetom Avanto MR scanner with up to 76 Tim coils, which can perform a whole-body scan in 15 minutes, plus other models such as the Magnetom Espree, which has 102 receiver coils, a 70-centimeter bore and a length of only 1.25 meters. The large diameter of the bore and its short length are very helpful in scanning very obese or claustrophobic patients. Tim has meanwhile become the platform on which an entire range of Magnetom systems are based.

Tim can scan several organs simultaneously without the need to reconfigure the coils. Since whole-body studies are not very common, Tim is mainly used to achieve shorter scan times or better-quality images. Today Tim also supports the much more frequent diagnostic use of 3D reconstructions. Users report that both the speed and the accuracy of their diagnoses have been improved enormously.

August 28, 2003 was a day to remember. At 11 p.m., Krieg became the first person to be placed into the new scanner's bore for a whole-body scan. A few days later, a touch of star power was added for the press when world-class swimmer Hannah Stockbauer took her turn in the scanner bore – an event that many newspapers and tabloids celebrated by publishing images of her internal anatomy (see page 201). Krieg still grins when recounting one aspect of the story. It turns out that the images of the heart and blood vessels in these pictures didn't really belong to the Olympic and world champion. Instead, images from Krieg's examination were pasted into the published version. But ultimately, there wasn't much alternative, given that nobody was going to inject sports star Hannah with contrast media.

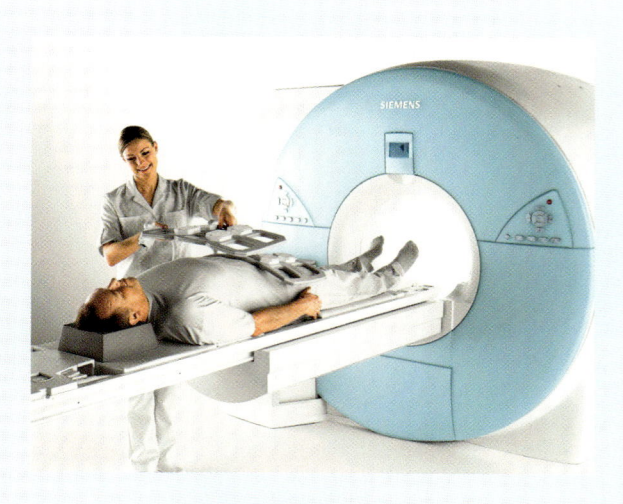

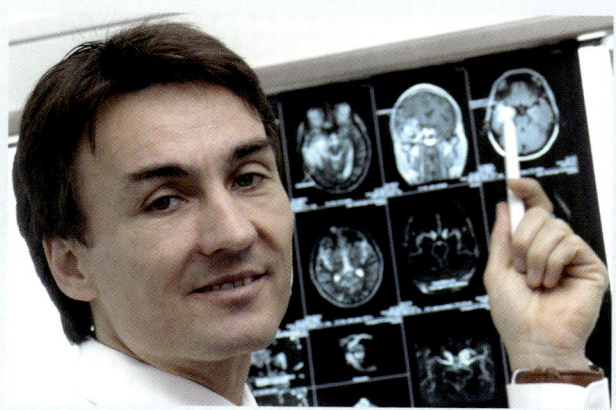

Tim technology. Body coils placed directly on the patient provide better-quality MR images than ever before – and it's possible to scan several organs, or even the whole body, at the same time.

Structured Processes Save Time

The whole process from the initial development of the Tim concept to the finished MR scanner took three years – too long in the opinion of several in-house critics, who considered the cost of the conjoint analysis and the Quality Function Deployment a waste of money. Krieg disagrees completely. "The structured processes ultimately saved us time," he says. He's also a great believer in carefully recording all decisions. "Project managers and employees change," he says. "A few years down the road no one knows why a certain decision was made." Krieg himself has meanwhile taken on a new assignment and is now in charge of molecular imaging with magnetic resonance processes.

The use of a highly professional communication approach also contributed to Tim's success in the marketplace (see also "The Yin and Yang of Innovation"). Early on in the development, test installations in medical centers produced the first clinical images, which were actually used to promote the system at a trade fair. The operators of these test systems were so enthusiastic that they offered to support the market introduction by giving presentations. In a new development, the system's benefits were described in the customer's language rather than in technical "jargon." For example, the marketing experts had fun with the acronym Tim: "Have you met Tim yet?" "Do you realize what Tim can do for you?" The trade press raved about Tim – as did the popular press. Even competitors started using the term, thereby unintentionally helping to promote it. As a result, Siemens gained recognition not only as an innovator but also as a trendsetter.

Getting the Green Light

Intensive internal communication meanwhile helped to keep the team's hundred or so members on the right track during the lengthy development period. One internal tool was the monthly "Traffic Light Check." At these meetings, each working group had to evaluate its own progress and report its findings to the executive management. Sometimes intense arguments had to be resolved. After all, it wasn't always easy to establish if a working group's traffic light was green (everything on track), yellow (behind schedule but still manageable) or red (impending disaster). "Some situations required the use of subtle psychology," relates Krieg. "For example, what do you do when one particular working group declares that it has fulfilled its tasks to date, but other colleagues are convinced that it is going off track?" That's where the leadership qualities of Krieg and co-director Werner Friedrich were indispensable. Having two project leaders was in itself a novelty, but proved very advantageous: "He was an excellent sparring partner, and between the two of us we always managed to find good convincing arguments before discussing an issue with other colleagues," says Krieg. Yes, the project had had to overcome some crises, but Krieg considers the group members' solidarity exemplary to this day. A certain family spirit was also fostered by barbecue parties and breakfast meetings organized by an executive. Due to the time pressure, these occasions invariably turned out to be a mixture of work and pleasure.

The Traffic Light Check had another benefit. It attracted the attention of senior management. At these monthly meetings, divisional managers were able to see for themselves that the group was working professionally and with dedication on a pioneering innovation that would pay major dividends for the entire company. Krieg believes that it was only possible to complete the entire Tim development project so quickly and without

Lessons learned	Robert Krieg's advice for innovators
• Offsite workshops and team-building measures can resolve an innovation dilemma. • In the early product definition phase it's important to include as many sources of ideas as possible. These may include customers, suppliers and even patients who have no immediate influence on the purchasing decision. • A structured process also makes it possible to define even very complex systems without weaknesses. • The use of tools such as QFD and requirement databases saves time and makes results more easily reusable. • A monthly "traffic light" review of the progress status with executive management fosters team spirit, makes it clear that each individual's contribution counts and supports efficient problem resolution by shortening communications paths.	• The initial project vision has to inspire employees to rise to the challenge. It's better to say "Let's build the world's best MRT" than "Let's achieve a 30 percent cost reduction." • Foster enthusiasm among participants, otherwise they won't deliver top performance. Every project needs to be marketed internally as well as externally. • Ensure a structured process and transparency so that employees and managers alike can fully understand how decisions have been made. • Include customers throughout the entire innovation process – in other words, from the first ideas to the marketing stage. • Make it clear to every customer what is novel about your innovation, and set new trends.

glitches because Siemens practiced a philosophy of developing highly innovative technologies in-house. Only a few components, such as the patient support, were built by a supplier. Competitive manufacturers of MR scanners, on the other hand, outsource as much development engineering as possible and consequently struggle to deal with enormous inefficiencies and longer development times. Krieg is convinced that what he calls "the Siemens approach" is one of the chief reasons why the company has increased its technology lead in MRI to at least two years.

In the end, the great endeavor has paid off. The goal of building the world's best MR scanner has been achieved. All other previous models were partially characterized by a list of weaknesses. Such a list does not yet exist for the Avanto model series. Not surprisingly, customers are enthusiastic about the product. In fact, some of them actually insisted on helping to promote the Siemens MR scanner marketing campaign by acting as reference contacts.

Christian has listened carefully to John's tale. "I like this mix of clearly structured methods and pragmatic implementation. I'll start using the traffic light progress status review in our department too. The project reporting scheme we're using now is so involved that even I, as a business manager, can barely understand it. Using traffic light checks seems a lot simpler and more supportive of teamwork."

Walter agrees and adds: "What I find so fascinating in this story is how well revolutionary new ideas and a very structured approach go together. I guess it doesn't always have to be creative chaos that produces brilliant ideas." Christian laughs: "Well, after all, creative brainstorming gave birth to this idea too. But then Robert made sure that the revolution proceeded according to an exact plan, using the best innovation management methods available. It was a true textbook innovation, in which detailed customer surveys were conducted in advance. The results were also linked to what's technically feasible and underpinned with highly sophisticated mathematical analyses. And, of course, a thoroughly thought-out marketing strategy was employed from the very beginning."

"I've got another example of how to implement an innovation in a well thought-out manner," says Walter. "It's from an entirely different field – electric power transmission – and it demonstrates the cumulative power of small steps..."

Reactive Power Counts Too – New Solutions in Power Transmission

Most people would agree that a child's upbringing has a big impact on his or her career. Had this common knowledge applied to Michael Weinhold, a leading innovator at Siemens Power Transmission and Distribution (PTD) in Erlangen, Germany, he would now be working in the automotive industry. A native of Rüsselsheim, Michael is a descendant of several generations of Weinholds who worked for automakers. "However, as a schoolboy I wanted to learn about – and improve – other technologies as well," says Weinhold describing his early interest in innovation.

As it turned out, he wasn't destined for a career in the automotive industry. But he never lost his passion for making products and solutions more efficient, which accompanied him during his studies in electrical engineering. After just a few semesters at the University of Bochum, the young student was offered an assistantship by Prof. Manfred Depenbrock, holder of the chair in electrical power generation and distribution, who would later become Weinhold's dissertation adviser. The digital revolution of the mid-1980s brought great changes. The converter controls used in power engineering, which relied heavily on analog electronic circuits, were particularly affected. Huge development leaps were about to occur. At the same time, converter technology was being used in increasingly high output ranges and for new applications. Transistor-powered drive engineering, for example, was developing at a rapid pace. This was in fact the area Weinhold addressed in his master's thesis in 1988, focusing on variable-speed electric drives.

When it comes to understanding the world's power grids, few people can match **Dr. Michael Weinhold's** knowledge. In working to ensure a secure and reliable power supply, Weinhold doesn't only aim for great technological leaps, but also optimizes the efficiency of power transmission and distribution in small steps. His innovations in the area of power electronics have greatly helped to shape the products and solutions portfolio at the Siemens Power Transmission and Distribution Group.

As a young research assistant, Weinhold then got his first chance to work on a groundbreaking development in electrical engineering – and this time not only in the practical but also in the theoretical domain. Based on Prof. Depenbrock's preliminary work, the DIN standard 40110 was created to define power variables in polyphase systems, including the term "reactive power." Since then, this standard has become recognized worldwide and serves as a basis for further developments in electrical engineering – and not only in the field of power transmission and distribution. Weinhold's intensive study of reactive power gave rise to key questions that would have a formative effect on the engineer's subsequent research. Reactive power is power that is present in a power transmission line but doesn't involve the transmission of any active current. "Many textbooks and publications contain inadequate definitions of reactive power," says Weinhold. "The exact definition is given in DIN 40110." In AC grids, reactive power sustains the high voltage, and reactive power must be fed into the power grid in order for electricity to flow efficiently, particularly over long transmission distances.

Stable, High-Output Power Grids

To make power grids more stable and to increase their transmission capacity, Weinhold sought control methods for generating reactive power in these networks. "I wanted to find out how to improve the operation of power grids by using power electronics-based systems that generate the right amounts of reactive power," he says, recalling a main area of inquiry in his dissertation. Developments in power electronics coincided with advances in microelectronics. Both technologies are based on the material properties of silicon. Unlike microelectronics, in which bits and bytes are switched to transmit data, power electronics involves the flow of larger currents as a means of transmitting power. This technology's main advantage is that it can be used to convert current in a low-loss, maintenance-free manner (for example, alternating current into direct current). It is also associated with much higher efficiencies than the transformers that were prevalent until the early 1980s, or the mercury vapor tubes of an even earlier era.

In October 1993, the month in which he was awarded his doctorate, Weinhold began working at Siemens – and started an impressive career as an innovator. His first patents were registered in his early days at Siemens – and the first commercial developments followed quickly. The SIPCON (Siemens Power Conditioner) is a system for optimizing distribution networks. It serves as an active filter for preventing undesirable oscillations in the grid voltage, such as those resulting from short circuits. Weinhold was awarded his first patents during this period.

He also contributed many inventions – which would later be patented – to the development of FACTS (Flexible AC Transmission Systems). Using sophisticated power electronics, these systems can control one or more parameters in three-phase power systems. By making power lines more stable and controllable, FACTS enables operators to exploit the lines to their physical limits – in other words, to transmit more power via existing lines. FACTS systems thus improve the reliability of power supplies and voltage quality during transmission and distribution in a targeted manner. This is particularly important for not only interconnected grids – such as the European UCTE grid, in which cross-border energy trading is increasing – but also less well-developed grids, for example in emerging economies like that of India, which need a stable power supply to drive their economic growth.

Optimization instead of Quantum Leaps

The innovative FACTS technology is among the top products from Siemens PTD, with reference systems in all of the world's growth markets, including South Korea, China, India, Europe, North America and South America. FACTS is the product of a long series of small development steps in which Weinhold played a major role with his many patents. His formula for success is highly effective yet simple: "I don't aim for quantum leaps but simply try to improve things. I optimize, and that's what customers need in order to master the challenges they face." FACTS is a good example of this approach. After all, utility companies need to better exploit the capacities of their power grids. Companies that achieve this goal can avoid the need to build new overhead power lines. With his 130 patent applications, Weinhold, 42, made a vital contribution to Siemens PTD's success with FACTS, so no one was surprised when he was honored as one of Siemens' "1997 Inventors of the Year" for his work on this development project.

While still a boy at home, where sales statistics for new car models were often a topic of conversation, he learned there's no guarantee that an invention will be a good product or a market success story. For Weinhold, close observation of the marketplace is always the top priority when it's time to decide whether to move forward with an innovation. After all, there's certainly no scarcity of ideas for improving power supplies. In his approach to innovation, the electrical engineer always asks himself:

"How can power electronics-based products and systems be used to improve something?"

One answer to this question became apparent in the mid-1990s: by using direct current. Back in 1975, Siemens linked the Republic of South Africa and the Cabora Bassa hydroelectric power plant in Mozambique using the world's first HVDC (high-voltage direct-current) transmission system, which featured thyristor technology. By virtue of its physical possibilities – especially its minimal transmission losses compared to those of AC transmission – this technology is particularly well-suited for transporting large amounts of energy over longer distances. Twenty years later, advanced power electronics opened up new opportunities – in terms of increasing the efficiency of HVDC systems and the prospects of transferring the concept to distribution networks.

And so Weinhold – true to his belief in making things better and not just different – first developed a medium-voltage (1 – 52 kilovolt), electronically controlled system for DC transmission. This system – the Siemens Multifunctional Power Link (SIPLINK) – has practically no competitors on the global market for power transmission and distribution. SIPLINK can be used to link smaller interconnected grids with one another, or to couple three-phase power systems with different frequencies. Ships, for example, often have on-board power systems that operate at a frequency different from that available in their ports of call, which is why their enormous engines have to run while the vessel is berthed. That's an inefficient solution that also generates pollutant emissions. With SIPLINK, however, a ship's energy needs can be supplied by the port's power system. This system also makes it possible, for instance, to link the interconnected grids of smaller utility companies to one another, eliminating the need to purchase energy from another supplier at expensive peak rates. In other words, making better use of existing technology benefits customers.

Power for Metropolitan Regions

At the high voltage level, it became possible to use direct light-triggered thyristors – the core elements of the electronics – to greatly boost the performance and efficiency of direct-current transmissions. Thanks to this innovation, PTD customers can achieve low-loss power transmission over much more than 1,000 kilometers. This is an important step forward in terms of meeting the basic needs of entire regions or urban centers that use large amounts of power. Since 2003, for example, a 2,000-megawatt HVDC system has been supplying the industrial region around Bangalore in southern India with power from the Talcher power plant complex, which is located 1,450 kilometers away in the eastern state of Orissa. And since 2006, a 600-megawatt submarine HVDC cable link has been delivering environmentally friendly power from hydroelectric plants on the island of Tasmania to the Australian state of Victoria.

As the head of the Technology and Innovation department, Weinhold has been working since 2004 to ensure that all of PTD's new products and

Earthquake-proof installation. Gigantic thyristors (top) are converter valves that enable high-voltage direct current to be transmitted from Tasmania to Australia via the world's longest submarine cable link.

solutions satisfy current, and future, customer requirements. Achieving this feat demands good communication within the Group, which is operating in more than 70 countries. "In particular, the exchange of ideas with customers worldwide is essential," says Weinhold. "Innovations don't simply happen in a vacuum; they grow out of dialogue." This is why he ensures that as many PTD innovators worldwide as possible not only take part in trade fairs, exhibitions, congresses and customer workshops but also play an active role in shaping the scientific discussions. He also says that it's important for innovators to experience at first hand how the products and solutions are actually used in everyday practice. "That's how we get direct feedback from the customer. You find out very quickly whether or not a product or solution really deserves to be called an innovation. As a rule, this work at the customer's locations is a valuable stimulus for further developments."

International Networks

Weinhold himself sets a good example in this regard. As an innovator, he has overseen the start-ups of a number of FACTS and SIPLINK systems at various locations, including Seoul, South Korea, and Ulm, Germany. At the IEC (International Electrotechnical Commission), he is the German spokesman for the use of power electronics in power transmission and distribution applications. He is also active in leading power transmission industry associations and organizations, including CIGRÉ and the IEEE, as well as in a variety of working groups in the worlds of politics, business and higher education. His commitment is necessary because, just like in the field of communications, having a voice in establishing industry standards is also important in the energy technology sector. In addition to the leading role it played in developing IEC 61850, the communications standard for power systems, Weinhold's team is now working intensively on the "SR+" initiative, which calls for PTD to monitor and optimize standardization measures worldwide.

For this engineer with a passion for networking, innovation is not only a matter of products and solutions but also processes. His colleagues in the divisions who are responsible for research and development meet regularly for discussions and to stay up to date on the latest issues. "That pays off in many ways," says Weinhold. "We always know what's going on and we have been able to put together a number of cross-divisional collaborations." Subsequently, the latest developments are presented and discussed by a large group of participants at the annual Innovation Day. Weinhold has always regarded Dr. Jürgen Schloß, the president of the engineer's Group, as a role model, especially when it came to exploiting innovation processes. Schloß taught him to determine the essential factors of technological requirements and to rapidly implement needed measures.

Weinhold is convinced that power electronics will be a future focus of innovation activities: "This area holds the key to the further development of smart grids," he says. Here, he's referring – in a nutshell – to self-optimizing and self-repairing power supply grids that can precisely transmit energy supplies to where they are needed. What's more, such power electronics systems respond to short circuits by isolating parts of grids, ensuring that power outages are confined to small grid sections. Many of Weinhold's new ideas for using energy more efficiently occur to him when he's vacationing, for instance when he's hiking in the mountains. At present, he's contemplating several very concrete concepts for innovations, especially for low-loss power transmission. Although Weinhold isn't ready yet to reveal his ideas, one thing is certain – power electronics will be playing a very big role.

Lessons learned

- Every idea counts. New insights, regardless of how small or insignificant they might seem, can turn out to be important "building blocks" in the process of developing solutions.
- International projects require an international exchange of ideas.
- If they are understood and analyzed, even mistakes can lead to a positive result.
- In-depth discussions with customers are particularly important sources of ideas.
- A similar knowledge base among all development partners is a good foundation for success.

Michael Weinhold's advice for innovators

- Instead of always striving to discover the next revolutionary idea, try to achieve continual improvement.
- Wanting to make something better is preferable to trying to do something different.
- Being your own toughest critic boosts creativity.
- A network of innovators is the most fertile environment for an innovative idea.
- Don't forget to leave work behind in the evening – relax, maybe over a cold beer, and recharge your batteries.

"It's better to improve something than to always try to do something new – that's an interesting motto," says Christian after Walter has finished telling his story. "Exactly. Being innovative doesn't mean always coming up with a revolutionary idea," Walter adds. "Essentially, succeeding in consistently providing gradual improvement can bring customers just as much benefit as some great new idea. A key is being able to listen very carefully to customers and to develop a sense of what their problems are. That was a point that Weinhold emphasized. Working on site at the customer's location, the global exchange of knowledge, continually studying the market..."

"... and I heard about another interesting aspect for the first time here, something that I believe is crucial in many cases," says Stacey. "What was it?" asks Matthias. "Serving on committees that determine international standards. Professionals who take part in such activities often benefit by staying a step ahead when it comes to gaining access to valuable knowledge, and they can also contribute their own developments. This is true for a wide range of fields – for example, for transmission standards in mobile communications, the formulation of environmental regulations and, of course, power transmission."

The others nod in agreement. "Stacey has hit the nail right on the head," says Bao Jun. "Being active in standardization organizations is another important key to success. And by the way the recommendation to keep your ears open for the customer's needs reminds me of another good example ..." he says with a grin. "And here we can really take this motto quite literally – as it's about hearing aids."

All Ears for Customers

When asked to name his weaknesses, Torsten Niederdränk immediately says, "impatience" – especially when faced with communication problems. "I get fidgety if people don't speak up and say what they mean," he explains. Luckily, that's not the case today. Niederdränk is sitting in the students' area of Siemens Audiology Group (S.A.T.) in Erlangen, patiently telling us about himself.

He's no student, though. Niederdränk is the managing director of Siemens Medical Instruments in Singapore, and it's easy to forgive him for stealing a glance at his watch every couple of minutes. After all, he's only going to be in Germany for three days. This is where he came up with 55 inventions between 1999 and 2004, and applied for patents for them. And it's also where he turned a workspace for students into his own working area, because it was the first unoccupied desk he could find.

Occupation: inventor. It's not a profession that can be learned; instead, it's all about creative thinking. "Either you have an idea or you don't," Niederdränk says. And he's had plenty of them, the most recent being the development of the Acuris hearing aids, which are worn in pairs, one in or behind each ear. The two instruments communicate with each other via radio signals and exchange control signals. Let's imagine an Acuris user chatting to a friend at the corner of a busy street. The user wants to concentrate on the conversation, but he or she also needs to be able to localize passing cars without having difficulty understanding what the friend is saying. The signals received by the two hearing aids are continuously assessed and compared by special software. With the help of a decision matrix, the signals are synchronized in order to produce a three-dimensional sound experience for the user.

Torsten Niederdränk, managing director of Siemens Medical Instruments in Singapore, has often asked himself what he can do to make life easier for the hard of hearing. This question has been the inspiration for his 55 inventions to date, which are a key factor behind the success of the Siemens Audiology Group.

As Niederdränk explains how the Acuris series works, he walks over from the students' area to a conference room where all of the hearing aids supplied by the Audiology Group are on display, including the Acuris systems. We catch a glimpse of the child in the man as he enthusiastically explains all about the in-the-ear and behind-the-ear instruments and their specific features.

From Beer Testing to Hearing Aids

Niederdränk was born near Düsseldorf in 1967 and grew up in the Cologne area. Even from an early age, he was fascinated by anything to do with sound. "I started out by playing around with loudspeakers, but soon I wanted to go further," he says. After graduating from high school and completing his military service, he took a degree in electrical engineering at the Aachen University of Technology. One of his main areas of interest was technical acoustics, and in 1993 he submitted his doctoral thesis, titled "The Origin and Analysis of Acoustic Cavitation in Liquids."

It was during this period that Niederdränk came up with his first inventions. He was motivated by development cooperation with the Krautkraemer company, which is known for its solutions for nondestructive materials testing. One of his inventions was a highly dynamic ultrasound system for measuring the maturity of beer. "When freshly brewed beer matures, you get gas bubbles that reflect the sound waves emitted by the system," he explains. "So the reflected sound signal tells you how mature the beer is." Niederdränk also supervised a number of cooperation projects in other areas, including the automotive industry and in medical technology at Siemens. In September 1998 he applied for a position at the Siemens subsidiary S.A.T., because he wanted to "gain an insight into the field of audiology as well."

Niederdränk quickly became interested in developing hearing aids, and he still vividly recalls an occasion that was to make a great impression on him. A month after he started his new job, he attended a trade show for hearing aid acoustics in Nuremberg. "I was talking to a man who was hard of hearing, and he told me about his problem," Niederdränk says. "I suggested a few hearing aids that I thought might meet his needs. Two months later, he called and thanked me for helping him to lead a full life again." This experience spurred Niederdränk on and gave him the motivation to push ahead with his work.

Ever since then, Niederdränk has been asking himself how the hard of hearing can be helped in the most effective way possible. Direct contact with customers is a vital source of new ideas. "There's no point in hiding in your ivory tower," he smiles. That's why he founded Hörtech in 2001, following several years of cooperation between S.A.T., the University of Oldenburg, and other partners in the German city. Among other activities, this Center of Competence tests hearing aids on people who are hard of hearing. "One of the things we found out in tests is that diminishing dexterity makes it much harder for people to operate hearing aids as they get older," reports Niederdränk. Out of this finding, the first ideas for the Acuris series were born.

Shortcuts to the Ageing Process

Niederdränk even conducted tests on himself to find out how it feels to no longer have the dexterity that younger people take for granted. By donning a special suit, the 39-year-old "aged" 30 years in a matter of minutes. "The gloves I was wearing had Velcro fasteners on the fingers for simulating difficulties with fine motor skills," he explains. "I also had a pair of yellow-tinted glasses that made it harder to see. I became tired very quickly, and then I could really empathize with what it's like to be someone in our target group. It makes you think completely differently about what a hearing aid must be able to do." The end result of this experience was a fully developed version of the wireless hearing aid, complete with a remote control and automatically synchronized controls for the hearing aids in or behind the left and right ear.

Niederdränk's head of development was enthusiastic about the idea, and the go-ahead for initial tests was soon given. But it rapidly became clear where the first problems would be encountered: in incorporating a sender and a receiver into a chip that was small enough to be built into any type of hearing aid. Niederdränk and his colleagues on the development team knew how tricky this work at such a small scale would be, and some people believed it could spell the early end of the project. "Luckily, however, our supervisors were happy to let us experiment," recalls Niederdränk. "They were on our side and encouraged us to keep looking for solutions."

By "us," Niederdränk means himself and his first team member, who had been with him right from the start of the project. Rather than being discouraged by their colleagues' skepticism, they were spurred on to continue. Gradually, more and more people began to voice support for their work, and the growing team spent six months researching and developing a demonstrator, which they then presented to the management. "With that demonstrator, a relatively simple circuit arrangement that already consumed very little power, we made it possible for signals to be transmitted wirelessly over a distance of 12 centimeters," Niederdränk explains. "That was already nearly the distance from one hearing aid to the other." The executive managers were convinced, and gave the green light for further development.

It wasn't all smooth sailing, however. Unforeseen problems emerged often, especially at the system integration stage. One of the toughest challenges was to reduce the current consumption to no more than 100 microamperes, to ensure that the hearing aid batteries would last as long as possible. But in spite of his impatience, Niederdränk didn't give up.

"At difficult moments we sometimes felt like we were up against a brick wall, but ultimately the problems became challenges that we wanted to overcome."

When faced with tough situations like these, Niederdränk knows the importance of separating work and leisure. He relaxes and unwinds by spending time with his wife and two children, or by going sailing. Afterwards, he finds it easier to tackle a problem again, or to remember that he and his team don't have to start over from scratch. The "not invented here" syndrome doesn't apply to him. "I always think about whether the problem we're facing might have already been solved in another technical field," he says. "That way, we can sometimes incorporate existing ideas into our work and develop them further." Each small success motivates him to carry on and master the major challenges.

Teamwork and Kayaking

The idea of creating something that seemed a very remote possibility to others, inside and outside of the company, was in itself motivation enough for Niederdränk and his now 14-member team to develop the Acuris system. In the course of their work, the boundaries between private and professional life became blurred at times. "We sometimes worked 48 hours at a stretch, but we also spent our free time together," recalls Niederdränk. "Group kayaking trips, hiking tours and concert visits were some of the activities that helped to bond the team."

And clearly these efforts were successful: In October 2004, the Acuris family of hearing aids featuring the e2e wireless system was launched on the market. "It really made us feel elated, particularly since our competitors have been trying for years to develop a similar system, but without success," says Niederdränk. Recognition of the system's excellence was soon forthcoming from the competitors as well, although indirectly. According to Niederdränk, experts from the competing companies began testing the device soon after it was introduced. Although their aim was to find its weak points, they soon had to concede that it worked flawlessly.

But far more important is the fact that the new technology soon won over the people for whom it was conceived, as well as other hearing-impaired individuals whose fine motor skills are not hampered and who select a hearing aid solely on the basis of its sound characteristics. "We have sold more hearing aids than we originally planned," says Niederdränk elatedly. Even though Niederdränk's invention has secured the

Acuris series a momentary monopoly on the market, the developers are unwilling to rest on their laurels. "By the time our competitors introduce a similar system, we want to be another step ahead," he says.

Room for Creativity

These days, Niederdränk is leaving the system's further development to others. That's because he was offered a position in Singapore a few days after the device was launched on the market. He now manages 80 employees who work in product development and on the creation of new manufacturing processes. According to Niederdränk, his new position has effectively ended his life as an inventor engaged in technically detailed work. "As the boss, you shouldn't interfere too much in your employees' development work," he says. So Niederdränk now sees himself as an advisor and an initiator of ideas. It's a lesson he learned from his former supervisor at the Acoustics Institute in Aachen. "He always gave his people a free rein and paved the way for their progress," Niederdränk says. "For their part, though, they were responsible for staying on the

Lessons learned	Torsten Niederdränk's advice for innovators
• Don't get discouraged! • Unnecessary time pressure is risky because you might lose sight of your objectives. • You should always be able to take a step back from your work in order to see the current situation from a different perspective. • Don't try to force anything. Planning is crucial, in development and other areas. • Always bear in mind that a similar problem might already have been solved in another field.	• You can't force inventions. There's a right time and a right place. Ideas often emerge from a particular situation. Take notice of, and exploit, such situations. • Don't be afraid of taking an idea to experts and talking to them about thoughts that might at first seem far-fetched. • Check existing patents and find out the current status of things. You'll always find something that can help you with your own idea. • Be patient. If you get stuck, always remember that there may be an alternative approach. • That's why it's also important to gain as much knowledge as you can and to remain curious and open-minded.

right course and making sure that they actually reached their goals." Niederdränk is trying to live this leadership style as well, because he knows from his own experience how important it is for a team to have room for creativity, despite ongoing projects and upcoming product launches.

Although he himself no long has much time for coming up with spectacular new inventions, he gladly gives his colleagues ideas for their work. But since creative approaches and innovative thinking are also needed in his current position, Niederdränk has transferred his experiences and skills as an inventor to his new tasks. Shortly before he left for Singapore, Niederdränk was voted Inventor of the Year 2004 for his development successes. The award is the highest honor that Siemens presents in recognition of its creative minds. In 2005 he received the Siemens Med Innovation Award for the e2e system, which is now used as standard in all of Siemens' premium hearing aids.

Noticing Stacey's barely suppressed smile, Bao Jun asks her what's so amusing. "Niederdränk's trials on himself, when he made himself 30 years older in order to test his hearing aids," she replies. "This seems to be done fairly frequently in medicine. Have you heard of Barry Marshall and Robin Warren?" The names aren't familiar, the others say. Stacey continues: "They're two Australians who won the Nobel Prize in Medicine in 2005. Marshall theorized that the bacterium Helicobacter pylori might be responsible for many ulcers. But since nobody believed him back in the early 1980s, he swallowed a nasty mix of bacteria – which not only gave him a bad stomachache, but also enabled him to prove that the condition could be alleviated with the help of antibiotics."

"Yeah, I also know some examples," interjects Matthias. "Max Pettenkofer imbibed cholera bacteria; Jonas Salk tested a polio vaccine on himself; and Werner Forssmann pushed a catheter into his own ventricle in 1929. He then walked to the X-ray department with the catheter hanging out, to show it had in fact reached his heart. For this feat he later received the Nobel Prize." "That's risky business," says Christian, shaking his head. "It's often the most idealistic doctors who conduct tests on themselves when they've reached a dead-end," replies Matthias. "It's not that they're naive; they are so well aware of the risk involved that they're unwilling to put anyone else in danger and will only test it on themselves."

"But that just shows how very determined, maybe even obsessed, they are when it comes to finding a solution," says John. "But let's get back to Torsten Niederdränk. I found two things he says particularly interest-

ing: One is his emphasis that the 'not invented here" syndrome doesn't apply to him. A similar statement came from Maximilian Fleischer, who said that an innovator shouldn't be afraid to take up existing ideas and improve them if necessary. During my career as a consultant, I've experienced cases in which quite the opposite was done and many developers insisted on reinventing the wheel – due to obstinacy, deliberate ignorance or excessive self-confidence because they think they're smarter than everyone else. The second thing that impressed me was that the members of Niederdränk's team also went kayaking or hiking together during their free time …"

"It was definitely a close-knit team," says Bao Jun. "But you always have to be able to let go of such a project – which is what Niederdränk managed to do. In his new position he's less of an inventor than a coach." "To do that you need a certain amount of equanimity," says Stacey. "You can also see this in his advice that 'You can't force inventions. There is a right time and a right place for them'. Many managers might find that hard to accept, because they are under enormous time pressure to be first on the market."

John agrees: "In that regard I think the saying 'Take the time to sharpen your axe before felling the first trees' is very pertinent. People who say they don't have time to sharpen the axe because they need to chop down the whole forest are slower than those who make sure they're well prepared. Speed won't help if we can't think because we're rushing around so much."

"That makes sense to me," says Christian. "And it applies to a former colleague of mine, who first thinks things through before going on to do the right thing. I recently visited him in his office."

"Let's sit here on this bench – the view of the lake is fantastic from here. It'll help us to concentrate on what Christian has to say."

Analysis Instead of Spontaneity – Innovation Steps for Gas Turbines

Klaus Riedle walks to the window of his large, bright office at the Siemens Research Center in Erlangen, Germany, and points to a concrete tower several hundred meters away. "That's the simulator for a pressurized water reactor," he says. More specifically, it's a simulator Riedle himself designed and built in the mid-1970s to study the impact of accidents at nuclear power plants. The simulator is still used today – but not by its designer. After spending several years studying accidents, Riedle, now 65, decided he would rather work on power plants that operate smoothly. As it turned out, Siemens benefited greatly from that decision. Following a stint as director of a nuclear technology lab, Riedle began developing fossil fuel power plants in the mid-1980s. This move marked the beginning of the success story of Siemens gas turbines, which today are among the best in the world.

Patents? Riedle, a mechanical engineer, only has a few. Spontaneous ideas? He admits these aren't his strong point. As an honorary professor at the University of Erlangen, he's spent the last 25 years teaching basic physics subjects such as thermodynamics and power transmission. So what's the secret of his success? It's his ability to recognize complex interrelationships and break them down into individual problems, which he gradually solves – all the while paying close attention to what happens if you change an apparently insignificant factor. This may sound unspectacular in an era in which companies constantly try to outdo each other with sexy ideas. Nevertheless, it's exactly the right approach for a technology as complex as the gas turbine. "Gas turbine technology has been around for a hundred years, and customers tend to be very critical and quality conscious," says Riedle.

Guest Worker from Innsbruck

Indeed, no one in Erlangen expects to see a spectacular innovation catapult gas turbines in a new direction over the next five years or so; too much time has already been spent on developing turbine engines and stationary gas turbines. Instead, innovations will most

Reaching even higher operating temperatures and raising efficiency by another tenth of a percent – these goals drive the daily activities of gas turbine innovators. This type of painstaking work, coupled with thorough analyses, holds the key to conserving resources and making our energy supply as environmentally friendly as possible. **Prof. Dr. Klaus Riedle** is an expert in the field. In fact, he has made Siemens gas turbines among the best in the world, an achievement for which he was awarded the Global Energy International Prize – a sort of Nobel Prize for energy technology. Riedle shared his prize money of one million dollars with Russian Nobel laureate Zhores Alferov.

likely focus on turbine blades made of ceramic materials that can withstand higher temperatures, and thus achieve higher efficiency ratings. "Innovations in this field are rarely due to spontaneous ideas but are instead the result of continuity and persistence," says Riedle, who originally hails from Innsbruck and therefore jokingly refers to himself as a "guest worker" from Austria. Riedle demonstrated his persistence back in the early 1980s, when he was assigned the task of building a catalytic converter for reducing nitrogen-oxide emissions at power plants. At that time, the relevant technology patents were held almost exclusively by Japanese companies. Riedle was patient, however, and eventually found a way to develop a catalytic converter that also set new technological standards.

However, this doesn't mean that everything related to gas and steam turbines, an area Riedle also recently assumed responsibility for, runs according to a long-established plan. The developers in Erlangen and their colleagues at Siemens Westinghouse in Orlando, Florida, must constantly make sure that they don't "over-engineer" by developing technically superior turbines that no one wants to buy. The market is changing rapidly and customer expectations have risen. The latest trend, for example, involves gas turbines with extremely short run-up periods. These

High-tech applications for power generation. Flow simulations on computers, smart cooling techniques, special materials and ceramic coatings are transforming gas turbine blades into high-tech products. The newest turbines, which must be able to withstand temperatures in excess of 1,400 degrees Celsius, operate at close to the speed of sound.

turbines can be used to bridge a break in power generation, for example when wind plants cannot deliver power due to weather conditions. Companies unable to supply the right product in the time available quickly lose market share.

It's Okay to Make Mistakes – as Long as You Learn from Them

That's why no one develops gas turbines today until customer requirements have been fully clarified. In Riedle's case, this means meeting with salespeople from around the world once a year, who explain exactly what their customers want. Specifications are not defined until after this meeting. Such rigid procedures are extremely important for the innovation process, says Riedle, because they help prevent expensive mistakes: "With development times of three to four years, it's almost impossible to change things if you discover you're moving in the wrong direction." At the same time, occasional mistakes do happen, says Riedle, so "you should never expect to always make the right decisions."

One such mistake involved a new generation of gas turbines that will be launched on the market in 2007. The turbines boast a world-record output of 340 megawatts. Back in 2001 the plan was to equip them with a ring-shaped combustion chamber, as is common practice at Siemens. The chamber contained up to 24 burners arranged in a circle, and the design had already proved its worth in many other gas turbines. Problems cropped up during development, however. Specifically, it was very difficult to predict the behavior of a new and larger gas turbine with a ring-shaped combustion chamber using computer simulations. Many real tests therefore had to be carried out on test rigs, at a cost of triple-digit millions of euros. Individual burners housed in bag-shaped chambers, which some competitors use, can be assessed more quickly and effectively – and at a lower cost. Siemens therefore pulled the plug on the project and used the individual burner concept instead.

As Powerful as 13 Jumbo Jet Engines

The turbines are now back on track for their market launch. In fact, the first of the record-breaking units is currently being built at the gas turbine plant in Berlin. It will be used at a power plant that will be operated by E.ON in conjunction with Siemens in the Bavarian town of

Irsching. The joint operation concept is also a novelty in the industry. The goal here is to determine the optimal operating conditions for such a plant. The gas turbine will initially be tested alone, and will subsequently be utilized in a combined-cycle power plant, where it will help the plant to achieve an overall efficiency of 60 percent, also a new world record. The output of the gas turbine alone is equivalent to that of 13 jumbo jet engines, or 1,100 Porsche turbo vehicles. The 340 megawatts it will produce could satisfy the power requirements of 620,000 three-person households – in other words, the inhabitants of a city the size of Hamburg.

One instrument used to prevent development errors from occurring is benchmarking – comparing yourself with the best in the industry. Under Riedle's guidance, the development team members have become expert users of this tool. "Benchmarking is good for both products and costs," says Riedle, whose work in this field has impressed other Siemens Groups. In fact, several have invited him to lecture on methods for comparing one's own products with the best the competition has to offer. Benchmarking has a long tradition in the gas turbine business, which is marked by a neck-and-neck race for technological supremacy. The first turbine benchmarking project was conducted in 1993 under the direction of Dr. Klaus Kleinfeld, who was appointed President and CEO of Siemens in January 2005. A benchmarking team of 20 to 35 employees gets together for up to six months every three or four years to collect information on the state of development at competing companies. The team members analyze turbine designs – for example, when performing contractual maintenance services on competitor products. They then calculate how much money they would require to produce such a turbine, in order to get a feeling for where they stand. The team also assesses competitors' business processes by studying how development or sales are organized at the competing company. In addition, it evaluates financial reports, media coverage and the results of technological conferences. Competitors do the same things, of course; everyone knows everyone else, and everyone is familiar with the "rules of the game."

Benchmarking Against the Best

Innovation benchmarking is a new tool developed by the Siemens-wide top+ Innovation program. The idea is to not only compare products and costs but also innovation processes. The resulting information is used to systematically draw up plans for the future. To this end, one job carried out by Riedle's team is to assess the likelihood that postulated trends will become reality. "Will there still be a market for gas turbines in 2020?" might be a relevant question here. Incidentally, the answer is "yes," as some €10 trillion will be spent on the construction of fossil-fuel power plants between now and 2020. Less certain, however, is the design of their turbines. Experts are therefore now defining the most likely trends, and the 700 employees working in turbine development will incorporate the results into actual products.

Designing such development activities on a long-term basis – and ensuring their application on both sides of the Atlantic – is the job of the Product and Development Control department, which coordinates the contributions made by all development and production units involved in the process. The department creates proper structures, analyzes even the most minor development steps, and uses balanced scorecards to determine the extent to which results correspond to plans. Riedle admits that he and his team had to learn project and risk management the hard way. But they eventually got things under control to such an extent that Siemens Groups such as Transportation Systems and Industrial Solutions and Services now utilize the tried and tested management methods from Erlangen.

Riedle's team also has to make sure that the various mentalities function together. That's something he knows about from his two years of postdoctoral work at Carnegie Mellon University in Pittsburgh. Here he learned that a situation described as a "serious problem" by a German engineer would be referred to as a "challenge" or at the most an "issue" by an American colleague – even if a project was about to fail. Here, Riedle sees his strength in his ability to ask the right questions and get to the bottom of things.

Equally importantly, Riedle is considered to be a fair boss – an evaluation his secretary, Brigitte Streit, is quick to confirm. He only gets annoyed if someone uses a meeting to blow his own horn. Other than that, his team members are given the same freedom to develop that Riedle himself had. "I was pleasantly surprised by how much freedom I had at Siemens," he says, adding that freedom is important for people determined to achieve things. Without adequate freedom, they won't be willing to share their knowledge, he maintains. Riedle himself shares his knowledge not only with Siemens employees and students at the University of Erlangen but also with other companies. For example, he acts as a consultant for the Russian company Power Machines, in which Siemens has a 25 percent interest.

"Nobel Prize for Energy Technology"

Riedle's achievements were rewarded in St. Petersburg, Russia, in June 2005, when he received the renowned Global Energy International Prize – a type of "Nobel Prize for power technology" and one of the most highly endowed awards any Siemens employee has ever been given. He shared the prize money of one million dollars with Russian Nobel laureate Zhores Alferov, using most of his half to establish a foundation at the University of Erlangen that supports an exchange of young scientists with their counterparts from the Power Engineering Institute in Moscow.

Although still blessed with tremendous energy, Riedle decided in July 2006 to "cut his output in half," as he jokingly stated on the invitations to his retirement party. The invitation also says that the conventional

Lessons learned	Klaus Riedle's advice for innovators
• The combined-cycle turbine business is rarely marked by sudden leaps of innovation. That's why it's so important to always be at the forefront of developments in its individual technologies.	• Analyze customer requirements and formulate goals for the product innovations that will help you to meet them so that you know the direction that has to be taken for each individual technology.
• The energy market changes rapidly and mistakes can be costly. That's why systematic innovation benchmarking is important. It helps developers make the right decisions.	• Tasks must be clearly structured and carried out. • Managers must also have the courage to admit mistakes.
• Errors can never completely be avoided. You must therefore have the courage to stop a development project if necessary.	• Choose your team members carefully and don't go for cheap solutions when it comes to highly qualified people.
• The competition never sleeps. It's therefore necessary to use benchmarking to become as familiar as possible with the technologies and business models used by competitors.	• Let your colleagues know that you're always available for discussion.
• Mentalities vary in international development teams. Reconciling differences and ensuring that everything runs smoothly are two major challenges every team leader faces.	

fuel consisting of responsibility and determination to perform well will be replaced by a new mixture of relaxation and leisure, with a little Tyrolean mountain air thrown in. His wife and four children hope that the newly freed-up energy will be channeled into their network of family and friends. So, will their wish be fulfilled? Only to a certain extent, as Riedle also plans to provide consulting services to universities such as Graz University of Technology and a college in Malaysia. He'll also remain active in various organizations such as the Association of German Engineers.

"For me, this clearly shows that your approach to innovation must be adaptable in order to meet the requirements of the area you're currently working in," says Matthias. "Riedle's method of breaking down complex interrelationships into individual problems, which he then gradually solved, is perfect for gas turbines. He also uses the right management tools, especially benchmarking, which is like a fitness test for an athletic-style innovation competition."

"Exactly," says Christian. "And Riedle also wants to learn new things and is always trying to find out what the customer really needs. In addition, he's active at science-industry interface. It just goes to show: You don't win the so-called Nobel Prize for power technology without a good reason."

"A willingness to learn is definitely one of the keys to success," says Walter. "Did you know that the history of the gas turbine is one of continual expansion? For example, the Berlin plant produced about ten gas turbines a year in the 1980s, but today it builds about five times that number each year. This progress is clearly the result of all the innovations that have occurred in this field."

In the meantime, the beautiful fall weather has got Matthias all excited: "Look how blue Lake Starnberg is and check out how clearly you can see the Alps in the distance," he says. "And the color of the trees and the light mist over the meadow – it's simply gorgeous here!"

"You're a romantic," Walter laughs, and then changes the subject: "Did you know that many of our innovation projects also have environmental goals? Besides economy and reliability, projects are often geared toward reducing the costs of power production, conserving electricity and the resources used to produce it, and lowering pollutant emissions. The supposed contradiction between economy and ecology actually doesn't exist."

Christian looks a little doubtful, but Walter continues: "The piezo injectors, power transmission and gas turbines all show that. But I've got an *even better example: Recently I met up with a new colleague, Henrik Stiesdal. His company was acquired by Siemens, and his innovations bring both ecologic and economic benefits. He works on wind power plants."*

Harnessing the Wind

The designation "Director of Special Projects" is usually reserved for managers whose best years are behind them. In most cases, the "special projects" are so special that their failure won't negatively affect company performance. In rare cases, however, the individuals given such a designation have served their organizations well, possess a wealth of ideas and are therefore allowed a great deal of freedom. Henrik Stiesdal is a case in point. So what exactly does he do? Stiesdal, 49, cannot provide a precise answer to this question. Instead, he describes his role as being a creator of ideas, departmental director, idea-development coach, problem solver and patent manager. He is all of these things – and much more. Above all, however, he is the force behind Siemens Windpower, which is based in Brande, Denmark, and was known as Bonus Energy up until two years ago, when it was acquired by Siemens.

Creator of new ideas, innovation manager, patent manager and much more – **Henrik Stiesdal** is the force behind the innovation factory that is Siemens Windpower in Brande, Denmark. The company, which is one of the world's top five firms in the booming wind energy sector, is the global market leader for offshore wind power plants. Stiesdal's most important goals are to optimize electricity yields per year and achieve the highest possible levels of reliability and quality. "We always recognize problems before our customers do," he says.

The fact that Stiesdal, who studied biology, would end up building wind power plants is surprising. But then so too is the story of his company, which went from a sprinkler manufacturer to one of the best-known producers of wind turbines in just 25 years. The man and the company thus suit each other perfectly, although Stiesdal's career path was subject to many twists and turns. Shortly after graduating from high school in 1976, Stiesdal built his first wind turbine for use on the family farm. He then produced a commercial version of his turbine in 1978, licensing it out one year later to Vestas, a company that went on to become the world's largest producer of wind turbines. Stiesdal also went to work for the company, and back then the young action man began studying medicine as well, later switching to biology and physics. Stiesdal left Vestas to concentrate on biology after the company began experiencing financial problems. However, he couldn't stay away from the wind power action for long: "After three months, I just had to get back into it, so I started working at Bonus Energy."

Today, Siemens Windpower is one of the world's top five manufacturers of wind power plants, although it's still quite a way from becoming the market leader. However, it is the world market leader for offshore windparks, and also stands alone when it comes to reliable technology and satisfied customers. "Bonus had an excellent reputation, its business was solid – and that's what made it perfect for Siemens," says Stiesdal, who is married and has two daughters. The parent company in Munich is indeed happy with its Danish subsidiary, whose 1,200 employees, 800 of whom work in Brande, will continue to provide customers with quality "made in Denmark" for a long time. Siemens' various contacts around the world have been a big help here, enabling the company to increase its market share, which now stands at just under ten percent and continues to grow rapidly. Between 2004 and 2005 sales nearly doubled, and the installed power reached more than 630 megawatts. What's more, after selling some 350 wind turbines in 2005, the company sold around 500 in 2006. Bonus Energy's founder, Palle Norgaard, is confident that this dynamic development will continue: "As a member of the Siemens family, we will become a leading manufacturer of wind power plants."

Never a Complaint

The success enjoyed by Siemens Windpower is closely linked with Stiesdal's strategy of placing top priority on reliability. Some manufacturers seek to squeeze out tenths of a percent in efficiency; others have tried to be the first to market gearless turbines. The Danes, on the other hand, prefer to optimize electricity yields per year, the most important performance measure for the customer. Stiesdal likes to tell the following story, which illustrates the company's diligence when it comes to quality: During acquisition negotiations, Siemens representatives asked to see a list of customer complaints, a common request in such a situation. Bonus Energy didn't give them a list, however – not because they had something to hide, but because there had never been a complaint. "We always recognize problems before our customers do," says Stiesdal.

That's easier said than done, as the huge turbines can't be tested as complete units in a lab. Only after a plant has been built can you determine whether it can cope with the prevailing weather conditions. Moreover, such conditions differ from region to region around the world. Expertise must therefore be gained in this area – but without causing customers problems. To this end, data such as wind, rainfall, temperature and lightning strikes is collected at 25 selected facilities equipped with Siemens wind turbines around the world. Evaluations are also carried out to determine how these facilities are affected by the elements. Moreover, turbines at all other facilities continually send their key operational data to Brande. Here, Siemens Windpower is consciously pursuing a more sophisticated strategy of its own. "We don't outsource – we insource," says Stiesdal. Nearly all of his competitors hire consulting companies to conduct field tests, so the expertise gained never flows back into the continual development process. Stiesdal prefers to keep such technical expertise inside the organization. That's why the company employs 18 people to conduct lab-based quality tests and field tests, while an additional six employees monitor turbines for customers around the

World's biggest offshore windpark. The 72 wind turbines located ten kilometers south of Nysted, Denmark, have a combined output of 166 megawatts (peak power) – enough to power a city with 145,000 households.

clock, solving problems before there's a noticeable drop in power generation.

Complete Rotor Blade as a Single Component

Siemens recognized the value of this approach. Instead of cleaning house, as is common in takeovers, they chose to keep established structures intact at Bonus Energy – and even hired new employees. But Siemens Windpower's focus on reliability does not mean stubbornly sticking with old technologies. On the contrary, its centerpiece unit is the Integral Blade, a rotor blade made without glue, which is much lighter and more robust than competing products. It is produced in a vacuum by spraying epoxy resin into a mold that has been lined with glass fiber. A type of inflatable balloon is used here to shape the contour inside the hollow rotor blade. Stiesdal has a display of sawed-out segments from different rotors in his office – and even the untrained layman can see the difference between the Integral Blade with its smooth surfaces both inside and out, and conventional blades that look like a giant jigsaw puzzle. The Integral Blades used with a 3.6-megawatt turbine are 52 meters long and weigh 16 metric tons. Their great rigidity is demonstrated in a bending test carried out behind the factory hall, where they are made to oscillate by a hydraulic arm. During the test, their edges bend up or down by as much as ten meters. A total of four million oscillations over a period of two months simulate the stress of 20 years of actual operation.

The company's success didn't come easy; above all, it required a great deal of patience. Back in the early 1990s, it became apparent that new manufacturing techniques would be required to build bigger and bigger rotor blades. Rotors provided by one manufacturer were increasingly displaying stability problems. However, due to its virtual market monopoly, the manufacturer had no interest in solving the problem, and even allowed some research results obtained by Bonus Energy to be leaked to the competition. In response, a concept for a "Bonus Blade Project" was developed between 1996 and 1998 with the goal of having the company build its own rotor blades of the highest quality. The first windmill equipped with the new blades was built in 2000. Series production of the component was launched in 2001, and maximum production capacity was achieved in 2003, when a new plant went into operation in Aalborg. That same year, Bonus Energy built the world's biggest offshore windpark near Nysted on the Danish coast. Its output of 166 megawatts impressively demonstrates the robustness of the rotor concept.

Development of the Integral Blade was not without its setbacks, of course, recalls Stiesdal. For example, the polyester resin initially used was unable to meet the company's stringent health-protection requirements, which is why it was replaced by epoxy. Visitors to the production hall in Aalborg today are surprised that they can't smell anything there, which is rather unusual for a factory that laminates glass fiber components.

More Powerful Windmills

Stiesdal has always had a good sense of which way the wind blows in his business – or at least almost always. Once, at a conference 15 years ago, he made the prediction that wind power output would never exceed half a megawatt. Today, Siemens Windpower builds turbines with an output of 3.6 megawatts, and is already working on a new model that will boast

Lessons learned	Henrik Stiesdal's advice for innovators
• Reliability and high energy yields are more important features of wind power plants than sophisticated technologies and maximum efficiency.	• Stay in shape mentally by seeking out challenges in everyday activities – even those that have nothing to do with your actual work.
• It is difficult to make predictions about future wind turbine performance levels. The output limits forecast in the 1990s have long since been surpassed.	• Give things time to develop. If you can't come up with a solution to a problem immediately, you're sure to find one later.
• A convincing concept and satisfied customers will serve to maintain the reputation of a company even after it is integrated into a major corporation like Siemens.	• Accept the fact that the innovation process is marked by both periods of creativity and times when relatively little is accomplished.
• Every project needs to have a goal that will continue to be pursued even when problems are encountered or new ideas come up.	• If you can't seem to solve a problem, find yourself a "sparring partner" to inspire you.
• Whenever possible, it's important to identify problems before the customer does.	• Accept the fact that most of your ideas will be rejected. This is the downside of the innovation process, but it also provides the incentive to go out and do something better. So get to work on the next idea!

much higher performance. So how powerful will it be? "Why don't we just wait and see?" Stiesdal says with a grin.

Afterwards, Stiesdal plans to remain active in the field. As he says, innovation has always been a lot of fun: "When you're trying to solve a difficult problem, you can't think about anything else. You constantly assess the various possibilities, but you don't always find the solution immediately, even though you're under tremendous pressure from customers to do so." Stiesdal says he has never suffered from a lack of ideas – only from a lack of time to implement them. That's because his days are often filled with routine work, making the innovation process seem like a roller coaster ride. He says it's good to have a motivated and well-oiled team with which to discuss the feasibility of new ideas. In such a setting, there's no need for formal processes. You just throw out the problem and begin talking about it, says Stiesdal. Sometimes when he runs into a problem, he'll call a colleague and explain it to him or her. "Basically, I need a sparring partner," he explains. However, all the effort is worthwhile. At some point the solution suddenly becomes clear in all its details. "When that happens, it feels a little like falling in love," says Stiesdal.

> *"You were right, Walter," Christian admits. "That's a great example of how products that are environmentally friendly can also be very profitable. Stiesdal's innovations have generated lots of added value – for Bonus Energy and now for Siemens too. Unfortunately, we economists still find it difficult to measure the return on innovation investment. Of course, this is because R&D expenditures take a long time to pay off – in many cases, only after years of work that entails quite a bit of risk. In the process, many things can go wrong – things that have nothing to do with R&D. If production processes are too expensive or inflexible, for example, or if sales methods don't function efficiently enough, or the marketing campaign takes the wrong approach to the customers, even the best R&D work can lead to a flop."*
>
> *"But when everything clicks, innovations can increase a company's value tremendously, as we've just heard," adds Stacey. "Exactly," says Christian. "R&D expenditures really have to be treated as an investment in the future instead of simply being written off as another cost of doing business. At the same time, return on innovation investment isn't really easy to measure if an innovation results not only from R&D input but also from the necessary interplay between production, marketing and sales. By the way, I found it remarkable that although Stiesdal was trained as a*

biologist, he was able to contribute in another discipline and help develop wind power plants."

"That shows once again that the area in which an expert was originally trained is by no means crucial. Instead, it's often more important to have a passionate interest in a topic, the ability to persistently pursue solutions and the determination to keep moving forward despite setbacks," John says. "And of course you have to know what the market requires. Stiesdal recognized that the key factor in the wind turbine business is electricity yields per year – and that's exactly what he and his team are optimizing. And let's not forget the emphasis on quality and reliability, insourcing instead of outsourcing, and using remote diagnostic methods. It's also great the way they recognize potential problems before their customers do. Virtually every product is at some time the subject of a customer complaint.

The others nod in agreement. A look at the clock tells them it's time to head back to the Management Center. "You know," says Christian, "yesterday evening when we were swapping stories about out-of-the-box thinkers, I realized that I wasn't one and doubted that I could contribute much to the cause of innovation. But hearing today's stories has given me a new perspective. After all, the question of how continual development and the optimization of processes can generate earnings is important for me personally. I'd like to determine which projects I can contribute to as a 'sparring partner' and thus help to move specific innovations forward. What's more, I really believe you can also adopt other approaches to innovation..."

The generally reticent Bao Jun cuts in. "You're absolutely right, and the same thought has occurred to me. That's why I'd like to suggest that we all meet again this evening in front of the fireplace." A wide grin spreads across his face as the others respond enthusiastically.

Space for your own thoughts

Which areas of existing businesses can you strengthen by implementing process innovations?

What has been running successfully for so long that new developments will probably lead to further improvements?

How can you help innovators successfully implement their ideas?

Siemens and the World

Regional Innovations, External Partners,
Spin-ins, Spin-offs

*T*his time, Bao Jun kicks off the talk around the fireplace. "The aspects we've looked at so far have been really fascinating, but I'd like to touch on another area that could help to broaden our perspective a bit. I think Stiesdal's story is pretty remarkable. As far as innovation processes are concerned, we usually assume that progressing from the original idea to its implementation takes place entirely within a company. But that's by no means necessarily so. Inspiration can come from many different directions. Henrik Stiesdal, for example, had his idea for the wind turbine while he lived at his parents' farmhouse. Maybe that was because they weren't connected to the power grid – but they did have plenty of wind. Then, Bonus Energy proved to be the ideal environment for further development. And now Siemens, a global company, is playing a vital role in the next step. The same applies to Bernd Gombert. The new brake he invented can be marketed much more effectively by Siemens than by a small company – worldwide and in many areas of application. That's why I think the focus of our talk this evening can be summed up with the words 'Siemens and the world,' to show that we need to extend our field of vision beyond our own company. We should move on from the traditional approach to inventions, in which everything must be discovered and realized in your own company..."

"You're right," says John. "We're also seeing this trend elsewhere. I recently read an article in Harvard Business Manager about Procter & Gamble, for example. In 2000 the success rate of their innovations was only 35 percent, and the Procter & Gamble share price dropped from $118 to $52 due to the company's declining competitiveness. Then, Alan G. Lafley, the new CEO, called for a reinvention of the innovation model, relied on Open Innovation and announced a goal: 50 percent of the innovations should come from external sources. Today the success rate of the company's innovations is twice what it was before, and the share price has also risen sharply."

Bao Jun regards these comments as a green light to proceed. "OK, why don't we sum up how innovations can be successfully further developed and promoted beyond boundaries, in order to network faster and more effectively with suppliers and inventors from outside a company. I have a good example to begin with. I'm referring to an innovator who started out with his own company, like Bernd Gombert, and then integrated it into Siemens, as a way to secure a bright future for his innovations. He's Italian, and his field is manufacturing automation..."

The Future of Manufacturing Execution Systems

One might well wonder what this man has to do with yogurt tubs and pressed steel, pillboxes and cookie tins. His stylish tie might be from a fashion shop in Milan, his striped shirt fits as if he were a model for an exclusive aftershave, and his suit looks far too elegant for a software engineer.

Giorgio Cuttica could pass for a gentleman of independent means or a sophisticated art collector. But his passion is for yogurt tubs, pressed steel, pillboxes and cookie tins – or rather, for the intelligence behind them. That's because Cuttica develops the control software for modern factories that manufacture such products – and because his Simatic IT software is so pioneering and such a departure from old paradigms that one could almost claim that he develops the software for the factory of the future.

"With Simatic IT, we integrate all of the functions that are relevant to manufacturing – the data of the numerous small units that control the individual machines. This allows the customer to optimize the entire process flexibly, even when it's running," explains Cuttica.

In fact, hundreds of so-called programmable logic controllers (PLCs) are often at work in modern production plants. They receive data on the status of individual machines, process this data, compare it with the desired values, and give new instructions for their individual small steps in the process. But if the control units aren't networked and working together in a common IT system, the production managers can't obtain an overall picture of the process. "That makes it more difficult to react to errors, and particularly hard to adjust production quickly and flexibly to changing requirements," explains Cuttica.

Until the mid-1990s, **Dr. Giorgio Cuttica** was the head of a company in Genoa, Italy, with 350 employees that developed solutions for plant control systems. In order to conquer the world market, he sold his company to Siemens in 2001 – and is now well on his way to achieving his goal.

The Future of Manufacturing Execution Systems 123

And exactly this flexibility is increasingly important in mass production. Because competitive advantages in the globalized economy are based more and more on minimal efficiency advances – especially in manufacturing – this factor can be decisive for a company's prosperity. This was demonstrated impressively by the Japanese automotive industry in the 1980s and 1990s.

Standards Instead of In-House Solutions

But software solutions that coordinate the process data of hundreds of individual manufacturing steps are still usually patchwork creations. "About 70 percent of the solutions installed worldwide for these so-called manufacturing execution systems (MES) are homemade," says Cuttica. "This means that the factory manager has commissioned some programmer to write him some software. And if the product line changes after three years, often even the original programmer no longer knows his way around his own software."

Meanwhile, companies worldwide are trying to standardize their manufacturing processes. A factory in China should manufacture in the same way as a plant in India or Germany, and should be able to change over its production just as quickly and flexibly. Whereas the motto for production managers until a few years ago was still "Never touch a running system," today it is vital to be able to react to changing customer desires and tastes faster and faster – whether it's in the production of mobile phones or of automotive accessories.

Cuttica saw enormous market potential in this field. But ten years ago he would never have dreamed that he would conquer this market as a Siemens employee. At that time, he was running his own company, ORSI, which he had founded in 1982 with four other young engineers in Genoa. "We started off by developing control units at the lowest process level, directly connected to the machines. Later, in the 1990s, we started writing software that helped these units to work together better," remembers Cuttica. But in the middle of the 1990s the idea crystallized that has been on his mind for the last decade: enhancing worldwide manufacturing efficiency and quality with just one software platform that customers can easily adapt to their own needs using a graphic interface. Cuttica calls it the "SAP for manufacturing processes."

In 1995 – still as the boss of his own company – he participated in a meeting of the Instrumentation Society of America, a standardization organization in the United States. He wanted to base his product on the MES standards approved in the US, which have since then been accepted all over the world. He regarded the fact that his company was small as an advantage. This enabled him to go through the first innovation and development stages quickly and flexibly. "But there came a point when we understood that our lack of size was a disadvantage, a serious disadvantage. We would never have had the sales power to market a successful standard solution worldwide. Someone would have stolen our good ideas and done the big deals."

An Entrepreneur's Company as Part of a Global Enterprise

So together with his partners, he decided to sell the company to Siemens. "To the benefit of everyone involved," says Cuttica. "We had the know-how to help Siemens expand its successful business in industrial automation, with technology that focuses on a higher level of value creation. And our 350 employees at that time, the engineers and programmers, were able to continue working on their project in Genoa – with a good chance of becoming the market leader worldwide." Following the sale of the company at the beginning of 2001, Cuttica could of course have retired completely and devoted himself to his hobbies: more sport, traveling and collecting classical works of art – which indeed is one of his interests.

However, his aim was not only to develop good ideas, but to make them successful in practice worldwide. So he accepted the offer to continue managing his team, which today comprises some 500 people, now as General Manager of the Siemens MES division. And today, Siemens solutions have already achieved a share of about five percent of an extremely fragmented market and are thus one of the market leaders for MES. The coming years will show which supplier will succeed. To make sure that Siemens is the one, Cuttica has to do something that he actually enjoys very much: traveling a lot – though now it's a little more than even he would like. He travels in order to meet customers in the United States, Brazil or Africa, confer with colleagues in Germany at Automation and Drives (A&D) in Nuremberg, or visit one of the other development facilities in Belgium, for example.

Management by Walking Around

"He's seldom here – that's the kind of job he has," say the staff members in Genoa about their boss. "And when he's here, there's a long line of people who want to speak to him." Cuttica knows the problem – and solves it in his own way. "Management by walking around" is his motto. When he walks up the narrow white marble steps to his office on the second floor, he answers employees' questions in passing, and wherever he turns up he hears the same two words: "Ciao, Giorgio."

Giorgio Cuttica is on first-name terms with his young team, on average in their late twenties. Although this is more common in Italy than at A&D in Nuremberg, for example, it's still all a part of his style. He has a natural approach, rather than being artificially polite. And the genuine compliments that he gives have the effect of making him even more popular with the staff members, who look forward to his visits, both at his headquarters in Genoa and at his other locations in California, Belgium and Nuremberg.

But the friendliness he encounters should not disguise the resistance he has had to overcome – for example, when he had to convince his German colleagues at A&D of the virtues of his product. After all, their success, especially with PLCs, has been absolutely phenomenal. In the past, even Cuttica has often asked himself whether he was really on the right track in wanting to expand a key area of A&D's business model to include software solutions.

Meanwhile, the Siemens newcomer has no more doubts – and he expends his energy on winning over the people who are responsible for business in all of the regions worldwide. Many of them would like to sell the new software packages with the assistance of the sales team for the conventional hardware, the PLCs, even though these salespersons don't always find it easy to get to know the new business model and the way the software works. Some competitors in the MES market have produced nothing but software for a long time now, and know more about their customers' specific programming problems.

A Mission to Promote an Innovation

In order to transform Siemens' technological lead with innovative MES systems into market success, Cuttica has to convince a large organization, or, as he says, "go on a mission." The top-management support that he can be sure of at Siemens provides him with important help in this task, or, to put it in Cuttica's not always diplomatic words, "This support ensures that your ideas aren't immediately killed by middle management." This is not a careerist speaking, but someone who sees his specific goals and pursues them single-mindedly: "I wasn't socialized in the Siemens universe so I still don't know many of the unwritten rules.

That makes me a maverick, a nonconformist. But this has the advantage that I can allow myself to say what I want. And it has the disadvantage that I sometimes do myself harm." Cuttica takes that as part of the deal – in order to advance his team's ideas.

Cuttica emphasizes one thing: "I'm not a one-man show. My team does the work – by now they've clocked up several hundred man-years. I just manage them." And if his system succeeds, the idea that emerged in the 1990s could become a billion-euro business for Siemens. Global sales of MES solutions already add up to more than one billion euros a year.

These are the big issues he thinks about – which are only remotely related to yogurt tubs and pressed steel, pillboxes and cookie tins. When Cuttica needs time to think, or to talk to someone without being disturbed, he just walks a few hundred meters through the back alleys of Genoa and sits down on the terrace of a pizzeria – with a view over the sea and the Gulf of Genoa. He came to this city on the Italian Riviera at the age of eight, studied engineering here and built up his company here.

Lessons learned	Giorgio Cuttica's advice for innovators
• The moment you think you've almost reached your goal is usually the point at which the real problems start.	• We should regard ourselves not as researchers and developers but rather as entrepreneurs.
• If you have the impression that management is heading in the wrong direction, you have only two options: leaving or following instructions. If you choose the second strategy, you should document everything and keep your documentation. That's because there's always the danger that if things go wrong later on, people could try to shift the responsibility for failure onto the person who carried out the instructions.	• We should never embark on project development simply because we enjoy grappling with a concrete technical challenge. Development begins when there's good reason to assume that the result will be a commercially successful product.
	• Geoffrey Moore's book Crossing the Chasm should be your personal bible when it comes to implementing development strategies.
• Siemens is an extremely complex organization. If you want to launch a truly innovative product on the market, you should look for very broad support above and beyond the members of management who are directly in charge. It's absolutely essential to reach a consensus with company headquarters and with the management of the regions.	• The real key to success is having the right team. Only if all the appropriate capabilities come together does the product have a chance of becoming a success. Behind every successful product is a successful team.

The Future of Manufacturing Execution Systems

And now at the age of 53, it's here that he would like to make Siemens a champion in a key area that is significantly accelerating the integration of global markets.

While the sea breeze tousles his hair, Cuttica puts down the pen he has been using to cover the paper tablecloth with production routines. Which experience of recent years, during his time at Siemens, was the most important for him? He silently considers, as though to emphasize what he's about to say. And he says just one word: "Patience".

As a connoisseur of ancient statues, he must be used to thinking in terms of long periods of time. But on the other hand, anyone who collects unique works of art in his private life while working on optimizing mass production must be allowed to live in two worlds.

A grin creases Matthias' face as Bao Jun finishes his story: "A classic example of the perfect combination of Italian elegance, sophistication and a razor-sharp, analytical entrepreneur with an eye for his own business interests. Cuttica recognized clearly when it's better to operate with a small company, and at what point it's smarter to integrate the enterprise into a big corporation. I'm sure that this insight is enabling him to reach his goal – to ensure that his innovations are successful in the international marketplace."

Bao Jun mentions another important aspect: "And he's a very independent-minded thinker who's not afraid to say exactly what he thinks. Sometimes that doesn't win you any friends. The fact that top management backs him up shows they are courageous and far-sighted. And that's crucial. As Bernd Gombert said: New, exotic plants need care, protection and good nourishment. And that applies all the more if they come from outside the organization."

"That can be difficult at times," says Walter with a nod of agreement. "Let's look at this topic from another perspective: So far, I've heard lots of comments on optimization of the value chain, but the focus has been only on the purchasing of materials and components. Actually, though, a company also can optimize innovation processes if it carefully considers what it should purchase from external suppliers and what it should supply internally. What do you think? Can – and should – ideas be bought?"

"Yes, definitely," says Stacey. "Especially with radically new ideas it's good to look beyond your own company, because every organization suffers from tunnel vision sometimes. That's one of the most important reasons why many companies put so much emphasis on building networks with other companies and suppliers, and between science and business. Every

year, for instance, Siemens launches about 1,000 partnership projects with universities and institutes worldwide. And at some locations, for instance in Berkeley, there are technology-to-business facilities that aim to transform external ideas into business success stories. Here's one example..."

I-WLAN – From University Research to a Global Product

Raymond Liao's story of how he got his first job sounds like every young person's dream. "I had been doing research at Columbia University in New York for five years, and the work for my doctorate was just about finished. And then a stranger called me out of the blue and asked if I'd like to work for Siemens." Raymond said yes, because the job offered him the opportunity to turn his research on quality of service in wireless networks into a Siemens product. "What I still like best today is seeing how advanced research leads to something that brings other people practical benefits – and generates good business for Siemens," he says.

Raymond received his doctorate in electrical engineering, and today he works at the Siemens Technology-to-Business Center (TTB) in Berkeley. He's constantly on the lookout for innovative ideas generated by outstanding young research scientists. Siemens TTB was established in 1999 to search for groundbreaking innovations that had been developed at universities or start-up companies and to make them commercially viable for Siemens. From the researchers' point of view, this means taking advantage of Siemens' potential for product development, market-

Raymond Liao, PhD, from the Siemens Technology-to-Business Center in Berkeley, California, achieved what many university researchers only dream of: transforming their ideas into products made by a global company. Liao's research generated Industrial WLAN, an innovative radio technology for industrial applications that is currently being offered on the world market only by Siemens Automation and Drives.

ing and sales to help transform these pioneering ideas into commercial breakthroughs.

Raymond came on board in the third year of the TTB's existence and is now one of its Directors of Venture Technology. His research generated a successful product some time ago – but it was quite different from his original plan. "Researchers have to stay flexible when it comes to the applications of their work," he says with a smile, pointing out that the potential of many great ideas has remained dormant because the imagination needed to transform them into products was lacking. In large organizations, such ideas can sometimes get bogged down in hierarchies and authorization loops or be ignored because of people's narrow-minded focus on what they already know or wariness of changes caused by innovations.

Big Opportunity: The Burst of the Dot-com Bubble

Initially Raymond wanted to market the results of his doctoral thesis research together with Siemens in the telecommunications industry. But the bursting of the "dot-com bubble" in 2000–2001 reduced the investments of network providers to nearly nothing, so Raymond and his TTB colleagues looked frantically for other fields of application. Just at that time, there was a need in the booming industrial automation segment for reliable WLAN (wireless local area network) solutions for factories and assembly lines. Wireless communications offered tremendous advantages for the control and supervision of machines such as driverless vehicles that receive their control commands via radio. In dusty or humid areas such as paint shops, there's no longer a need for expensive special cable insulation if the data packets are transmitted as radio waves, and cables aren't suitable for rotating machine parts in any case.

"In those days, the manufacturing sector customers understood the benefit of wireless and mobility, but they were concerned about moving their mission-critical applications to wireless. Even though the high-end industrial WLAN products could promise high profit margins, no WLAN vendors could meet the requirements of these demanding manufacturing plants," Raymond explains. That was because the fast and deterministic cycle time for communications could not be guaranteed using the WLAN solutions then available on the market. However, it's precisely this exact knowledge of the cycle time that makes it possible to reliably control industrial machines, many of which require millisecond precision. If control commands take too much time to travel through the data network, the result may be an expensive chain of errors, which in the worst case could bring the entire production process to a halt – and the more valuable the products are, the more costly the downtime will be.

"Together with colleagues at the Siemens Group Automation and Drives (A&D) in Nuremberg and Karlsruhe and marketing and sales experts, we then went to work to clearly define what customers want. If our industrial WLAN (I-WLAN) can guarantee the cycle time, then we've got a unique selling point that sets us apart from our competitors," explains Raymond. Exactly six months after the project began, the prototype was ready – thanks in large part to Raymond's doctoral thesis – and six months after that, the finished product was released.

Industrial WLAN in action. At a VW plant in Emden, Germany (top) and a Siemens plant in Amberg, Germany radio networks are improving production processes, which are now more flexible and efficient thanks to wireless data transmission and management.

Hunting for Applications

Raymond is proud of this achievement: "If we had insisted on offering our solution only to telecommunications providers, we wouldn't have been able to strengthen Siemens' position in the fast-growing I-WLAN market (which had an estimated total market volume of €100 million in 2005) with such lasting effect. Today we're ahead of the competition in the premium segment for I-WLAN, and Siemens revenue from I-WLAN products continues to grow, currently by 200 to 300 percent annually!" According to Raymond, this illustrates one of Siemens' special strengths. The company's extensive portfolio of products and solutions makes it easier to roll out certain innovations across the groups – and if implementation of a certain application reaches a dead end in one group, in many cases a surprising number of promising areas of application open up elsewhere. "Looking for a possible product application for an innovation is real detective work – but that's exactly what I like the most about my job," he says.

Managing the actual development projects is very hard work, however. Together with his colleagues from the Siemens A&D groups in Germany and India, Raymond is developing his I-WLAN projects step by step with international teams. He gets up early in the morning for the daily telephone conferences, and his colleagues in Nuremberg and Karlsruhe work longer shifts in the evening – given the nine-hour time difference, there's no alternative. All the same, e-mails make their cooperation easier. Raymond sends e-mails out regularly, even from the plane on the way to Germany when he's on his way to the indispensable face-to-face meetings that take place roughly once a month. After all, using WLAN is a matter of course for today's air travelers – at least for business travelers – and Siemens helped to make it so.

By the time Raymond shows up for his meeting at the A&D unit south of Nuremberg, one of his colleagues, such as product manager Martin Kunz, has already printed out a stack of messages containing new ideas that were sent to him by Raymond during the long flight from California. In the evening, Raymond sometimes accompanies his German colleague on a tour of the Nuremberg pubs – even though not all of the establishments measure up to his San Francisco standards. "With international projects running on a tight schedule, it's very important for the team members to have regular personal contact. Otherwise, the researchers on different continents won't feel they're part of a team – and that would put the project's success at risk," Raymond says.

There's just one thing he doesn't understand, he says with a grin as he wipes his brow on a hot summer's day in the Nuremberg office: "Why don't they have air conditioning in Germany?" Actually, he ought to be used to hot summers: His home town, Wuhan in central China, is known as one of the country's "three ovens," with temperatures regularly climbing as high as 40 degrees Celsius in the summertime. But despite the heat, Raymond persevered and received his university degree in information theory and electronic technology in China. After that, he earned a master's degree from the University of Toronto in Canada in telecommunications networks and a doctorate from Columbia University in Manhattan.

It's Hard to Let Go

Today, at 36, Raymond says that his personal goals have changed. Initially he aspired to be a brilliant researcher and possibly a university professor, but later he realized he was having more fun developing marketable products that had a positive impact on the operating business. "Of course that meant making a lot of compromises," he says. "First of all, it wasn't easy for me to distance myself from the results of my Ph.D. thesis. I had spent six years working on it, and suddenly it was a mass of raw material for the team to take apart."

Today, he tries to help young researchers to cope with some of the hard lessons he himself has learned along the way – for example, that they have to set priorities when schedules are very tight, or that it's sometimes better to ignore the particularly challenging research issues that might lead to a comprehensive solution and simply address a small part of the problem or to save effort by avoiding the issue altogether. According to Raymond, young researchers also have to be marketers of their own ideas. "If you can't sell your idea effectively, you're facing an uphill struggle, because before an idea can become a successful product, it has to be sold to development managers, product managers, marketing experts, sales people, controllers, and ultimately the customers," he says.

Many researchers have a lot to learn in this regard, says Raymond, who has attended inter-personal communication training sessions in order to get where he is now. In some cases, he suspects that a researcher's passionate devotion to technical problems leads to a lack of interest in inter-personal skills. But the products that ultimately result from this process are meant to benefit people, and they can only be created through the cooperation of all the members of a team.

People and Technology

"I've learned a lot. And over time I've become a lot more communicative. When I arrived in the USA from China 15 years ago, I was too shy to look my fellow students and colleagues in the eye – until someone told me that this irritates most people. I had to learn it the hard way," he remembers. He believes this is the most effective way of learning things,

Lessons learned	Raymond Liao's advice for innovators
• People who have earned a doctorate have learned to be critical thinkers. But we have to be careful. If we tear unconventional ideas apart too soon with our negative criticism, we'll prevent some great ideas from being born. • We should accept the less glamorous development work on innovations as well and follow through our projects to the end. Those who can describe their visions in grand terms should also be prepared to do all the hard work involved, from start to finish. • Anyone who wants to inspire others with their complex ideas – and most innovations initially appear to be complex – should present them in a way that's easy to understand. Physical concepts of a product are tremendously valuable and helpful, even before the prototype phase. • Only those who understand a company's business process and appreciate the business experience will be able to direct their research work consistently toward the successful products they are aiming for. • When we are evaluating a technological innovation, we should first look at all of its possible fields of application. Sometimes an exciting idea will make economic sense in a completely unexpected context.	• Balance your life. Those who do nothing but work will soon be unable to produce any good results. • Technical people should truly master their own fields of specialization. Nothing can make up for an inadequate grasp of one's specialty. • Every presentation has to be matched to its audience. If the presenter bores a group of marketing specialists with the technical details of his or her standard presentation, the audience won't be enthusiastic about the product. • An innovation manager seems to fall outside all the standard job categories, so he or she has to understand the roles of development managers, product managers and sales specialists in an innovation project, and develop appropriate incentives for each of them to contribute. • Those who are completely devoted to research should ask themselves whether they can deal with people as well as they can with ideas. Sometimes communication training sessions can make a tremendous difference.

even though he would like to save his young colleagues in Berkeley from a similar fate.

Many of the young researchers who work for him come from the elite universities, such as nearby UC Berkeley, and they're accustomed to the breakneck pace of Silicon Valley. "The people here work day and night," Raymond says. When asked if that applies to him as well, he hesitates before admitting with a smile, "Yes, it does. That's why I tell the young researchers, 'Balance your life.' If they burn out at a young age, nobody benefits." Raymond married a college classmate. They have two children, a 3-year-old daughter and another baby girl, born in October 2006.

Two years ago he was approached by a young man who had developed a tool for placing WLAN radios in rooms so as to get ideal network coverage. By chance, he had found out just a short time earlier from his colleagues in Nuremberg that some customers were desperately looking for exactly such solutions for their interconnected factory halls. Raymond recruited the young man to work for Siemens and a few months ago the product was released. But in his search for talent he doesn't rely on chance encounters alone: "We read through the papers given at conferences, and if something interests us we get in touch with the authors directly. By now our reputation is spreading and people send us unsolicited summaries of their papers," he says. But these summaries rarely contain the really exciting innovations, so Raymond prefers to do the searching himself. Sometimes, he says, he feels like a prospector panning for gold – but the nuggets he's looking for are ideas. And sometimes he's the stranger calling up a talented student out of the blue – with a job offer at Siemens.

"I'm sure that story will strike a chord with lots of university researchers," says Matthias. "If you've spent years researching in a particular field, it's not easy to let go and be flexible when your ideas are implemented."

"Yes, that's what Raymond Liao says, too," agrees Stacey. "If one path doesn't lead anywhere, you have to try a different one. Switching from telecommunications to industrial automation, for instance, means you have to change your way of thinking. And then he also understands how important communication training can be for researchers and developers – not everyone does."

While Stacey was talking about Liao, John had been gazing thoughtfully into the flickering flames of the open fire. Turning toward the others, he says, "The innovators we've heard about so far had their ideas outside of Siemens and then turned them into reality within the company. But plenty of development projects have arisen in cooperation with universities or research institutes as well. Lots of them were supported by the Ministry *of Research or as part of European Union projects. Let me tell you about an innovation that, just like piezotechnology, received the German Future Prize – the highest award for innovation in the country."*

The others lean back in their comfortable armchairs by the fireside, and John begins his story.

Biolab on a Chip

Asked about the significance of his team's innovation for society as a whole, Walter Gumbrecht hesitates and frowns. "I'm always a little reluctant to evaluate my own work," he says. Gumbrecht is slim with very short hair and a cropped beard. Today he's wearing jeans with a shirt and tie, and there's a pair of narrow sunglasses tucked into his shirt pocket. He's a sporty, alert man who has a keenly critical eye. Gumbrecht is constantly questioning things, especially things that affect him directly. So what, in his view, marks an innovation? He stares at the floor and thinks for a moment. "The invention of the transistor many years ago was a true innovation – perhaps even a revolution," he says. "But between major innovations you also get inventions that help to advance society in smaller steps." No, he wouldn't describe his own innovation as revolutionary.

The judging panel for the German Future Prize took a different view. In 2004, German President Horst Köhler presented Gumbrecht and two partners from the Fraunhofer Institute for Silicon Technology (ISIT) in Itzehoe and Infineon Technologies in Munich with the most important award in Germany for technology and innovation, which is endowed with €250,000. Together, the three

According to **Dr. Walter Gumbrecht**, the way to overcome difficulties is to persevere and be self-critical. With these qualities and the help of strong external partners, he developed an innovation that was awarded the German Future Prize in 2004: the first electric biolaboratory on a chip.

Siemens and the World

researchers had developed an electric biochip for detecting and analyzing pathogens, proteins and DNA sequences. The chip is equipped with receptor molecules that can bind to specific substances in blood or other bodily fluids – such as proteins, which accumulate in the blood when a patient is suffering from heart disease or infections. A tiny electrical pulse is emitted when the substance docks onto the receptor and the chip sounds the alarm.

From Days to Minutes

Gumbrecht and his team from Siemens then built the chip into a miniature laboratory the size of a credit card. Known as the *quicklab*, this type of card will enable doctors to make analyses in their own offices in the future. Because the lab on a chip processes and displays diagnostic information electrically, it's faster and more robust than conventional visual analysis systems. In these systems, the docking of a substance results in light signals that have to be evaluated by means of relatively complex technology. Such tests are currently carried out in large laboratories, and it often takes several hours or even days to produce a result. Depending on the type of analysis, the *quicklab* will make it possible to do the same task in a short time – anything from a couple of minutes to no more than an hour – thereby speeding up the patient's treatment and saving costs.

"Winning the Future Prize generated a lot of publicity for us, both externally and internally," recalls Gumbrecht. The innovation, which he invented with Dr. Rainer Hintsche from the Fraunhofer Institute for Silicon Technology in Itzehoe and Dr. Roland Thewes from Infineon Technologies, was featured on TV and in several newspapers. Infineon withdrew from the biochip development shortly afterwards, but, as Gumbrecht explains, "the Future Prize made Siemens so enthusiastic about the biochip that the Medical Solutions Group (Med) decided to take over the Infineon biochip technology." To date, no other company has built a biochip that uses electricity so comprehensively.

Despite the team's accomplishments, Gumbrecht "wouldn't dare" to call *quicklab* – the market-ready, enhanced version of the biochip – an innovation. That's because it still hasn't been launched or achieved commercial success. "We've only produced prototypes so far," he says. At the same time, he's working hard to ensure that the product's market success isn't left to chance. "I've invested years in the development of this technology and would obviously love to see it used in a successful market product," he says. What's the essential driving force behind Gumbrecht's

A lab the size of a credit card. A single drop of blood will be enough to perform examinations and DNA analyses completely automatically in the various channels and reaction chambers of the *quicklab* system.

work? "It might sound like a cliché, but I think that it would be wonderful to contribute toward something that ultimately helps people."

At the start of his career, however, Gumbrecht never would have expected his contribution to be a biochip. After studying chemistry and earning a doctorate, he joined Siemens in 1985, long before the company was doing research in biotechnology. His initial task was to establish a small Microsensors working group in the central research department, which later became Corporate Technology (CT). The aim of this group was to develop an online blood-monitoring system for intensive care units that would measure chemical parameters such as oxygen and blood pH values. Gumbrecht had received a job offer from a chemical company at the same time, but he chose Siemens because he was excited by the interdisciplinary approach involving chemistry, biology and electrotechnology; the chip was to be made of semiconductors. As Gumbrecht explains, "Working with teams from other disciplines is what makes my job so exciting."

The Risky Side of Autonomy

Gumbrecht was surprised at the amount of leeway given to him by his supervisors, who had realized that microsensors were an upcoming trend. "There were no constraints about the kind of chemosensor we were supposed to develop, so we had a great deal of freedom right from the beginning." Gumbrecht got to work, combing through journals and other industry sources for recent publications and the latest information. After six months he developed his first clear ideas of how the microsensors could work. He began cooperating with what was then the Siemens Semiconductors Group, Siemens Med and various universities. "It was a fantastic environment," he recalls. "We were given complete freedom and didn't need to be afraid of making mistakes." In the end, however, Med didn't take up the technology, and the Patient Monitoring business area was spun off. That put an end to Gumbrecht's field of research and to the chemosensor, although the technology behind it was later spun off in an external company. Gumbrecht changed direction and started developing power electronics based on silicon carbide. "That was exciting too, and I could have seen myself spending more time in that field," he reports.

But it wasn't to be. With the rapid advance of genetic technology and biotechnology in the late 1990s, developers from four Siemens Groups, including Med and CT, founded a working group of around 20 people in order to assess the potential harbored by biotechnology, especially molecular diagnosis. Gumbrecht was asked to join this group. "We meet every four weeks or so," he explains. "Our discussions of the new technology and its opportunities were very lively at first. Some people backed it, but a few of the supervisors had reservations." Gumbrecht and his fellow supporters persevered, and in the end their viewpoint prevailed. The committee decided to take part in a project sponsored by the Federal Ministry of Research (BMBF) to develop a fully electrical biochip. "The BMBF covered half of the costs, which made it easier to get people on our side," continues Gumbrecht. The management of CT and Siemens Med agreed to meet the remaining costs. At that time, nobody knew whether the investment in the new research field would pay off – and certainly nobody could have predicted that the company's decision would later lead to the Future Prize. Gumbrecht had now reached the end of a difficult period in which he had often questioned the reasons behind his work. "When you keep being told, 'What you're doing is great, but...', you constantly have to rethink your objectives," he explains. "You start asking yourself if you're being pigheaded, or if you might be wrong after all."

Diplomacy and Single-Mindedness

But keeping a critical eye on your work also has advantages. Gumbrecht firmly believes that his "obstinacy" was one of the key characteristics that spurred him on. After all, the "normal" processes that companies use to drive innovations ahead did not apply in his case. This time

Gumbrecht and his team were working on something completely new, and the company didn't even have a business area for it yet. There were no strategies for marketing or patenting, and it wasn't until some time later that the Siemens Patents department had somebody who was familiar with biotechnology. But Gumbrecht never lost heart, because he had strong partners in the BMBF project. They were old acquaintances and, like him, they believed in the value of the work. He had known Hintsche, a researcher from Itzehoe, for years from conferences and occasional work meetings. Hintsche was contributing his knowledge of microsensors to the project, in areas such as the analysis of environmental toxins. The other partner was Infineon, which evolved from the Siemens Semiconductors Group and had been involved in the project right from the start. Also working alongside Gumbrecht were developers from three CT departments and Siemens Med. As the coordinator of this "huge project," Gumbrecht was in charge of pulling all the threads together. He regarded himself as an intermediary between the specialists from various disciplines, ranging from CMOS chip experts to electrochemists and biologists. "To fulfill that role, you need a clear idea of how you want to achieve your goals, as well as plenty of diplomacy to put your ideas into practice," he says.

With the project up and running, Gumbrecht had an idea: to fit the chip on a chip card with not only a microfluidic system of small channels for transporting water and bodily fluids, but also tiny chambers that contain all of the necessary biochemicals. The concept behind the *quicklab* was born. Luckily for Gumbrecht, his supervisors at CT approved additional funding because of the progress made in the BMBF project. Gumbrecht was asked to work on the *quicklab* concept in parallel with his other work. He teamed up with an engineer and a biologist from his working group and decided that the mini laboratory had to be small, inexpensive and, above all, fast – which is how the *quicklab* name originated. In terms of the format, a chip card seemed to be the best option. "Lots of people already have chip cards from their banks, for example," explains Gumbrecht. "They're quick and easy to use, and handy as well."

Then, however, came another financial setback. Although the BMBF project had concluded successfully and Gumbrecht was working hard on the *quicklab*, the decision-makers at Med – still Gumbrecht's most important customer – could not yet approve the funding. But six months later, in November 2003, they reconsidered and agreed to continue supporting the microfluidics concept. The defining moment came the following year with the Future Prize 2004. This external award showed even the doubters that Gumbrecht and his colleagues had backed the right horse. With the major obstacle removed, the *quicklab* was about to be transformed from a concept into a real product. A clear project agreement was drawn up between Gumbrecht and Med, setting out the objectives, milestones and timeframes for the next development stages.

For Gumbrecht, that was the right approach. "I was heavily involved in the research for a long time," says the 54-year-old. In the future he'd like to spend more time on product development so that his idea can become a market success as quickly as possible. "We're very close to the final product now, and our main focus is on the manufacturing technology," he explains. At the moment, more of his time is taken up with business plans and analyses of production costs than with working in the laboratory. When it comes to technical development, his team includes many people who, in Gumbrecht's words, "are fantastic at what they do." He has also recently recruited new biology experts for his eight-person working group. "It's a great team and we have a good working environment," he continues. "I like to think that I can motivate people."

Time to Relax

But what about relaxation? Gumbrecht draws strength by separating his work from his private life, although he often finds it difficult to switch off from his job because he's preoccupied by some tricky problem. "But when your family starts griping because you're still thinking about work, you soon realize that things have to change," he says. Gumbrecht relaxes by playing the guitar. Every two weeks, he meets up with a friend from his old school band to rehearse Simon & Garfunkel songs. "We have 25 songs in our repertoire, and we have to keep rehearsing them so that we don't forget the lyrics or the arrangements," he smiles. They perform in public around four times a year, or more often if people ask them to. Gumbrecht appreciates having regular rehearsals that take him away from his work. "Some days I really don't feel like rehearsing, but by the time I get home afterwards, I'm completely relaxed. It's important to be able to switch off from work, otherwise your performance suffers. That's something to bear in mind when you're at work, too. I find that after around 6 p.m. my concentration level falls and I can't work so effectively. And if you're having problems in your family life, you can't put in your best performance in the office." Gumbrecht's other mainstay is living in Franconia; he was born and raised there, studied locally and decided to stay in the area and work for Siemens in Erlangen.

At the moment, Gumbrecht is configuring the *quicklab* to detect DNA sequences, with the aim of identifying genetic predispositions toward certain diseases before those diseases occur. The chip captures strands

Lessons learned	**Walter Gumbrecht's advice for innovators**
• Having too much leeway at work can be unsettling, but it's important to exploit it. • Being able to work without the fear of making mistakes boosts creativity. • Setbacks are painful, but they're a good opportunity to change direction. • Successful cooperation requires diplomacy and the ability to communicate clearly. • It's essential to have a clear objective for day-to-day work – for example, the aim of developing a commercially successful product that benefits people.	• Persevere. • Be diplomatic. • Be self-critical, keep assessing your own work, and set new goals when necessary. • Keep your work life separate from your private life and take time to relax. • Have the courage to disagree, but behave fairly.

from the patient's blood that contain genetic sequences characteristic of the disease. That makes it possible to determine whether the patient is at a higher risk of thrombosis or of cystic fibrosis – an illness that causes thick mucus to accumulate in the respiratory tract. "Genotyping will be our first *quicklab* application," Gumbrecht explains, although many other uses are possible. Theoretically, the *quicklab* could help to detect antibiotics in milk or to track down suppliers of rotten meat, for example. It's potentially a molecular diagnostics platform that can serve a whole host of purposes. In that sense it has something in common with its creator. Over the years, Gumbrecht has above all learned the importance of flexibility – and of continuing to set new goals.

"It'll be interesting to see whether quicklab really will be ready to launch soon, or whether there'll be more obstacles along the way," says Matthias. "But it's a fascinating idea. I'd love it if my doctor could do a quick test to find out if I had a normal cold or a dangerous attack of the flu. The problem at the moment is that tests have to be sent to a special lab, so it takes days to get results."

"Yes, quicklab is a valuable innovation," John agrees. "But to return to Walter's comment about the value chain, there are major differences in the analogy with suppliers compared to 'purchasing innovation.' When you

buy a product, you know exactly what you want. 'Open innovation' is much more difficult, because although you can define your goals and interim results, they're often moving targets. You never know exactly what's going to happen. Especially with radical innovations, you're bound to face surprises and delays."

"You're right," says Christian. "That's also why Gumbrecht finds it so important to be diplomatic and to keep scrutinizing his own work. Any radical innovation is primarily a learning project with lots of trial and error, guided by the methods of innovation management. Just as Gumbrecht said, there was no business unit for his new technology, and there were no marketing or patenting strategies. What's more, it was an interdisciplinary project that involved coordinating chemists, biologists, electrical engineers, various Siemens departments, external institutes and companies. It could hardly have been more difficult."

"But it's the complexity that made the project so exciting and so challenging for Gumbrecht," replies John. Bao Jun adds, "I can think of one other aspect that can make innovation processes even harder: having to coordinate teams from different cultural backgrounds, like China and Germany. Let me tell you about the Somatom Spirit and the innovator who followed in the tradition of Confucius."

Recipe for Success from China

"To learn and from time to time to return to what one has learned – isn't that a pleasure?" Although Jun Kong prefers to venture into the unknown rather than repeatedly return to what he's already learned, quotes from Confucius like the one above still have an effect on him. After all, Siemens researcher Jun Kong is a direct descendant of Kong Zi (Master Kong, or Confucius), and that's an honor only few others in China share. The teachings of Confucius, formulated around 2,500 years ago, are considered the foundation of the Chinese ethical system. Jun Kong looks at it more pragmatically, however. He says: "The philosophy of Confucius has strongly influenced my management style. My main concerns in my daily work are honesty, trust and perseverance. The good results I achieve are directly related to that." The success of the Somatom Spirit computer tomograph, which he and his team developed in China, seems to confirm this. The device has been a huge sales hit. About 400 orders had been received by mid-2006. Three out of four orders for the tomograph are from abroad, as health care providers around the globe are coming under increasing cost pressures, and that makes favorably priced diagnostic devices very attractive.

Jun is just another example of how China can be an excellent location for research and development. The country has enjoyed a reputation as a land of inventors for thousands of years. It was responsible for inventions such as noodles, printing and gunpowder, which were just a few of its most famous innovations. Jun's idea was also a big bang, as Somatom Spirit utilizes proven, state-of-the-art Siemens technology but is geared toward the needs of the so-called entry-level market – not the top segment but instead wherever costs are crucial.

Trend toward Second Units

"In China, the market for top-of-the-line computer tomographs, like the ones that deliver three-dimensional images of a beating heart, is relatively small," Jun explains. "All the important hospitals already have high-end equipment, but many of them still need to acquire lower-priced secondary devices for less complicated procedures such as lung examinations." The numerous small hospitals in this vast country are also interested in obtaining an entry-level model so as to be able to perform CT scans themselves.

Executives in Forchheim, Germany, quickly realized that Jun Kong was the right person for the two-year assignment to develop such an entry-level device. It was because he had previously proved himself by enhancing the image quality of the predecessor model, Somatom Smile. Afterwards, he spent two years visiting customers throughout the world, providing training and technical support. "In some remote Chinese hospitals in small cities, my colleagues even had to

Proof positive that China can be an outstanding research and development location comes from **Dr. Jun Kong** and the Somatom Spirit, a Siemens computer tomograph that was developed in Shanghai. Originally designed for customers looking for a robust, affordable entry-level device that's easy to operate, the Somatom Spirit went on to become a worldwide best seller. Today, three out of four orders for it come from outside China.

explain how to use a computer mouse," he says. "However, during such visits we learned a great deal about what customers in an up-and-coming market like China actually need."

The knowledge and experience he gained as a result flowed into his later development work. Together with the sales and marketing teams, Jun clearly defined the strategy for the follow-up device from the beginning: Somatom Spirit was to be cost-efficient, highly reliable, easy to use and quick to recoup the customers' investment costs. In the end, even Jun was surprised by how quickly the initial investment can be recovered. "Some European hospitals scan 20 to 30 patients per day with one device, but I visited hospitals in China that handle more than 100 patients per day with our unit," he says. The maximization of efficiency is really necessary, however, as the Chinese government sets the prices charged for such examinations in order to provide good diagnoses and treatment to as many people as possible.

No Overengineering

That's why Jun wanted to make sure from the beginning that there would be no "over-engineering" in the Somatom Spirit. It was therefore decided not to include any technical features that go beyond the basic functions, especially since the customers would not want them anyway. To ensure that Jun's team of approximately 100 Chinese engineers would completely internalize this attitude, he decided to get them closer to their customers by sending them to hospitals and encouraging them to talk to doctors. In fact, it's obligatory for them to do so at least one day a year.

"Ultimately, the key to success is communication – with customers, within the team, and also with Siemens Medical Solutions Computed Tomography headquarters in Erlangen and our top developers in Forchheim, Germany," Jun explains. Somatom Spirit ended up being developed by an international team that Jun managed out of Shanghai. Jun says he's certain they never would have been so successful if not for a highly precise process management system and the clear monitoring of all milestones. Even more important, however, was the fact that the Chinese and German engineers spoke English equally well and were able to overcome cultural differences.

Jun's younger colleague Jian Du knows a lot about such differences. The 29-year-old engineer spent six months working in Forchheim before returning to Shanghai to take over his own project team. "I was pleasantly surprised by the directness of my European colleagues," Jian says.

"It's often the case in China that people say 'yes' but definitely mean 'no.' I never experienced anything like that in Germany, though, and these kinds of differences are what make collaboration such a cultural challenge."

Jun knows this too, as he learned about Western styles of work and communication early on. After completing his bachelor's program in just two years, he obtained a Ph.D. degree in medical technology in Hangzhou, China. The special thing about the program was that most of the books and much of the instruction was in English, and some of the teachers were from the U.S. After finishing the program, he spent time as a research assistant in Hong Kong, and was then hired by Siemens.

This experience of expanding his horizons helps him to mediate between his employees and their colleagues in Europe. "In the beginning, I was an engineer and researcher, but I gradually became an innovation manager," Jun explains. Those who observe him in his work quickly realize that he's also become a coach as well as a mediator. He chooses to work with his team in an open-plan office because issues can be clarified more quickly that way, he says. He maintains continual contact with his project teams, for example by having lunch with them.

Other Peoples' Cultures

Jun recalls with amusement the first problems that came up early on in his project. There were some occasions when the Germans would just keep on talking during videoconferences and the Chinese, polite and shy as they tend to be, couldn't get a word in edgewise. "When it was over, the people in Germany had the impression that the Asian engineers either had no desire to contribute anything or else were incapable of doing so," Jun explains. "The Chinese, on the other hand, thought that the Germans just couldn't stop talking."

Jun encourages his people to act a bit more forcefully and communicate more with each other. "He says to us: 'Be straightforward, and aggressive where necessary,'" Jian explains. "He also hands out criticism but it's always directed toward the issue at hand; it's never about an individual." Jian and his colleagues appreciate this, while Jun himself feels that he sometimes expects too much from his employees. "But maybe that goes with the territory," he reflects. "On the other hand, I certainly don't want to expect too little of them. After all, our rapidly developing low-end market shows no mercy to those who move too slowly." Jun was always fast – in his studies and in his career. However, he says that since he became a father a little less than two years ago, he's come to understand just how much responsibility he bears – toward his employees as well, some of whom are only a little younger than his 35 years.

Young university graduates in particular (those who have not yet been exposed to the slow-moving state-run companies) are attracted to Siemens by its fast pace and its open communication style, which is rare at traditional Chinese companies. This becomes clear during a walk through the production hall, which is located directly below the research laboratory. Most of the workers here are in their early 20s and highly motivated. Their workstations are more or less the same as those of their German counterparts who assemble high-end tomographs in Forchheim. "Whenever we offer a job here, we end up with a ton of applications in the human resources department," says Jun, as he proudly runs his hand across a nearly finished CT. Although it's "only" the entry-level model, it's already won several design awards.

It's not always easy to hold on to good people. This is a big challenge for Jun, who has to be creative in order to get the best people into his department and keep them there. That's because many talented individuals receive lucrative offers from abroad. Moreover, the local subsidiaries of Siemens' competitors in the market for medical systems are only a short drive away, and some are also located in Pudong. "So I have to be a good motivator," says Jun.

Parties, Incentives, Plaques

He does in fact do whatever it takes. For example, once a month he turns the canteen into a giant party room. "We discuss the progress being made on all our projects at the monthly meeting because it's important to have responsible employees who have an overview of what's going on throughout the department, rather than focusing solely on their own individual projects," says Jun. After the meeting, there's a party in honor of everyone whose birthday falls in that month. "That's really a big boost," says Jun. "Everyone can talk in a relaxed atmosphere and has a feeling that's important for many Chinese people – the feeling that 'my company is there for me.'"

Jun also offers rewards to his researchers. Those who register a patent, for example, will have their portrait put up in a special place of honor located near the entrance, making clear to visitors and employees alike that this is a research department where people work hard and are very successful. Patents are also rewarded with bonuses that can total up to one month's salary. The bonuses have been increased recently, which made Jian happy, as he's set to receive a check for his first patent soon.

Jian, however, wishes to make clear that although everyone is happy with the incentives, "if we constantly needed a motivational coach, we'd be in the wrong job. I'm here because I enjoy my work and because it's a job with a future." Jian is already working on the next-generation Somatom Spirit, which will offer much better performance but will also be favorably priced. The difference with regard to functionality and performance between Somatom Spirit and devices developed and produced in Germany will remain noticeable, however.

Jun has given this difference some thought. "Of course every researcher dreams of working on high-end products," he says. "However, our job is to cover a different spectrum of innovation, and we've been very, very successful doing it." Still, who knows what the future will bring? Next year, for example, a larger building will be opened in the Shanghai Inter-

Lessons learned	Jun Kong's advice for innovators
• Always keep in mind customer requirements and customer utility. • Research and innovation in China can be tremendously efficient and profitable – but it can only function well with the full support of management, locally and at company headquarters as well. • Those who seek to develop innovative products in cooperation with local suppliers in China must pay close attention to quality if they want to avoid unpleasant surprises. • It is very difficult to recruit, develop and hold on to excellent employees in China. In some areas, the market for highly qualified specialists has already been swept clean. • All members of international project teams must speak the same language – and this refers not only to English but also to the creation of a common cultural foundation. Stringent processes can further improve cooperation once this cultural foundation has been laid.	• Research conducted outside an international company's headquarters has led to impressive successes around the world. Allowing for even greater individual freedom and independence can only enhance dynamic developments here. • Challenge your people. If you expect too little, you'll also get it. • Learn English. If language barriers are eliminated, cooperation can be as fruitful as we want it to be, and as the competitive environment requires. • Don't neglect advance development. Successful products like the Somatom Spirit are based on state-of-the-art technology that didn't just drop into Siemens' lap. • Pursue even those ideas that initially sound crazy. The path to excellence doesn't always appear rational. When my employees approach me with a crazy idea, I allocate them a limited budget for a specific period of time.

national Medical Zone. The building will house almost all of the Siemens Medical Solutions departments based in Shanghai. The business is expanding.

China is where the customers of the future are. The country's market for medical systems is growing at a rate of over ten percent per year – faster than anywhere else in the world. Those who want to know the needs of the customers of tomorrow would do well to develop products for them in the places where they live. That means Jun can expect more such assignments – which may include development projects for top-of-the-line products. Until then, he will maintain his passion for, and enjoyment of, his work, along with a good old Confucian virtue: patience.

After listening attentively to Bao Jun, John speaks first. "I think the story of the Somatom Spirit is a great example of how innovations are increasingly emerging out of the global division of work these days, just like lots of other parts of the value creation process. The key success factor was the smooth collaboration between the high-end developers in Germany and the local specialists," he says.

"Don't forget that the innovation wouldn't have been born in the first place without Kong's close ties with the customer," adds Christian. "From Germany it probably wouldn't have been possible to recognize the real needs of the customers in China so accurately, or to find out which innovations are required to meet those needs. I think the importance of that aspect is often underestimated. Innovations aren't always just about the best technology. In countries like China you often achieve your objectives for completely different reasons."

"Robust, inexpensive and easy to use," sums up Bao Jun, repeating what Kong had said. "And as it turned out, those were the key factors behind the innovation's success not just on the Chinese market, but also in many other countries around the world – including hospitals in highly developed industrial nations looking for inexpensive additional equipment."

"I guess the global success came as a very pleasant surprise for the developers," states Walter. "Companies that push ahead with innovations should remember not only to do so at their own headquarters. It's definitely worthwhile to get input from other countries and to exploit the dynamism of rapidly growing economies like those of China and India."

Stacey nods. "That reminds me of another example where the development was deliberately conducted abroad in order to exploit the strengths of a dynamic market and also to avoid stagnation at home," she says. But that wasn't in an emerging country, it was in the U.S."

Recipe for Success from China

Simplicity as a Principle – Telephoning via Cable Networks

The fact that her unit's technology makes the business models of billion-dollar companies obsolete does not move Eve Aretakis to tears. She has actually been greeted with the words "Your Softswitch is ruining our industry." But Aretakis remains calm even when faced with such accusations. "If we hadn't revolutionized the technology of switching telephone calls, someone else would have done it, only a bit later. And Siemens would be trailing behind the competition today," she says. Instead, Aretakis and the company she manages – Siemens Network Convergence (SNC) in Chelmsford near Boston, Massachusetts – is far ahead of the field.

Her successful product is easy to understand. It's a small box that replaces the wardrobe-sized switchboxes that were previously used to switch phone calls. All of this has become possible thanks to voice-over-Internet protocol technology (VoIP). "You could put our Softswitch on your washing machine at home and start your own phone company," says Aretakis with a smile.

The image with the washing machine appeals to her, because Aretakis loves simplicity; after all, the world is complicated enough anyway. The 46-year-old innovation manager explains that her products have the task of controlling complexity for her customers. And her job as a manager is to reduce complexity for her team so as to make tasks feasible.

Of course that's easier said than done, because although the basic idea for VoIP switching servers was thoroughly convincing, there was great resistance to the technology

Voice-over-IP, telephoning via Internet protocol technology, is currently one of the most important trends in telecommunications. **Eve Aretakis** wrote a success story with it in the U.S. The Softswitch technology developed by her team enabled cable network operators to enter the lucrative telephony business and offer their customers not only TV but also telephone services. Aretakis' company operates like a small flexible David among the telecommunications Goliaths – and Aretakis enjoys the benefits. Lots of freedom, simplicity, close contact with customers, and a team consisting of like-minded colleagues – those are the secrets of her success.

from competitors as well as from managers within the company, which for a long time had generated high revenues and earnings from conventional digital telephone switching. But a few years ago, the industry had the idea that instead of conventional switching technology, phone calls could be routed through the Internet – and that this would be easier and less expensive. This paradigm shift turned out to be a massive threat for suppliers of the old technology – because the flexible Internet technology is cheaper and faster for most applications than conventional switchboxes. On the other hand, it also had a lot of teething problems to overcome with regard to reliability, sound quality and convenience.

David and Goliaths

"We played the role of David with our ideas, while the Goliaths of the industry, each one of them a hundred times bigger than us, watched us suspiciously and laid obstacles in our path," remembers Aretakis. These Goliaths, including Siemens Communications Group itself, didn't make her life any easier – and they had good reasons not to do so, at least according to the logic of their current business. They didn't want their major customers at that time, primarily the telephone network operators, to be irritated by the additional offer of new switching technology – the new product from SNC in Massachusetts was not to be allowed to cannibalize a successful business. Yet SNC had been founded in the year 2002 as a Siemens start-up subsidiary in order to identify important trends for Siemens Communications – flexibly and fast – and to make use of them.

Eve Aretakis and the Fixed Network sales group arranged a deal: Existing customers would continue to be supplied by parent company Siemens with conventional technology as long as that was practical. Aretakis ambiguously describes the old technology as a "legacy." In return, her company, a 100% Siemens subsidiary, would enter new markets and develop its own customers there, of course with the cooperation of selected sales/solutions teams. "We accepted the challenge. And we soon found out that the operators of cable networks, which had previously mainly been used to carry television channels, were ideal partners. They already had large customer bases, already were pursing broadband IP data services, and could add another service to their offering without much expense: telephony via Internet protocol."

In April 2003, the first agreement was concluded with Cablevision, one of the biggest TV cable companies in the United States with a customer base mainly in New York. Meanwhile, more than a million subscribers pay a flat rate of $39 a month to use SNC's VoIP technology to make fixed-line phone calls – now free of charge within the U.S. Aretakis enthuses about the additional gimmicks that are particularly popular with customers, such as personalized messages and customer flexibility. "Unwanted callers' numbers can be blocked so that they don't get through. Or you can set the following message for phone calls from your mother-in-law: 'We have relocated and can no longer be contacted at this number,'" she jokes.

Surviving with Speed

However, during the incredibly short development time, Aretakis and her team didn't have much to laugh about. They set themselves two years as a maximum time to market – the period needed from the beginning of a product's development until the first delivery. They really did have to be quick, because in 2002 the first competitors also discovered the market for VoIP telephony. Another factor was that evolutionary cycles in the telecommunications industry were getting shorter and shorter. "The time is long past when a technology firm's development engineers could talk to a customer and leave him or her with the words: 'Great, I understand what you need. I'll come back in two years with the finished product,'" says Aretakis.

In order to meet their deadlines, the development teams made increasing use of freely available components such as open-source codes for software, or licensed technology; they didn't feel the need to invent everything themselves. And for the hardware, Aretakis' team only used components that were already on the open market, instead of spending lots of time creating proprietary hardware. This also brought another advantage: "It means that we can always build our solutions on the latest platforms and take advantage of platform innovations – so, in a way, a part of our development work is outsourced, permanently and free of charge. But the software and the total package offer a solution that is only available from Siemens in this quality," Aretakis points out. The product functions as a network-independent control-and-connection interface, routing incoming signals like an intelligent switchboard.

Getting Customers Involved in Product Development

Pilot customer Cablevision worked hand in hand with the SNC engineers in Chelmsford and Siemens USA during the incremental development in a gradual process that had a major impact on the solution's functionality. These close customer contacts were a new experience for some software engineers. Some team members needed to buy new suits and for the first time spend serious time with the customers, "so that they could learn what our customers really need in order to be successful in their market," says Aretakis. "After all, in our industry, you won't do any business if your solution doesn't offer the customer either significant revenue growth or long-term cost-cutting potential."

The success of the solution, according to Aretakis, should be linked to that of the customers. For each new subscriber to VoIP services, Siemens receives a one-time payment from the cable network operator ranging between €20 and €50, depending on whether Siemens supplied individual components or a complete solution, for example with a service agreement. If Cablevision had flopped with its extra VoIP service, VoIP-Softswitch and SNC would have flopped too. "We were aware that we were taking this risk," states Aretakis. "because on the one hand we had to position a completely new product, so it was important for us to demonstrate our commitment. And on the other hand we also wanted to participate in our partner's revenue growth since this was a software business model. Pay as you go – pay as you grow."

This methodology has paid off. Meanwhile, Aretakis, her team and Siemens are also developing VoIP solutions for large companies that use Softswitch to become less dependent on their telephony providers and route a lot of their phone calls through the Internet themselves. Together with the cable-network operators, this adds up to an annual market potential of around $6.5 billion for the VoIP infrastructure alone. But the technology from the U.S. is also in use in Europe, for example in Hungary, the Netherlands and Switzerland – everywhere that cable networks have large numbers of end customers. Aretakis' team is expanding the business not only in regional terms: "Our engineers continue to talk with customers about the needs of the end users, so we can often identify helpful applications, which we can then sell on top. These are added to the Siemens LifeWorks concept," explains Aretakis. One example is managing and optimizing how subscribers can be contacted. For instance, messages are passed on to them no matter where they are or which channels they are using, whether by fixed-line telephone, mobile phone, e-mail, text message, fax or answering machine.

Small and Flexible – Yet Part of a Larger Whole

The fact that in this case a good idea led to high-revenue business – Eve Aretakis is firmly convinced of this – was partially due to the favorable environment. "If we had been part of Siemens itself, it wouldn't have worked out. We needed a level of autonomy, we needed the risk, we needed our independence. But afterwareds, we needed the sales power of a large organization to make our product a success in the marketplace," says Aretakis. Her company's location in Chelmsford – and its branch in Boca Raton, Florida – are like a sort of incubator. "There's no wearying office politics, no permanent coordination and decision processes – that's what I like. I worked for Siemens, the parent company, for a long time. But since getting to know the speed with which we can now implement decisions here at SNC, I don't want to go back. And I hope we've shown we can take the best of both worlds – the start-ups are fast and flexible, but it takes the depth of Siemens to provide quality, reliability and market reach," she explains.

Many of her approximately 350 research and development staff don't want to leave either, although there are plenty of very good job offers for well-qualified software engineers in this area. This has a lot to do with the atmosphere the SNC management team has created: a flat organization with decision-making responsibility at the lowest possible management level.

Aretakis answers questions in monthly conference calls in which all her staff members can participate. Anyone who doesn't want to ask a question directly can submit it anonymously in advance.

In these calls, some issues that might otherwise develop into problems receive top-management attention. Aretakis remembers one occurrence that surprised her: "During the soccer World Cup, a lot of staff members were following the games on the Internet. Because this ended up blocking the corporate network, Siemens USA blocked access to the relevant websites. My people complained; the Brazilians in particular wanted to cheer on their team." So she had televisions installed in the offices, because she's convinced that only satisfied employees work well. And if they are happy with their work, they do more than they would otherwise – they go the extra mile, which can make the crucial difference in the fight against the competition.

Wanted: Team Players

Aretakis and her management team pay "bounty money" to help her find excellent employees. Anyone who proposes a new co-worker who is then hired by the company receives a payment of between $2,000 and $5,000. This often saves SNC a troublesome and expensive search in the employment market. And not only software engineers have a chance – in addition to software engineering, Aretakis herself studied economics at a college in New York.

But interesting job offers at SNC are only made to real team players. Aretakis has learned from her kids why this skill is so important, on those weekends when she takes them to basketball and football games. Innovation manager Aretakis noticed how some teams lost although they had first-class players: "A superstar alone doesn't make a team. Often success goes to teams in which five rather average players coordinate their strengths and weaknesses," she observes. Of course she didn't have Softswitch, SNC's key product, developed by mediocre engineers. But no matter whether it's a super talent or a development engineer with solid

Lessons learned

- In highly dynamic markets, development departments have to maintain close contacts with the customers. This saves time and can be the crucial advantage for a product's market success.
- You will only make money if you have really understood your customers' business model. And if you cannot present your customer with plausible prospects of either lower costs or higher revenues, you won't sell anything.
- Good ideas have little chance of succeeding in large companies when they compete with existing portfolio products – an external start-up can be very helpful in such situations, even if it's "virtual," as in the case of SNC.
- Time to market – the rapid implementation of development targets – is enormously important nowadays. Incremental processes and proximity to customers can be very helpful in this context.
- For the implementation of innovative technologies in successful products, it is also important to have some experienced people on board. They know the rules of the business and make valuable contributions to the team.

Eve Aretakis' advice for innovators

- Never lose sight of the market opportunities of your own development work. The innovator of the future also has to think like a businessperson.
- Getting involved in office politics is a disadvantage in the long term. Avoid it whenever possible.
- Networking is tremendously important. Those employees who get into conversations with everyone, irrespective of age or position, gain enormous advantages for themselves and for the organization.
- Trying to gain praise by claiming other people's ideas as your own is an extremely short-term policy. Old-fashioned bosses who regularly do this demotivate their staff enormously.
- Whatever you do, it should be fun, because that's an excellent indicator of whether you're doing the right thing. If you're enjoying something you're usually performing well and achieving results.

capabilities, she likes to give everyone a chance to shine – so that everyone is highly motivated and can deliver the maximum added value for a virtual start-up firm.

Aretakis is laid back about the fact that suppliers of conventional switching technology are now approaching the cable-network operators. Actually, the Siemens team should regard that as a compliment for having discovered a new market segment. The giant Siemens organization now supports SNC with a highly effective international sales team. Ultimately, both companies together made Softswitch's market success possible: David and Goliath sometimes work hand in hand after all.

"Any developer whose innovation cannibalizes a successful business within his or her own company will always face great opposition from others in the organization – that's simply how it works," says Christian. "That why it's so important for top managers to create a niche for the new idea – if they don't, they could be endangering future business activities. A good solution here is to move ahead with the innovation in a different country and with a new customer base."

"You're absolutely right," John says. "The important thing is to select the right environment for each innovation project, and then let the innovators go to work to prove that they and their small, highly motivated team can attract customers with their new product, and that the product can be a financial success. After that, they'll gradually be able to influence the future course the organization as a whole will take."

"But what do you do if someone develops a product that simply doesn't fit in with the company's portfolio?" Matthias asks. "That's a good point," John replies. "In that case, you shouldn't just file the innovation away; a better idea would be to try to market it using a new start-up company. There really is a growing market for selling good ideas that can't be implemented in one's own company. Let me tell you about a spin-off called EnOcean, whose founders really showed a lot of courage."

An Ocean of Energy

"The learning curve at a new company is very steep and can't really be compared to anything else," says Markus Brehler. "In the beginning, there's nothing there – you've got to do everything, implement everything yourself. The range of decision making is huge, and so is the potential for making the wrong decisions. The list of tasks seems endless – develop an optimal business strategy, find the right employees and investors, locate affordable office space, get product development off the ground, acquire customers, and who knows how many other things. And you feel every mistake you make, like a brick falling on your foot." Don't expect long-winded explanations from Brehler, 43, on how to make a start-up successful. "Success is reserved for those who make more right decisions than mistakes – everything else falls under the category of 'numerous externally financed start-ups in Germany that slowly waste away and eventually disappear,'" he says.

The important thing, according to Brehler, is to openly discuss mistakes as a team and then work together to find a way to do things better in the future. Still, how do you establish such an open corporate culture? "It's all a question of leadership style," says Brehler. "The managing director serves as the role model for all employees. That's why the rugged individualist as a leader is just as bad for a start-up as an arrogant manager who tries to exploit his or her position and power and refuses to get involved with 'lowly' tasks. If you never put your coffee cup in the dishwasher, how can you expect your employees to do it? This also applies to the big picture. If I'm the CEO, I have to do things in a structured manner and bring order to the company. That's because everything I do will be observed and imitated, whether knowingly or unknowingly." Brehler says he's never been the "inventor type." Instead, he describes himself more as a manager with technical knowledge. "Inventing means investing money to generate a lot of ideas – but for me, innovation means making money from ideas, and that's what I do best," he says.

At first, conditions were anything but promising, to say the least. There was no financing, no product, no sales, and no customers. So who would be crazy enough to become managing director of such a company – and give up a secure job at a major corporation to do it? **Markus Brehler** did – but he wasn't crazy, just courageous. And he doesn't regret a thing. Brehler is passionate about turning outstanding ideas into business success. That's why he and two colleagues quit their jobs in November 2001 to join EnOcean GmbH – a Siemens AG spin-off in Oberhaching, Germany – just two weeks after it was founded. Three more founding members joined them at the beginning of 2002.

An Ocean of Energy

Searching for the Best Approach

Structured thinking and action have always been easy for Brehler. As a laid-back person by nature, he likes to think carefully about how to best accomplish whatever he needs to do. A communications engineer, Brehler also completed management programs at the Massachusetts Institute of Technology and Stanford University in the U.S., at the INSEAD Business School in France, and at the Indian Institute of Management. In 1989 he joined Siemens, where he successfully established new businesses, the most recent being for cell phone accessories. He then spent eight years working in research and development at Intelligent Traffic Systems, where his responsibilities included the development of traffic telematics systems.

In 2001, Brehler transferred to Siemens Technology Accelerator (STA), where he was responsible for preparing the launch of the spin-off company EnOcean. STA's mission is to rapidly transform innovative ideas from Corporate Technology – Siemens' central research organization – and from the company's various business units and external sources into entrepreneurial success stories. EnOcean's technology has broad applications; its business model could be described as that of a component company. As the 1990s came to a close, Siemens had made a strategic decision to spin off such businesses, as evidenced by the launch of Infineon and Epcos, so it was clear that the innovations behind EnOcean wouldn't be developed within Siemens. STA provided the new company with €100,000 in start-up funding, which was matched by the combined contribution of EnOcean's five founding members, all of them experienced Siemens managers. So while the company's start-up capital wasn't exactly mind-blowing, EnOcean did get a boost in February 2002, when it raised €5 million in venture capital in its first round of financing. The second round at the beginning of 2004 brought in €4.4 million, followed by €10 million in the third round in April 2005.

Speed before Perfection

"The trick is to balance technological progress with the cash burn rate," says Brehler. "When you start out with five experienced industrial managers, you automatically have a higher cost position than a spin-off from a university, which will have some employees who continue to work part time at their college. The rule of thumb at a start-up like ours is: Speed before perfection. This means that putting a product on the market that functions properly, but only does about 80 percent of what you're looking for, will leave you better off than if you launch something that's got everything packed into it. That's because the only really valuable input for determining the ultimate form your product should take is the feedback it gets from the market." Although Brehler admits that various market research techniques and prototype production can help minimize commercial risks, he says you only gain real knowledge when the product is on the shelf and available for purchase.

EnOcean (from "energy" and "ocean") specializes in the development of wireless, battery-less radio technology, which is based on an idea that originated at Siemens Corporate Technology. "We are more or less swimming in a sea of energy, and we need to learn how to utilize it intelligently," says Brehler. The idea behind EnOcean is akin to a rabbit pulling itself out of a hat. "Our wireless, battery-less, and maintenance-free sensors are equipped with tiny radio modules that can transmit data up to 300 meters away," Brehler explains. "They create energy seemingly from nothing: The slightest movement, briefest flash of light, or smallest variation in temperature is enough to generate power for our ultraefficient sensors to make their readings and transmit their results via radio." In the case of a wireless light switch, the pressure placed on the switch – or, more precisely, the electro-dynamic energy converter – is by itself enough to generate sufficient energy for sending a signal to a receiver in a lamp, which then turns the light on or off. In other words, neither a wire, battery, nor any other source of electricity is required to switch the light on and off, which means the switch itself can be placed anywhere and also moved around at any time.

Technology Pioneer

Several international awards have given the EnOcean team additional motivation to continue working hard. In 2002, for example, the company received the Bavarian Innovation Prize, which was endowed with €100,000. And it also was named a "Technology Pioneer 2006" by the World Economic Forum. In April 2003, EnOcean celebrated the market launch of its first product – a piezo-based switch module and corresponding receiver. The company uses existing sales channels, which means it doesn't sell its radio modules directly to consumers but instead to major established firms such as the electrical-device manufacturers PEHA, WAGO and Thermokon, who incorporate the modules into their designer lines. The three companies have in fact been EnOcean's leading customers since the beginning of 2002. Brehler considered selling the company's light switches at home improvement outlets under a consumer brand name, but quickly dismissed the idea as too costly: "We'd have to lay out €25 million to €30 million easily – just for the German market alone, and with no guarantee of success."

EnOcean has already sold more than 150,000 radio modules through its main customers to date, and the devices are also being used in building projects all over Europe. In addition, the company is expanding into the U.S. by opening a subsidiary there. The range of applications for EnOcean's wireless and battery-less devices is tremendous. "Whether it's in the home, the car, the office, or during our precious leisure time – there are always new applications for a new way to turn things on and off faster, or to detect states," says Brehler. "Light switches, industrial limit switches that register when a pallet passes by or a door is opened, thermostats, brightness sensors or a sensor that monitors the position of a window handle – we just keep launching new products on the market every month." The trend toward flexible offices is optimally serviced by portable sensors from EnOcean, which can be placed anywhere quickly and easily, and also moved around – all without creating any dirt or noise. Brehler and his team plan to gradually conquer world markets in the coming years by supplanting conventional products such as wired light switches. Market volume here is enormous, with sales for light and window-blind switches in building automation systems alone totaling €2 billion per year worldwide. To that can be added another half-billion to one billion euros for other sensors, including thermostats and brightness sensors. Brehler also anticipates excellent business in the area of tire pressure sensors, which in 2005 became mandatory in the U.S., where 20 million new vehicles are registered annually.

Why Start-ups Need Optimists

EnOcean currently has 30 employees and is headquartered in a rural setting in the town of Oberhaching, near Munich. For Brehler, it's a given that the team must occasionally overcome difficult times. "I don't know of any entrepreneur whose start-up ran completely smoothly," he says. "That's why the only people who should work for a start-up are those who can approach the future with optimism and are convinced that the company is their life. You also need to be stubborn and persistent." Brehler and his colleagues were in fact dealt a severe blow to their confidence early on, when the head of development at a major producer of switches and electrical sockets told them after analyzing their product that their battery-less radio technology "would never work" because "no one could possibly ever realize such a product." However, all that did was convince

Brehler that there was no point in trying to sell the model for production under license. "A licensing business model only makes sense if an innovation has already been taken to an advanced stage and a company has a dominant position on the market," he explains. "So at that point, we got down to work to develop and market our radio modules ourselves."

They also had to overcome (and still must) the opposition of established electrical installation companies, who have been successful with conventional solutions like wired light switches and are resistant to changing long-practiced methods of doing business. These days, however, many of the invitations to tender for the construction of big commercial complexes contain a clause stipulating that battery-less radio technology must be used, and achieving this change in attitude was a major success for EnOcean. It wasn't easy getting there, though: "The entire market segment is dominated by pragmatists, and we had to gradually convince these people that our innovation offered big benefits. We accomplished this through reference projects. In Germany alone, there are around 2,000 electrical systems planners who we've established contact with over the years, and we work to maintain these relationships. One of our reference projects is the administrative building of Bosch und Siemens Hausgeräte GmbH in Munich, which was equipped with hundreds of our radio switches and room sensors in 2003. When you go to trade fairs, you can really see how we've increased our presence on the market. For example, there were 50 stands at the light+building 2006 show in Frankfurt that featured products adorned with our logo, 'Enabled by EnOcean.'"

Such success more than compensates for the fact that the company was unable to maintain the original schedule for the launch of the second product generation, which had to be postponed for nine months. "Neither we nor our investors were happy about that, of course," says Brehler. "But ultimately, it also shows that an innovation process is different in reality than it is on paper. We need to learn from this experience so that we can do things better in the future, and that includes planning the phases for market launch in a more realistic manner." With all of his structure and professional dedication, Brehler isn't left with much time for his wife, two children, and hobbies, which include jogging, hiking and mountain biking. "My whole life is organized down to the last minute," he explains. "I couldn't get everything done if that weren't the case. Most of my energy flows into the company, and that's why it's important to carefully select the members of your team when you launch a start-up, since you're going to be spending more time with them over the next few years than with your family." One method Brehler uses here is to take prospective employees on a hike: "When you go hiking, you figure out

Lessons learned	Markus Brehler's advice for innovators
• Things always take longer than you think. • You need to have a lead customer who is incorporated into the development process, because the only useful feedback comes from the market. • Never get discouraged if you hear the words: "That will never work." • Management meetings in particular are the places where problems are discussed and solutions developed. It's crucial for boosting motivation to also review what has gone well. • Even a perfect manager capable of motivating employees can't ensure continuously high morale at a company. Business success is the ultimate motivator.	• Because things always take longer than you think, you need a "plan B." • The overriding goal is to launch a marketable product as quickly as possible, and speed comes before perfection here. • A company should quickly make a name for itself and establish a brand. Competing for awards, conducting extensive media work and establishing a solid presence on the Internet are very important. • Go to the customer! Every contact is also an opportunity. Never take "no" for an answer; often they simply mean "not yet." You need to be persistent, stubborn and optimistic. • The only people who should work for a start-up are those who can approach the future with optimism and are convinced that the company is a major part of their life.

pretty quickly if you're going to get along together – there's no getting around it." There's also no getting around the latest timetable Brehler and his team have drawn up: The entire schedule is full – and carefully structured.

John finishes his story, sipping his drink with a smile. "Wow," says Matthias. "That takes a lot of guts, entrepreneurial spirit and the energy to withstand the setbacks that are sure to come – to believe in an idea so much that you establish a company even though you have no product, practically no money, without any customers, and no guarantee you can get your old job back."

John gives a nod of agreement: "Especially when you're aware of how many start-ups fail – and not because they had a bad idea. What happens more often is that the people involved don't have the right marketing skills and sales talent. You also have to know the basics of business administration, and be able to find the right people to work for you – and customers who won't abandon you at the first sign of a minor problem. And sometimes, start-ups just have bad luck."

Christian finishes his red wine, casting a glance at the clock. "The stories I heard tonight were very impressive," he says. "I also think that the business world – and our own company – are much further along today than they were a few years ago, when we used to talk a lot about that 'not invented here' problem. Increasing globalization has made people much less afraid to get out and talk to other people. Think about it: You've got Walter Gumbrecht's research networks, Jun Kong's regional innovation ideas, Eve Aretakis' targeted innovation niches, spin-ins like the ones established by Giorgio Cuttica and Raymond Liao, and spin-offs like Markus Brehler's. All these are paths to innovation that are much more common today than they were in the past."

"You're right," says Walter. "It's just too bad that we don't have that much time in our daily work to reflect on what we do, why we do it and whether or not there might be another way. That's what I like so much about our get-togethers."

Everyone nods in agreement. Stacey's already on her feet: It's late and the Feldafing event is going to end tomorrow at noon. She turns to Matthias and asks: "Do you think you and your team could organize an event like our meetings, so that others can benefit from the exchange of ideas and the secrets of success? You can call it 'Executive Circle Innovation' – we'd all be paying customers if you could organize such a platform."

Matthias considers it for a moment. "Why not," he says, "I'll take care of it. Tomorrow, we all have to go to the airport after we're done here. Why don't we book a shuttle bus for the trip there?" "That's a great idea," says Walter, "then we can talk some more before we all leave."

Space for your own thoughts

Which people, organizations and networks outside your own company could you work with in the search for new ideas?

Are there any ideas that your organization has rejected that might be worth talking about in another region, or with other customer groups?

Which external partnerships could you intensify in order to move innovations forward?

Innovation Is More Than Technology

Innovation Management, Communications,
New Business Models

The management conference in Feldafing has come to an end. John, Stacey, Christian, Bao Jun, Matthias and Walter board the spacious shuttle bus. "Munich airport, please." The driver starts the engine and pulls away from the curb. "This morning," says Christian, "I was asking myself, 'What is management's main task, really, when it comes to innovation?' During our first discussions, I had lots of ideas on this point: fostering free thinkers, creating niches, remembering to look beyond the company, managing implementation, having the right project management and the best tools – all these things are necessary and helpful. But how do I create the right culture for innovation? How do I ensure a structure for my organization that makes it possible to achieve organic growth by means of a steady stream of successful innovations?"

"That's most likely the decisive question for management," says Walter. "In addition to a clear strategy covering portfolios, products, innovation and patents, which every business must develop for itself, innovation management is surely the most important factor. Managing the idea pipeline, knowing which are the key fields for new products, developing these products and using them to shape the market – that's the innovation strategy of a trendsetter, and we follow it. I'd like to start off with an example – another one from the field of medical technology." As the shuttle rolls through the idyllic landscape along Lake Starnberg, Walter begins.

Machines for People

He radiates genuine warmth, has a friendly smile and modest demeanor. He thinks before speaking, and he takes his time before answering. "My greatest motivation for working in medical engineering is that it enables me to use technical equipment to help people," says Dr. Thomas von der Haar. A doctorate in physics is only one of his credentials. While studying physics at the Universities of Münster and Tübingen, he also pursued a minor in philosophy, completing the intermediate examination. What interests him most is humanity. His studies included courses in anthropology, ethics and European intellectual history, including the works of Kant and Nietzsche.

"I wasn't satisfied with simply learning how the world functions from a natural sciences perspective," recalls von der Haar. "I was just as eager to find out if everything is really 'relative' – for instance morality." Although von der Haar works in the world of technology, it's very important to him that the machines he builds should have a positive effect on people's lives. He develops computed tomography (CT) scanners, which visualize heart disease and malignant tumors. These rotating x-ray systems take just seconds to produce cross-sectional images of the human body and process this data into three-dimensional pictures. The resulting computer image of a human organ can then be rotated and viewed from every angle – inside and out.

Von der Haar works in a bright, tidy office at Siemens Medical Solutions (Med) in Forchheim, near Nuremberg. The office's only decor is a large potted plant and, on one white wall, a big calendar with landscape photos. Two years ago, von der Haar, 43, became vice president of product portfolio management in the CT division. His department specifies the new properties that a new tomographic system should have – and must have, to be a commercial success. Core elements of any CT system are the x-ray tube and the detector, components that face each other from opposite sides of the circular gantry that revolves around a patient in just 0.3 seconds. Within a few seconds, the CT scanner snaps thousands of individual x-ray pictures – like a very fast strobe light – each with a very short exposure time. The computer then converts the resulting layer images or "slices" into the final 3D image.

The latest such system in the Siemens CT family is the Somatom Definition – a new scanner with unique features and capabilities. Unlike all previous CT scanners, this machine is equipped with two x-ray sources and two detectors. The axes of the two source-detector pairs are set at a 90-degree angle within the gantry. During each revolution, this arrangement allows twice as many x-ray images to be generated than ever before. The temporal resolution is substantially improved, while the x-ray exposure is reduced. Such high speeds are especially important in studies of a beating heart. This is the first CT system that can visualize small

Using technology to help people – that's top priority for **Dr. Thomas von der Haar**. And for many years, he's been very successful at doing precisely that. Von der Haar's innovations in computed tomography have contributed greatly to progress in medical imaging. His formula for success is to combine a number of good ideas into an optimized overall concept.

coronary vessels even when a patient's heartbeat is fast and irregular (see also "The Yin and Yang of Innovation").

The Key Question: What Gives Our Customers the Decisive Added Value They Need?

Von der Haar has been working on computed tomography scanners for 11 years, and the performance expected of these systems has changed during this period. Before, the main objective was to engineer increasingly faster CT scanners with higher and higher image resolutions. Now

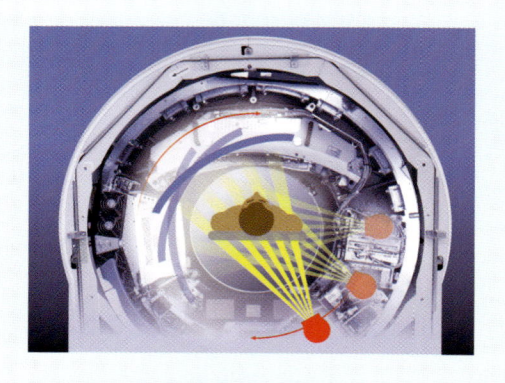

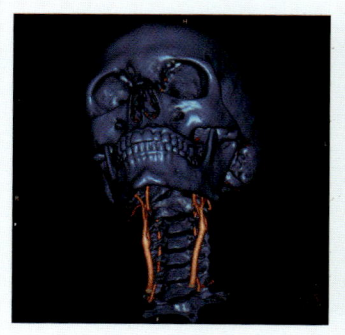

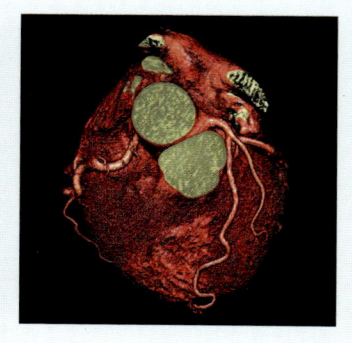

Three-dimensional views deep inside the body. In this computed tomography scanner, the X-ray tube rotates around the patient three times per second (top). The latest such system, the Somatom Definition, uses two X-ray tubes and two detectors. The result is images of unprecedented accuracy and the ability to freeze even rapidly beating hearts.

the trend is toward improving clinical workflow as well: The 3D image data should be immediately available wherever needed – not just, as in the past, on a computer workstation near the CT scanner, but also in the radiologist's office, in the radiology "reading room," and even to experts outside the hospital, via the Internet. In the reading rooms of today's radiology departments, radiologists can access only two-dimensional images. For a 3D view they have to go to a workstation, and that consumes valuable time. "But the radiologist is the limiting resource in the clinical workflow," von der Haar points out. And, all too often, radiologists are working near the limits of their capacities, so it's very important to them to be able to complete each case as quickly as possible.

"In engineering development, you've got to beware of tunnel vision. It can blind you to operational requirements while you're concentrating on improving the scanner," von der Haar explains. The overarching priority, he underscores, is to focus on what the customer wants. "Of course the customer wants superb image quality," he says. "But great images alone aren't enough." The scanner must speed up the entire process chain, from the actual scan to the completed report the radiologist enters into the Radiology Information System. "When it comes to workflow efficiency, Siemens is now a worldwide leader," says von der Haar. To fully understand users' needs, CT engineers engage physicians as consultants. Some of these doctors work in Forchheim for months on end, working intensively to address the engineering issues – and the end results are solutions that can be perfectly integrated into the clinical workflow.

Combining Good Ideas

But regardless of whether the issue is software that improves workflow or better hardware components – what ultimately determines the clinical and operational effectiveness of a CT system is always the sum of many good ideas, which means von der Haar always has to keep an eye on many different facets. "I really benefit from all the hands-on experience I've had with the machines," he says. He started at Siemens Med in Forchheim in the mid-1990s, when jobs for physicists weren't plentiful. Von der Haar sent out many applications to coincide with the completion of his doctoral thesis at the Max-Planck Institute for Biophysical Chemistry in Göttingen. The thesis was on the behavior of organic molecules subjected to energetic excitation. "That was pure, basic research, with no direct connection to any known application," von der Haar says. He missed hands-on practical work, so he took the initiative to apply at Siemens, although the company had no openings listed.

Von der Haar had a bit of luck and was hired for a job in Forchheim, joining a workgroup for detector technology. His first assignment was to introduce a new detector product to the clinical environment. While visiting many test installations in various hospitals, he learned a great deal not only about the reality of everyday clinical practice but also about what's really important to customers from the ground up. At the same time, his workgroup was exploring ways to improve the resolution of detector technology. "We were given a lot of leeway," he recalls. "At first there were no precise specifications regarding how the detectors should be improved."

Von der Haar had an ingeniously simple idea: Instead of improving the detector, he worked on the x-ray tube. In a CT study, the patient is slowly shifted longitudinally through the bore of the machine while the gantry revolves. The thickness of the x-ray beam's focus (the "layer" or "slice") determines the scanner's resolution. The premise of von der Haar's idea was: If the focus of the x-ray beam is shifted by one-half of a slice thickness within a fraction of a second, the emitted x-rays penetrate the patient from two slightly different angles. With this method, not just one but two adjacent slices are imaged – at nearly the same instant. This "shifting focus," also known as z-Sharp Technology, doubles the scanner's resolution without the need for major changes in the detector.

Initially, however, the z-Sharp concept was difficult to convert into a practical product, and it would be several years before it became a key competitive advantage. This was because the earlier x-ray tubes couldn't shift their focus as required. But von der Haar's work sparked the interest of divisional management, and he was appointed development manager at the Detector Center in 1995. He became responsible for restoring a high level of detector know-how at Med: Years earlier, the company had decided to de-emphasize detector expertise and to buy detectors from outside suppliers. Detectors were considered commodities. "That proved to be a mistake," says von der Haar. The late 1990s, after all, saw the market launches of multi-slice detectors that made not one, but multiple closely adjacent slices with each revolution. This markedly improved the resolution of CT scanners.

Leader in Detector Technology

Siemens executives realized that detector technology was developing into a core competency with a decisive impact on sales. "To successfully develop innovative products, you must clearly define core components and core competencies – and engage in a major build-up of the needed know-how," says von der Haar. In fact, he considers this to be one of his most important tasks. Von der Haar succeeded in hiring electronics specialists from other companies – for instance ASIC designers, experts in application-specific processors. And his team achieved a turnaround. "Today we're the leader in detector technology," he reports. His conclusion: "It's clear that even if you've been moving in the wrong direction, a lot can still be accomplished by providing the right resources precisely where it counts."

Ultimately, von der Haar's z-Sharp concept also contributed to this success. During the hottest phase of detector development, his colleagues on the x-ray side surprised him with the new Straton x-ray tube. It was considerably smaller and lighter in weight than prior models, making it an ideal x-ray source for his z-Sharp Technology. It was introduced to the market with the Somatom Sensation 64 in 2004. This new CT scanner's detector recorded 32 individual slices – and with z-Sharp, the resolution doubled to 64 slices. Before this development, nothing better than 16-slice CTs had been available on the market. The 64-line multislice scanner made a tremendous impact, becoming an overnight sensation.

"Components such as z-Sharp or the Straton tube are perfect examples of innovations," says von der Haar. "They're major technical undertakings that require long development periods and can't be imitated quickly by others." z-Sharp, for example, is still a distinctive feature of Siemens technology today. Equally important, though, are many minor software solutions that make up the product, and especially those that make it easier to use. Lungcare is a good example. This software automatically analyzes images of the lungs for tiny tumor nodules, making it easier for a radiologist to arrive at a diagnosis. Good suggestions for software improvements abound – and there are many discussions about which ideas actually can be implemented. "We simply don't have the resources to realize every good idea. That's when it really hurts to have to compromise."

Don't Burn out Innovators with Everyday Tasks

Von der Haar has always focused on finding "really good innovative people," and he takes special care to ensure that they get the support they need. "It sounds obvious, but innovative employees are simply the people that come up with good ideas." And good ideas ultimately come from just a few employees – a handful of individuals. He does his best to give them the freedom to think, to pursue their ideas. "You've got to be careful that employees like these don't become burned out with everyday tasks," von der Haar explains. On the other hand, you can't let these creative minds stray too far from reality, so involving them in day-to-day business is a good idea. "It keeps them in touch with real-world requirements and constraints," he says.

Siemens Med sells several thousand CT scanners annually. High-end devices such as the new Somatom Definition are manufactured in small series – the basic version costs more than one million euros. About 30 percent of all CT systems in the world are from Siemens Med. General Electric continues to be the worldwide leader, with a 35 to 40 percent market share – largely because the company is still the top dog in the United States, the largest CT market. Still, Med has gained ten percent market share in six years. "That's an enormous gain when you consider that the CT market is very conservative," says von der Haar. The best evidence of the success of Med's CT scanners is the fact that 13 of the top 15 teaching hospitals in the U.S. are now using Siemens CT scanners from Forchheim. "Of course that's going to have an impact," the innovator says.

Detector technology, software issues, market analysis – von der Haar has to deal with all of it. "So it's a good thing that I took the time to

Lessons learned

- To make an innovation successful, you've got to know what the customer wants.
- The right product can only be developed through close cooperation with the customer.
- If a development project has gotten off on the wrong track, much can be recouped by applying the right resources in the right places.
- Really good ideas come from just a few employees – but they can only be implemented by a team.
- Good innovators need the freedom to pursue their ideas.

Thomas von der Haar's advice for innovators

- Give employees plenty of elbow room to be creative.
- Make a persistent effort to find innovative employees.
- Focus on strengthening core competencies.
- Be willing to work with customers and other business units.
- Enjoy your work.

complete my basic studies in business management," he says. "Having a grasp of cost accounting, performance accounting and civil law makes my work a lot easier." And he believes that being a physicist also endows him with a certain proficiency in structured thinking – and with a good feel for many different subject areas, like radiation physics, electronics, mechanics and information science. "People say that a physicist can do almost anything – but nothing exceptionally well," says von der Haar. "And that's not entirely wrong." Engineers really apply their skills to concrete tasks. They have the detailed know-how to build a gantry, or develop an electronic circuit. "I can't do any of that," he says. Von der Haar loves his work and the creative, friendly atmosphere in Forchheim. "It's satisfying to see that a good idea actually makes it all the way to becoming a real product," he says. Maybe it's the idea itself that gives him satisfaction. "Inventing things is certainly rewarding in itself," he adds. "It's just plain fun to figure things out."

Von der Haar is the father of three children, the youngest of whom is just a few weeks old. He grew up in a small town near Münster, in the Westphalia region. After his studies in Münster and Tübingen he spent a year as a research assistant at the University of Denver, before earning his doctorate in Göttingen. "Sometimes I wonder if I've landed at Med because my wife and my sister have influenced me – they're both physicians," he muses. Then again, it may have been simply von der Haar's aspiration to make a difference in people's lives.

"Did you know that a complete 3D study of the heart calls for collecting gigabytes of data?" Walter asks his colleagues upon finishing his story. "And can you imagine the mechanical stresses on the components as the gantry revolves around a patient three times per second?" Without waiting for an answer, he continues: "Such a machine is a veritable hodgepodge of the latest technologies. It encompasses radiology, image processing, materials research, electronics and software. Someone like Thomas von der Haar must have a solid grasp of all these things to be able to make the right decisions. Certainly his broad-based training as a physicist is very helpful. So too is the fact that he himself has been an innovator and has a detailed understanding of this kind of equipment."

"At the same time, he has to use a very strategic approach, identify core competencies and rigorously build up the needed know-how," explains Christian. "And that's not all: He's got to be able to play devil's advocate regarding decisions that have been made, and if necessary correct them. And he needs a good feel for the best way to involve creative minds in projects

Machines for People

– with sufficient freedom to develop ideas, but enough grounding in reality to allow these ideas to become marketable products."

"That kind of innovation management is certainly a very complex assignment, but also a very satisfying one," adds Matthias. "I recently had an opportunity to learn how innovation-friendly structures can be specifically cultivated. The tips came from an innovation manager at a Group that has had to overcome difficult challenges in a very competitive market – telecommunications..."

The Power to Keep Ideas Alive

When asked why he chose this field of work, Tilo Messer smiles and says, "Because it's a lot of fun and I'm convinced that we really change things. After all, innovation means change. My job is to encourage employees to initiate change themselves and consistently continue down the path of innovation. Innovation management is about creating a framework for the processes required to achieve something new." Does that mean that all Tilo has to do is to surround himself with a group of creative minds, and the first drafts of prototypes will start landing on his desk?

While that view might appear naïve, it's actually not far from the truth, which is only a little more complicated. Messer and his four colleagues in the Chief Technology Office (CTO) at the Communications Group – or, more precisely, the part of that Group that has been operating under the direction of Siemens Networks since October 1, 2006, and

It's not enough for a company to have clever researchers. Without a solid innovation management system, their creative potential will go to waste. The process of creating and selecting ideas has to be just as systematically organized as does the promotion of an innovation within the company and in the marketplace. By providing inventors with support, innovation managers like **Dr. Tilo Messer** help to ensure that good ideas are transformed into tomorrow's successful products.

which was incorporated into the Nokia Siemens Networks joint venture in 2007 – regularly conduct "Innovation Summits" in various countries. These events are usually attended by around 40 people, including developers and representatives from business development, marketing and sales departments. The meeting offers the participants the opportunity to "try out ideas that they've had for some time," says Messer. The advantage is that participants receive immediate feedback from a larger group of colleagues than is normally the case, including employees who have close contact with customers. If these "sparring partners" like an idea, it becomes easier for participants to further pursue the topic at their own department etc., where it can be developed into a marketable product.

Diversity: The Mother of Innovation

Ideally, even more people should participate in the creation of ideas, says Messer. The input of men and women from different cultural and technical backgrounds, as well as academics from the humanities, psychology and social sciences is particularly desirable. Messer, 45, believes an intercultural and interdisciplinary team can produce the best results: "Innovation is teamwork – and good innovations are a product of diversity." It was teamwork that brought Messer, who hails from the city of Augsburg, Germany, and has a doctorate in computer science, to Siemens Communications in 1997. Previously he had worked at Corporate Technology in Munich, where he assessed and improved software development processes. Some of this work was conducted in cooperation with Communications, which was so impressed by Messer's commitment that it invited him to join the Group and help develop the software for the Gigaset cordless phone. It is partly thanks to Messer's efforts that Siemens cordless telephones – with all their complex features – operate so well. After working in various positions related to product management, Messer was offered a post in the newly established Chief Technology Office at the Communications Group.

One of his jobs at the office is to "link the vertically structured divisions – which operate very independently of one another – in selected topic groups. He also compares roadmaps, harmonizes product development, and provides the sales departments with information from the other divisions in order to ensure 'one face to the customer.'" According to Messer, the most important thing to do in an organization structured in such a manner is to "work horizontally as a means of creating new business opportunities for the company."

Diamonds in the Rough

This is no easy task, especially when you consider the complex demands placed on innovation managers. For one thing, they must be motivators and coaches. "The first thing you have to do is to make inventors aware of the value of their 'rough diamond,'" says Messer. "Then you have to make it clear that although grinding and polishing the diamond will require a lot of hard work, it will also be rewarding, because polishing will make the idea successful. The inventor then has to convince managers, marketing experts and sales staff that the idea will work. Once that's done, the foundation for the innovation has been laid."

Messer's job also requires playing the roles of investor, networker and entrepreneur. He's an investor because he provides funding to inventors at the Innovation Summits – money they can use to initiate a market analysis or draw up a business model. This "motivational capital" is linked to the condition that the inventors "...produce a detailed result in a reasonable amount of time. Then we can see what's become of the idea and better assess whether it makes sense to provide further funding."

Messer seems very relaxed sitting at his desk. In fact, even the construction noise from outside doesn't seem to bother him. A father of two daughters, he's good at integrating people, a trait he says is necessary to succeed in his job. Still, he's not driven by social ideals. Instead, it's the thrill he gets from being at the cutting edge of technology. He describes his job as "operating a business-driven system for bringing together innovators in order to generate extra value."

That's where the networking part comes in. After all, all this activity involves more than just being able to gauge trends. Messer's job also requires openness and friendliness in order to establish contact with the right people. It's easy to picture Messer employing his calm and professional demeanor to bring together colleagues who really need to meet one another. "Such encounters allow researchers and developers working on similar issues to learn and benefit from one another," he says. "Bringing innovators together can generate added value."

So what's the entrepreneurial aspect? "If you view innovation as a business, then my role is that of the entrepreneur," Messer says. "Innovations can't be planned, but the conditions in which they occur can – and my job is to create the right conditions." It's not enough, however, to simply create structures conducive to innovation. If an innovation is to be successful, someone has to decide early on which market is to be targeted and what type of business model should be used.

Developers and Entrepreneurs – Getting the Right Mix

And that brings us to the main difference between inventing and innovating: "A developer is not necessarily the ideal entrepreneur – you rarely find someone who can do both. To make an invention successful, it's therefore very helpful to put together a team that includes an entrepreneurial type who can help the idea evolve into a marketable product." In other words, inventors must learn to let go at the right time in order to focus on something new. They're still involved with their idea, since in the ideal case the innovation has already been protected by a patent.

The best scenario is when management is involved in the innovation process – or, even better, becomes the driving force behind it. "Management often faces a dilemma when confronted with radical innovations," says Messer. "That's because part of its job is to always make sure that resources and budgets are distributed with one eye on optimizing short-term business success. However, management can't neglect innovations, because they hold the key to future success." Messer therefore believes that it's not enough to rely on incentive systems that only reward the attainment of short-term goals.

He will leave the issue of incentives to others when the new structures for the Communications Group are finally in place. Instead, Messer will tackle the challenge of developing the newly founded European Center for Information and Communication Technologies (EICT) in Berlin, in which he serves as CEO. The founding members of EICT are the Technical University of Berlin, the Fraunhofer Society, Deutsche Telekom, DaimlerChrysler and Siemens.

The partners are dedicated to "linking fundamental and application-oriented research with industry in order to rapidly develop and implement new information and communication technologies." In line with this objective, the EICT will help initiate spinoffs and support new companies that wish to establish themselves with innovative products. The center also has the ambitious goal of "establishing a counterweight to the U.S. – and Asia as well in the future – so that we also have a role to play when it comes to shaping technological developments in the information and communications market." To achieve its aims, the EICT plans to drum up political support for its activities.

Messer's interpersonal skills will be of great use here. As EICT CEO, he will need to mediate between various interests and get all the partners to agree on a common approach. Although each member wants EICT research partnerships to improve its own competitive position, they all bring different corporate cultures to the venture. The challenge is

Lessons learned	Tilo Messer's advice for innovators
• Innovation is always about change – and sometimes it's an uphill battle. • Many obstacles are internal, which means they can be overcome internally. • Only the most completely thought-out ideas will succeed. • Ideas develop best in a protected environment. • The successful transfer of a prototype into the rough organizational reality requires support from management.	• Get top management involved in projects from the very beginning. • Create an innovation budget – especially for radical innovations. • Put together innovation teams consisting of members from different cultural and professional backgrounds. • Don't lose sight of the innovation's relevance to the business, especially with regard to technology-driven ideas. • Actively support and promote brilliant ideas.

therefore immense. "Ultimately, this is all about a better quality of life and greater security – and raising productivity by efficiently utilizing information and communication technologies," says Messer. "We want to demonstrate that all these things are possible."

Messer is thus once again being called upon to initiate change – which shouldn't be a problem, given his track record to date.

"It definitely makes sense to have an overall innovation management system that brings the right people together," says Christian. "It's also an excellent idea to have regular innovation meetings with interdisciplinary teams in different countries in order to generate new ideas, and then to give the innovators a certain amount of funding. The hard part is filtering out the good ideas and getting the right people together."

"It's just a shame that this innovation management system was launched too late to make a major difference for Communications," says Walter. "But their problems were of a totally different nature and had been going on for years..."

John agrees: "That's true, and it shows you the limits of what innovation managers can do. They can create structures conducive to innovation – but coming up with the right business and product strategy is top management's job. Hey, Matthias, what do you think about setting up a training program for innovation managers? A lot of them work alone and could use some help with methods. It would also be good for them to get together and exchange ideas."

"That's a good idea – but there's already a Community of Practice for innovation managers. Still, it might make sense to set up a further training program that covers the basics of innovation management and provides practical exercises with proven tools."

Stacey, too, has thought of something: "Innovation management has a lot to do with networking and team work – those are traits that people generally attribute to women. I know a woman who has brought these 'feminine strengths' into a very masculine technical environment. Her name is Tzoanna Ekaterinidi, she's from Greece, and now I'm going to tell you her exciting story..."

Software for a Global Player

Her firm handshake and warm look immediately generate an atmosphere of trust. It's easy to believe Dr. Tzoanna Ekaterinidi when she says that the Software Center is really one big family. "It's important to love people, to accept them with all their good points and their flaws, just like parents do with their children," she says. "And, of course, you have to educate them as well, so that you can build up a culture of objective self-evaluation." After all, she adds, it's only when you have a climate of trust that employees feel able to talk openly about their strengths and weaknesses. It's when they feel comfortable "that things start to happen, that they become more creative and productive."

However, this culture of self-evaluation is by no means imposed from above. It's something that Ekaterinidi, 47, embodies. "As someone in a position of seniority, I want to give my employees the feeling that I'm working for them and with them," she says. "This means ensuring that there is open feedback in both directions and that mistakes are discussed. I openly admit my mistakes. If we talk to each other openly, we can avoid errors and do things better next time. The one thing I don't tolerate in myself is making the same mistake twice."

This may well be the secret of success at the Software Center, where computer scientists, engineers and physicists not only develop software but also work on innovations and prototypes in three main fields: telecommunication networks, simulation technologies and security systems. Their work includes the further development of software, for example for UMTS (Universal Mobile Telecommunications Service) – the third-generation cellular phone system – or for the ultramodern C4I security and traffic surveillance system that was such a success at the Athens Olympics in 2004. Since then, Siemens Greece has developed into a global center of excellence for activities related to "security at major events."

Starting a Family and Learning How to Lead

There are now some 700 people working at the Software Center, although its beginnings were much more modest. "That was in 1990," says Ekaterinidi, who was born in Athens. "I had just started working as a software developer at Siemens Greece. Back then, 12 of us set about building up the Center." In fact, 1990 was the start of a second career for her. Before that, she managed her own company, which she had set up at the age of 24, two years after getting her degree. The company specialized in the design and engineering of electrical equipment. In between, she had started a family and devoted 12 months exclusively to childcare, following the birth of her baby son. "During that time, I learned a lot of things that have also come in very useful at work, like learning how to 'lead' other people and taking responsibility for both the good and the bad aspects of my leadership."

Even as a young child, Ekaterinidi showed a keen interest in technology. "I started to make things at a very early age," she says. "I thought anything connected with electricity was incredibly exciting." Back then, it was not unknown for a blown fuse to temporarily cut off the power supply to the family home. Her parents weren't at all concerned that she didn't fit the traditional picture of a little girl playing with dolls. "They just accepted me as I am." Her name, Tzoanna, is in fact a nickname invented by her father as an amalgamation of her two given names, Zoi and Anna.

Dr. Tzoanna Ekaterinidi already had an electrical engineering degree in the bag before she turned 22. For years, she ran her own company and studied physics on the side, eventually gaining a doctorate. She then gave up being her own boss to join Siemens in Athens as a software developer. Today, she is head of the Software Center at Siemens Greece, where she is responsible for 700 employees. Together with her talented team, she turns out a continuous flow of innovations.

The early start of elementary school in Greece and a 12-year schooling system meant that she had already completed her high school education at the German School in Athens when she was 17. For her parents and close relatives, many of whom were in the medical profession, it was completely normal that she should want to study a scientific subject. Nor did they object to her opting to study in Munich, Germany – a country to which she "always had an affinity." However, at the Technical University in Munich, several eyebrows were raised at the notion of a girl not yet 18 wanting to study electrical engineering. In fact, the idea was so exotic that it threatened to delay her admission. "Fortunately, I had a scholarship from the DAAD, the German Academic Exchange Service, so I was allowed to start right away," she recalls.

In the Germany of the mid-1970s, she was the only female student in a class of 500. But she found the course easy, and four and a half years later she passed with distinction. Normally, she would then have tackled her doctorate, particularly as she had already secured funding for a project in laser technology. However, during a vacation in Greece she met her future husband and stayed on to be with him. But this step didn't mean the end of her career. Showing a flexibility that she claims is one of the greatest assets of her employees and fellow Greeks, she set up her own company. "And in my spare time I studied physics and did my doctorate," says Ekaterinidi, who is now the mother of a grownup son. After eight years as her own boss, she decided it was time to take up an international career. So she wound up her company and joined Siemens.

More Women in Technology Companies

Has she ever encountered problems as a company manager or software developer simply because of the fact that she's a woman? No, she answers. "If you're good in your field and work professionally, that gets recognized," she says, adding that she would like to see more women in technology companies. "Software development is a highly analytical and precise type of work that is well suited to the female way of thinking. Obviously, men have their strong points too, and will tend to bring along a more practical way of looking at things. The best possible situation is a healthy mix of the two." And that's precisely what the Software Center has, with women making up almost 40 percent of the workforce.

When Siemens approached Ekaterinidi and asked her if she'd like to become Director of the Software Center in 1997, she had already climbed "all the rungs of the career ladder." For example, she had been a technical director, project manager and departmental head. She immediately took advantage of her advancement to give the center a more international focus. As a result, in recent years it has developed into an international research and development center that is responsible for realizing customer-specific projects in Europe, the Middle East and Africa. The objective is to provide end customers – in other words, international Siemens companies or Siemens Groups – with innovations that give them an advantage over the competition.

Ekaterinidi defines her own role as that of a "manager who continuously leads her team to new innovations." When she speaks about innovations, she doesn't just mean new products. "Innovation is all about taking an idea based on the recognition of a 'gap' – in other words, the recognition of a need – and turning it into something tangible." This need, she explains, might have its roots in the market itself, in which case innovation leads to new products and services. It can also be a need for a new technology or for greater efficiency and better organization, which then results in new processes. "Achieving innovation is particularly difficult when it comes to processes," she says. "Success here must be based on a culture and a strategy of objective self-evaluation and continuous improvement."

Open Communication Promotes Creativity

From day one, Ekaterinidi has gone to great lengths to cultivate an innovation-friendly atmosphere that "helps promote creativity among the younger software engineers, keeps people interested in their jobs and strengthens their identification with the company." She has always strived to ensure that the Software Center not only takes on development contracts, such as software modifications for the regional and international market, but also continually pushes ahead with the innovation process. Its activities therefore include developing prototypes – if appropriate, in cooperation with local and European research institutes and universities – and developing innovative services and products that Siemens can sell on the international market.

Free and open communication plays a key role in Ekaterinidi's culture of innovation. For example, during internal workshops she asks engineers, researchers, technicians, sales staff and customers to sit around the same table and form "communities." Likewise, nobody at the Software Center has inhibitions about thinking out loud at the brainstorming sessions. "People need to learn to express themselves freely," she says. "They shouldn't be embarrassed about saying something. No comment is stupid or wrong." And Ekaterinidi also encourages her employ-

Lessons learned	Tzoanna Ekaterinidi's advice for innovators
• Innovation is about recognizing a need and turning it into something tangible. • An innovation needn't be a new product; it can be a process or a service. • Generating innovations is an intellectual process that requires continuous stimulation and cultivation. • Obstacles can be overcome through determination, the right strategy, teamwork and open communication. • A global company should always involve its regional organizations in its innovation strategy, because they are the only ones who really know local customers' requirements.	• Learn to think openly and out loud. • Form communities whose members adopt different approaches but have the same objectives. • Work closely with the sales and marketing departments. This is the only way to find out what the market really wants. • Never let the flow of information dry up; stay in constant contact with fellow team members. • Hone your observation skills. Take nature as an example, and don't always search for the most complicated solution. The simplest ideas can generate the best innovations.

ees to keep things simple. "Sometimes our thinking is just too complicated. The simplest solutions are often the best."

Under her leadership, the employees have learned to discuss their ideas and also defend them against skeptics. "You have to be able to explain clearly the utility of what you're proposing. And you need to believe in your own idea and have the will to put it into practice," says Ekaterinidi, who admires people who are humble about their own achievements. As far as Tzoanna Ekaterinidi is concerned, her success speaks for itself. Thanks to her dedication and that of her employees at the Software Center in Athens, Siemens enjoys a leading market position in the region and has a first-class reputation as an innovative company.

> *"Love your employees just like parents love their children, and educate them," says Matthias with smile. "That's good – trust a woman to come up with such an excellent idea. The analogy between bringing up kids and managing a team of employees seems right on target to me. When a child learns to tie its own shoelaces or flies abroad for the first time on its own, it's entering completely unknown territory. Parents can show their kids how to perform simple tasks, but when things become complicated it's crucial to ensure that they have the self-confidence necessary to succeed."*

John nods in agreement: "That's right, the analogy's not bad at all. With innovation projects, management also needs to let employees try things out and learn, rather than simply penalizing mistakes. We know from numerous surveys of companies that over 90 percent of all new ideas never make it to market, and less than five percent are a real success. Therefore, instead of penalizing the failure of an innovation project, you should reward employees for quickly helping to clarify whether an innovative concept should be promoted or terminated. If innovators see how a colleague is penalized when something doesn't work out, they'll most likely concentrate on covering their backs. While risk avoidance involving many people, endless meetings and countless approval procedures might obscure blame, it doesn't promote genuine innovations. And that's true whether you're talking about politics or business."

"All this talk reminds of an idea of Dr. Michael Kaschke, the CFO at Carl Zeiss AG, who's also responsible for innovation there," interrupts Walter. The others look quizzical, so he continues: "Kaschke noticed that there was a strong culture of avoiding failure at Zeiss, so he introduced a prize for the most 'successful failure.' The aim was to reward innovation projects that provided important experience even though they were never implemented. Such an award emphasizes the fact that failure is also part of the business of innovation. Failing successfully can provide valuable know-how that might prove useful in future projects."

John is impressed. "Laying down clearly defined processes, dictating strategy and allocating resources – those tasks have always been the job of management. But innovation requires more. You don't simply have to decide whether to continue, modify or halt a project – you also have to create a culture of innovation on the emotional level. You need open communication and you need to remove people's fear of failure. And here I'm referring not only to product innovations but also to new processes and new business models."

Christian moves uneasily in his chair. "You're asking quite a lot there, John. As a businessman, it's usually my job to be cautious as far as innovations are concerned. Now I'm supposed to not only encourage a culture of innovation but also to start questioning the stability of our processes! But maybe you're right. There's certainly potential for innovation there. One example that immediately comes to mind involves the introduction of a new business model in an established market. In this particular example, we basically reinvented the way we make money – with energy-performance contracting..."

Financing by Saving

Ullrich Brickmann, head of Sales and Marketing in the Energy & Environmental Solutions division at Siemens Building Technologies (SBT) in Frankfurt am Main, Germany, is optimally prepared for his interview. He's got plenty of information material, brochures and newspaper articles – and his laptop, of course. However, he's a little uncomfortable about the fact that his achievements as an innovator are going to be highlighted. "You know, I didn't come up with this innovative business model by myself; we produced it together as a team," he says. It's true, of course, that innovations cannot be implemented by a single individual. Still, Brickmann played a key role in the development of energy-performance contracting and its implementation in Europe. He also continues to work on expanding the concept.

So what's it all about? Brickmann explains: "The construction of new buildings has been stagnating in Europe for some time, especially here in Germany, where the country has already been built to its limits, so to speak. Fewer new buildings mean more competition and lower prices, which is why the biggest and most attractive market at the moment is for maintaining existing structures. My colleagues and I therefore began searching for a new type of business model involving responsible, high-tech construction activities that would generate income." Their solution was the energy-performance contracting model, which aims at energy-efficient planning and construction through optimized systems for building automation, heating, air conditioning and ventilation, water supply, lighting and much more. However, energy-performance contracting also involves a completely new form of cooperation, whereby SBT assumes responsibility for the energy efficiency and economy of all construction activities and guarantees that building owners will recoup their investment after a cer-

Ullrich Brickmann has been practicing a novel form of cooperation in the building business for more than ten years. Known as "energy-performance contracting," it involves guaranteed energy savings that are used to finance the modernization of energy systems in buildings.

tain period of time. The refinancing of the applications is accomplished by means of a share of the energy-cost savings. As a result, the investment risk is transferred from the building owner to the service provider, which voluntarily delivers the project "up front."

Public-Private Partnership

In many selected projects, SBT also handles investment prefinancing, thereby making it possible to implement the project more rapidly. The innovation here involves not just state-of-the-art technology but also the new method of cooperation employed. "Energy-performance contracting is a variation of a public-private partnership," says Brickmann. "Instead of an adversarial relationship, you have an energy-conservation partnership between all parties in the construction project." Brickmann's enthusiasm for the concept can be heard whenever he talks about it, and you can tell he's an expert when it comes to working responsibly and in partnerships. He's a team player who has no desire to push people around.

Brickmann didn't invent energy-performance contracting – but he did adapt the model to Germany and launch it on the market, thereby helping to pave the way for the business model in Europe. This achievement goes together well with his motto, a quote from Aristotle: "We cannot direct the wind, but we can adjust the sails." The idea for energy-performance contracting originated in North America in the 1980s as a logical consequence of the first oil crisis. Brickmann heard about it back then, and was one of ten employees specially chosen to establish a Performance Contracting division when his former employer Landis & Staefa GmbH in Frankfurt am Main – a subsidiary of the Swiss company Elektrowatt AG – turned to the concept ten years ago. The industrial segment of Elektrowatt AG was acquired by Siemens in 1998 and became part of Siemens Building Technologies in 2003.

Getting back to the beginning, the first task was to analyze the market and set up a sales and marketing organization. "Our initial customer target groups were schools, colleges, athletic facilities, indoor swimming pools, public and private offices, hotels, hospitals and industrial buildings," Brickmann recalls. "Because of the long-term nature of the financing model, we were looking for customers with good credit and high annual energy requirements. We therefore focused on public clients such as cities, municipalities, counties, states and the German federal government. These target groups owned a lot of buildings that used a lot of energy and also required substantial modernization and financing."

Banking on Higher Efficiency and Lower Consumption

Brickmann's team was helped here by the German government, which was pushing for more energy-efficient forms of building construction and modernization. "Our energy resources are finite," says Brickmann. "Oil and gas reserves in the North Sea are being depleted, and Germany is dependent on energy supplies from outside the European Union for more than half of its energy requirements. The problems this can cause are the subject of much discussion at the moment, following the cutoff of gas deliveries to Ukraine by the Russian energy giant Gazprom. The fast-growing emerging markets also need more and more oil and gas. At some point, demand will be so great that not everyone will be able to obtain the energy they need. The German government therefore wishes to dramatically reduce energy consumption – among other things, by increasing energy efficiency in buildings."

Acknowledging its responsibilities as a major industrial nation, Germany has set ambitious climate protection goals for itself and plans to significantly reduce greenhouse gas emissions over the next few years. To this end, the government has implemented the Energy Saving Regulation, and the Energy Conservation Law. At the same time, the EU has enacted the directive on the energy performance of buildings, which defines criteria for the overall assessment of energy efficiency in buildings.

When establishing a new business segment, you need to have a competent team of people with knowledge in all the disciplines required for the new field. Implementation of energy-efficient methods of construction and building modernization requires expertise in a very diverse range of technologies and applications, including energy controlling and facility monitoring. "That's why instead of specialists, we needed people with a more general background who could look beyond their immediate horizons," says Brickmann. This required training people in completely new areas so as to enable energy engineers to conduct energy analyses and determine the level of energy savings that could be guaranteed, as well as demonstrating the overall economic feasibility of specific projects. In the same vein, performance assurance managers had to be able to ensure and validate the energy savings and handle the annual invoices for customers. Moreover, all the experts had to be competent in both technical and commercial matters.

Projects that Attract New Customers

The first reference project Brickmann and his team carried out was launched in 1996 while the business segment was still being organized. It involved renovating and modernizing 74 buildings in Berlin, including schools, kindergartens, gyms and administrative buildings. Additional contracts quickly followed. "Over time, we ended up modernizing around 200 buildings in Berlin in an energy-efficient manner," Brickmann says. "The total investment of €28.5 million was recouped through €5.3 million in annual energy savings." The team went on to conduct similar projects for municipalities, counties and hospitals.

"Our innovations weren't just theoretical – we constantly had customers we could point to, and therefore revenues as well," Brickmann explains. "As a result, we created a solid economic basis for building up the business segment. It's not always a given that a company will invest in a new business model. We, however, were allowed the freedom that you need to develop innovative solutions." As Brickmann recalls, the early days were marked by strong team cohesion and a euphoric mood. Cooperation was close, uncomplicated, free of bureaucratic constraints and without hierarchies. "Building up the business segment was a lot of fun, even though we had to work very hard and put in a lot of time," says Brickmann. "But everyone was completely focused; we all had our eyes on the prize."

There were difficulties as well, of course. After being incorporated into SBT, the new Energy & Environmental Solutions subdivision had to prove itself to already established departments, some of which dismissed the new model as a crazy idea or else feared its competition. The new team also had to be integrated into Siemens structures, whereby the original core team was broken up and incorporated into the regional sales organizations. What remained was a central competence center consisting of six members. Based at SBT headquarters in Frankfurt, it was assigned the task of managing and further developing the concept. Operating teams with a total of 50 employees were then assigned to the nine sales regions in the regional organization for Germany.

"Placing energy-performance contracting services on the market remains a very challenging affair," says Brickmann. "Even though the government is applying pressure here, many customers still don't really understand the model, and some fear the transparency involved or are turned off by the effort involved in project development." As a result, the market is developing more slowly than he would like – but it could be moving faster if building authorities were more open and flexible. A forecast by the Berlin Energy Agency reveals just how much economic potential the energy-saving modernization of existing buildings harbors: "The systematic dismantling of structural hurdles could create a market for energy services in Europe with an annual volume of up to €25 billion," says Michael Geißler, managing director of the Berlin Energy Agency.

A Market Worth Billions

The difficulties associated with establishing such a market were forgotten on May 31, 2006, when Brickmann accepted the European Energy Service Award for SBT as the "Best Energy Service Provider 2006." The

Lessons learned	Ullrich Brickmann's advice for innovators
• You need to have a vision, look beyond your immediate horizons, embark upon new paths, and have the courage to attempt completely new solutions. Don't just think about tomorrow – think about the day after tomorrow as well. Otherwise, your company won't survive for long. • To achieve this long-term vision, you must have innovative and creative employees and give them the freedom to experiment. That's because innovations cannot be developed with rigid processes. • A new project management system must be introduced if a new business model or service requires the integration of many new technologies. • It might make sense to remove experienced employees from daily operations for a while and put them to work at headquarters – and vice versa. The resulting exchange of ideas benefits both sides. • A team with a shared vision is unstoppable.	• Rigid structures and too much bureaucracy and hierarchy inhibit innovation. • Short-term thinking has fatal consequences. Innovations are often created in a process lasting several years, as they need time to mature. • New types of energy services require generalists, who can develop holistic solutions, rather than specialists. • Employees must be given the freedom to develop. • Managers must be able to think for the long term – and also have the courage to do so.

panel for this European Union award explained its decision to honor SBT by pointing out the company's "great willingness to take risks in order to enter new markets, and its drive to shape competition to the benefit of its customers." SBT is now the market leader for energy-performance contracting not only in Germany but also worldwide. By 2006, SBT had modernized energy systems in more than 1,100 buildings in Germany alone. It had also invested €70 million, but the results of its work had led to savings of €110 million in energy costs and a reduction in CO_2 emissions of more than 430,000 tons. SBT has also generated energy savings totaling $1.1 billion with some 1,000 customers in the U.S. since 1995. Double-digit growth is expected worldwide over the next few years as well.

These are impressive numbers, but Brickmann also has another point to make: "Our example shows that it pays for a company to be on the leading edge of a development. For this reason, I can only recommend that companies demonstrate courage by giving their employees the freedom they need to be creative and innovative. If you do that, there'll be no stopping them."

"Brickmann created a real win-win-win situation with the energy-performance contracting system," says Walter. "The customer's building is completely modernized – and he doesn't even have to pay for it because the costs are gradually covered by the energy savings; Siemens gets business, and the environment benefits as well. It's like a rabbit pulling itself out of a hat."

Christian laughs: "It just shows you how innovative new business models can be. Uh-oh – I think we'll have time to talk about other examples because it looks like there's traffic up ahead. How come we don't have air taxis? Now that would be an innovation that makes sense."

"Cars in the air?" Walter says. "It might not be that difficult technically speaking, but organizing it could be a problem, not to mention the legal ramifications and general acceptance issues. For example, the customers would have to trust the vehicles, which would have to be completely automatic. Laws would have to be changed and special air corridors set up."

John agrees: "Launching something like that on the market would be anything but easy. Professor John T. Gourville from Harvard Business School in Boston says that most market launches that fail do so because innovators overestimate the utility of their inventions, while customers also have an irrationally high opinion regarding the utility of the products they've come to trust. So if you're talking about personal air travel on a mass scale, your technical solution not only has to be objectively superior to the system currently used on the ground; innovators also have to convince customers that they would benefit from trading in their old, trusty cars that they operate themselves for an automated flying vehicle."

Stacey laughs: "If I had the choice, I'd give up my car immediately. But you're probably right: The utility of an innovation must be so clear to customers that they'll not only spend money on it but also go through the stress of having to change accustomed ways of doing things. As Gombert said, everyone '…demands innovation but is wary of change.' Speaking of which: I can't help us out with a helicopter, but a lot is happening in the big field of security technology. You all know about the requirements for biometric data in identity documents. Let me tell you about an innovative project in this area…"

Body Codes

Gerd Hribernig is so tall that he has to duck when he walks from one office to another at the Biometrics Center (BC) operated by Siemens Program and System Development in Graz, Austria. It's therefore no surprise that Hribernig, who stands around two meters tall, hardly fits into the small photo booth that his employees built for testing purposes. The booth, a camera, a PC, and a fingerprint measuring system are all components of the recently completed „Swiss Passport 2006" project.

In this project, the BC developed a forgery-proof passport that would meet the restrictive U.S. immigration regulations as well as EU requirements. "The U.S. requires biometric passports for all people coming from countries whose citizens do not need a visa to enter America," Hribernig, 42, explains, as he looks into the camera in order to be photographed by a colleague conducting a demonstration. "We therefore had to integrate the biometric data into the passport."

Hribernig likes to laugh – but now he needs to look serious, as international passport regulations require portraits with "a neutral expression and the mouth closed." The photos will be used for automated facial recognition and will later be printed on the inside of the new passports and stored as data on a chip embedded in the same. Now Hribernig places his right index finger on a fingerprint sensor. A gray image of his fingerprint appears on a monitor within seconds, and the computer immediately goes to work combining the characteristic patterns of the fingerprint into a reference data set that will be encrypted and stored in the passport. Immigration officials need this data set to confirm that a passport is genuine. In other words, travelers will only be admitted if the face in the photo matches their face, and their fingerprint matches the one stored in the passport.

Biometric Data on a Wireless Chip

The red Swiss passport with the white cross on the front is no different from any other passport in terms of its weight or thickness. That's because the data storage unit is an ultra-thin RFID chip integrated into the back cover. Immigration officials can read its encrypted data via radio in order to verify the identity of the document holder. Switzerland has also set up a special service for its citizens that was extensively tested by BC experts before being implemented. The service enables citizens to check the data stored in their passport at any time using "checkpoint" systems, which are special computers operated by national agencies. The Biometrics Center developed the complete biometric and application software for the system.

"Passports are just one of many applications for biometrics," says Hribernig, who studied electrical engineering at Graz University of Technology and began working with neural networks, fuzzy logic and image processing while writing his Master's thesis. In 1992, he joined Siemens PSE, where he was able to apply his knowledge to the development of biometric procedures from the very beginning. Hribernig became head of PSE's Biometrics Center in 1999 and has conducted numerous projects since that time. Since January 1, 2007, PSE has been a part of the new Siemens IT Solutions and Services Group.

Gerd Hribernig doesn't know how to sail, but he still sees himself as a steersman. His boat is the Siemens Biometrics Center (BC), which is headquartered in Graz, Austria, and has 100 employees worldwide. BC develops biometric procedures for a variety of applications, including everything from security to health care.

One of his projects involves a 3D face scanner that is being tested at the ultramodern Siemens Airport Center located in Fürth-Bislohe near Nuremberg. The 8,500 square-meter facility contains everything an airport does except airplanes and runways. The 3D face scanner offers a new way of verifying a passenger's identity – one that is based on a system developed by Dr. Frank Forster, who is with Siemens Corporate Technology (see "The Colors of Success"). With this system, a type of slide projector projects color strips onto a face, whereby the forehead, eye sockets, cheekbones, nose and chin deform the color strips and generate a unique pattern for each individual. A computer calculates the shape of the face based on the color data, and this information is then stored in a data set. The advantage of this system is that it can register in practically real time the three-dimensional form of a face from a single video image, regardless of the lighting conditions or head position.

Check-in and boarding procedures that utilize a fingerprint solution developed by BC and Siemens Business Services have already been tested by 400 Lufthansa employees at a real airport (Frankfurt). Lufthansa conducted the tests because it wanted to obtain initial experience with new systems as it pursues its goal of making check-in and boarding processes more secure and efficient.

Face access. Siemens is testing security systems for airports, like this 3D face scanner at the Siemens Airport Center near Nuremberg. A three-dimensional face is a much better biometric reference than a two-dimensional photo.

Body Codes

The Highest Levels of Security

The highest levels of security can be achieved using a combination of biometric procedures. An example of this is the "Intelligent Digital Passport" which Siemens developed for India's Ministry of Defense. With this system, a device records the voice of the individual in question, generates a digital image of their face, and also registers their fingerprint. The data is transferred to a chip card in compressed and encrypted form. If an employee of the ministry wishes to enter a restricted area, the reference data is compared to the parameters measured on site. This significantly reduces the danger of unauthorized persons accessing restricted zones.

Hribernig believes the market for biometric systems (fingerprints, facial imaging, voice recognition, iris recognition, signatures) will have a total volume of $4.7 billion in 2008, not including revenues from system service, rollout and operation. According to Hribernig, expertise in biometric techniques is the key to success in this attractive market, which is growing at an annual rate of 35 percent. Speed is also important, however, because "companies in the IT sector must be able to implement their ideas within a year's time." That's why it's also crucial to quickly market attractive solutions.

He sees five economic sectors in particular for which the Biometrics Center offers procedures and products: the public sector (solutions for electronic documents and e-government applications); the health care sector (administration systems for medical data); the travel and transportation sector (systems for screening passengers); the banking and insurance sector (to make administrative processes as secure as possible); and the leisure and gaming sector (products for amusement parks and casinos).

The driving forces of growth are increased security concerns on the part of governments and agencies and the desire of companies to achieve lower costs and provide greater convenience for the users and the people they scan. Such convenience is ensured because biometric systems require only a few seconds to do their job. The cost savings result from the fact that data is automatically analyzed, which reduces personnel costs and accelerates and improves processes.

Innovations Must Thrill Customers, not Developers

Hribernig has a clear idea of what an innovation is. "Innovation is not necessarily related to high-tech," he says. "In our case, the important thing is to simplify the human-machine interface. Technical innovations have to be linked with a 'sexy feature' – in other words, an application that is visible rather than hidden, and which makes it easier to use the system in question."

It's not always easy for engineers to focus on the customer, and Hribernig – who holds ten patents in the fields of image processing, pattern recognition and biometrics – is no exception here, as he readily admits: "I also started out as a technology freak. But what's the point of that when the customer doesn't know how to operate the technology? Besides, the most important question is always: Is the customer ready for this product?" Hribernig is referring here not only to psychological aspects but also to the customer's IT infrastructure and processes – which may not be as advanced as the technology Siemens is offering. "The best biometric access authorization system will be useless if it's not linked with firewalls, encryption and other security applications to form a complete system," he explains.

The Biometrics Center, which also has offices in Vienna, Zagreb, Split and Munich, does not wish to leave innovations to chance, which is why the people in Graz have been working according to a defined innovation process for a year now. This involves asking questions such as: "What type of innovation can still generate earnings?" "Which innovations have been exhausted?" "What will the customer be doing in five years?" In the latter case, staff members utilize scenarios known as "Pictures of the Future," which Siemens has developed for all business areas, in order to generate ideas as to what course future developments will take. They then attempt to come up with approaches for applying innovations in a targeted manner.

BC employees in Graz and at other locations certainly have plenty of ideas. In Graz, some 25 electrical engineers and computer scientists bring their ideas to Hribernig, who is on familiar terms with his staff and also regularly talks to all other employees. After initial discussions, the first question Hribernig asks his people is: "Is there a system that can be used to implement the idea more easily?" The employees, most of them 25–30 years old, are obviously taken aback by the question, but it's not Hribernig's intention to discourage them. Instead, his approach is based on the knowledge that "engineers tend to try to solve every problem using the tools available to them," he says. Comparing engineers to workmen, Hribering points out that "you can't always use a hammer or pliers for everything. For example, a hammer won't help much if you want to saw something. Successful innovations have to offer solutions for which there are no simpler technical alternatives."

Successful Marketing Requires Partners

As a result, only "five to ten percent of the ideas created at the Biometrics Center are actually realized." The most promising innovative ideas are first presented to a pilot customer. Then comes phase two, in which a workshop is held and the customer is asked to state his wishes and requirements. In the third phase, BC presents the refined innovation idea to Groups such as Siemens Building Technologies or Medical Solutions.

An example of an idea for the health care sector would be biometric authentication procedures for personnel who process and manage patient data or administer medication. Biometric systems simplify work processes for doctors and other medical staff, while at the same time leaving patients secure in the knowledge that only authorized persons will be able to access their data. One of the biggest installations is the Siemens ID Center used by the Susquehanna Health System's group of networked hospitals in Pennsylvania. A total of 3,000 staff members – doctors and clinical personnel – use their fingerprints to enter the group's network via PC, after which they can access the information that is relevant to their needs. Personnel are identified within one to three seconds, after which they are given access to information relevant to their jobs. Depending on their authorization, staff can then perform operations such as collecting and managing patient data, utilizing clinical programs, accessing illness reports and care and treatment plans, or administering medication.

The Biometrics Center does not market such innovative solutions itself, however, but instead offers them to international Siemens companies around the world. Hribernig says the important thing when presenting such solutions "is not to talk above the heads of people but to instead communicate the innovation in a simple and understandable manner. That's how we try to win over the product managers in the Groups." Once they've convinced their potential partners, they move into phase four, in which business and investment plans are drawn up, and phase five, which is implementation.

Determining the Limits of Action and Remaining Patient

Although it all sounds very simple, it's certainly not the case that BC never encounters obstacles or criticism. Hribernig is not easily discouraged, however. "I don't accept any limits without having first determined what they are myself," he says. Such perseverance usually enables him to find a solution, whether by searching for allies at the top management level, or implementing ideas using alternative methods. In the latter case, he'll always have a backup plan ready, even if that sometimes means taking a couple of steps backwards. After all, an innovator needs to be flexible and patient, as Hribernig points out.

"It's advisable to sail with the wind, by which I mean utilizing the strengths of the company and developing innovations for markets in which Siemens is already strategically active and well positioned," he says. Such markets for biometric applications can currently be found mainly in the U.S. and central Europe, and these will be joined in the near future by the Middle East and South America. Still, there have been occasions when a Group has been reluctant to get on board immediately because it first wishes to fully exploit a profit-making innovation – and thus fails to see the next one coming up on the horizon. The people in Graz manage to get around this, however. "We've always managed to obtain the resources we need one way or another – usually through regional, national or EU funding programs," says Hribernig. "If that doesn't work, we try to tap into the innovation fund at Siemens Austria. Such funding enables us to finance market analyses, feasibility studies and the construction of a prototype."

Hribernig is driven by what he calls "the joy of creating something new," and you can be sure that any biometric procedures that might be used in a few years to optimize the admission of huge crowds to sporting events and amusement parks will be based on solutions from the Biometrics Center. A system that combines fingerprints and admission tickets will allow easy access to the parks. Some entertainment parks in the U.S. are among the first to use this innovation, and others will follow.

The Biometrics Center is already working on other more sophisticated ideas, however. One of these involves using image processing software to automatically analyze video images recorded at the entrance areas to major events. The system can help identify suspicious objects or people (biometric identification) and also inform personnel of long lines so that they can open up additional entrance gates. Hribernig also has a plan to optimize the flow of visitors at trade fairs by using video cameras that record the flow of people and then send data to a system that uses special algorithms to analyze it. "You'd then be able to see through color codes which exhibits attracted a lot of people and which did not," Hribernig explains. "Red markings, for example, would indicate a large number of people, and areas with few people would be marked in blue. This would enable trade fair organizers to plan future exhibitions more effectively."

Hribernig obviously still gets a thrill out of "creating a good idea myself – at least until I can find someone who understands it and can run

Lessons learned	Gerd Hribernig's advice for innovators
• Technology alone does not make for an innovation. A new product or system must be easy to operate and fit in well with the customer's existing infrastructure. • Think about the future and anticipate what the customer will be doing in five years. • Develop a sense of when the time is right to launch a new development on the market. • Utilize the strengths of your company, and sail with the wind. • Criticism is to be expected, so frustration must be avoided and patience maintained.	• Always ask yourself if there isn't a simpler technical alternative to your innovation. • Try to gain support from management. • Don't talk above people's heads; explain your ideas in a simple and understandable manner. • Don't rely on a single plan; make sure you always have a backup plan ready. • Maintain flexibility so as to be able to react to external changes.

with it." That's not a problem, as he has 100 talented individuals working for him around the world. He therefore often travels for his work – but his weekends and vacations are spent with his wife and three sons. The family likes to go on bike trips, often traveling 60 to 80 kilometers in one day. Hribernig says it's important for him to give his sons a chance to prove themselves – something he also does with his employees, for whom he strives to be a mentor and teacher. "I didn't have that kind of support when I started out," he explains. "There was no one who took me by the hand, which is why I fell on my face a few times with my innovative ideas."

Such statements illustrate the fact that Hribernig has long ago given up playing the role of inventor. As director of the Biometrics Center, he's now more like a traditional innovation manager – but he doesn't particularly like that description because he says it makes him sound like he's only there to collect ideas and keep processes running. Instead, Gerd Hribernig sees himself as a steersman of innovation ships, which he guides safely to their destinations.

"The innovation manager as a steersman; that's a pretty good analogy," says Matthias. "He's right – it doesn't make sense to sail against the wind.

You've got to harness the power of the wind – whether in the form of the strengths of your company or the changes that occur on the market – to accomplish what you want to do. Prof. Claus Weyrich, who was head of Corporate Technology until the fall of 2006, likes to say: 'When the wind of change blows, some people build huts to protect themselves and others build windmills.' I think I'd rather be one of those who build windmills."

"OK, welcome to the innovators' club," says Bao Jun. "What you said almost sounds like Eastern philosophy."

Matthias isn't sure whether Bao Jun is making fun of him, but when he looks at him he can't see anything to indicate that he is – even though some of the others are grinning. But Bao Jun continues in a serious tone: "Hribernig runs his innovation ship very strategically. He always looks ahead and tries to figure out the best route to take to get to his destination. And he's always got a backup plan prepared."

John agrees: "He also searches for simple solutions because he knows that innovation doesn't always involve the most sophisticated technologies but rather those that benefit customers the most. I also think it's interesting that he asks himself if the customer is ready for the product. That's like what we were talking about before: Only those things that customers view as innovations – and that fit in with their business environment – will be successful."

Walter nods in agreement: "In the end, it all comes down once again to how tremendously important communication is, especially between innovators and customers – but also within one's own company. I can give you another good example of that, one you're already familiar with: the story of computed and magnetic resonance tomography – but this time from a marketing perspective..."

The Yin and Yang of Innovation

As you step into Bernd Montag's office, you realize at once why they define a whole body here as exactly 2.05 meters tall – and where the marketing idea of a basketball player in the MR core originated. Montag is exactly that size, so his elongated figure would fully occupy the maximum scanning length of the Magnetom Avanto scanner series. And he was not only tall enough but also good enough to play on the German Junior National Basketball Team and then in the German National Basketball League. A landscape-sized poster on the wall – of an airborne basketball

How tall is a "whole body"? That's a question the Siemens engineers who developed Tim technology must have asked themselves often before the rollout in 2003 of the first magnetic resonance tomograph capable of imaging a whole human body in a single scan. Perhaps 1.78 meters? That's the size of an average German man. Or a nice round number like 2 meters? That would have sounded good in any Total Imaging Matrix (Tim) ads. The number ultimately chosen was an imposing 2.05 meters. – which happens to be exactly the height of **Dr. Bernd Montag**, the former marketing chief for Siemens magnetic resonance tomography business area. Montag is the person ultimately responsible for the fact that whole-body tomograph examinations of tall basketball players and other tall athletes were for years the subject of newspaper and magazine articles all over the world.

player with his arms spread wide, titled "Wings" – dispels any doubt that the man in this office is accustomed to thinking on a monumental scale.

Montag's career proceeded in the fast lane. Now 37 and a father of three, Montag – then a theoretical physicist – earned his doctorate at the Friedrich Alexander University in Erlangen-Nuremberg with a thesis on metallic clusters and then joined the Medical Solutions Group (Med) at Siemens in 1995. After several assignments in the quality and processes departments, in export sales for audiology systems, and as product manager for CT scanners, he was appointed marketing manager of the Magnetic Resonance Tomography division in 2001 – exactly when Tim technology was conceived and developed to the production level (see also "Revolution According to Plan – Whole-Body MR Tomography"). This imaging technique makes it possible to scan a patient's body in a single sweep. The successful rollout campaign of Tim, which used orange as a dominant color and focused on the technology and its benefits rather than on the device and its features, would have been inconceivable without Montag.

A Message Based on KISS

"I was dead certain this campaign was going to work," Montag recalls. Most of his colleagues believed the campaign was dead wrong: A vote on his concept among his colleagues in management came out 3 in favor versus 15 opposed. The prevailing opinion was that such an unprofessional approach just wouldn't do. Yet what Montag was proposing had already become an established practice in other industries: the strategy of the trendsetting innovation. This approach mandates a compelling

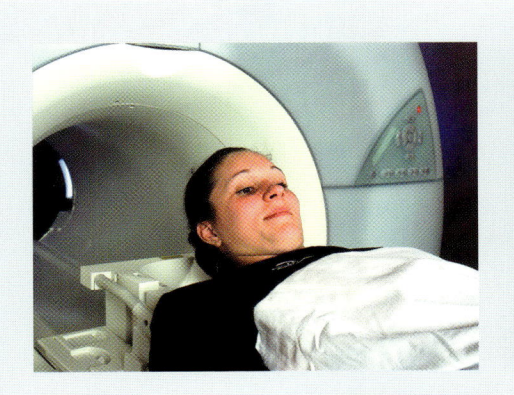

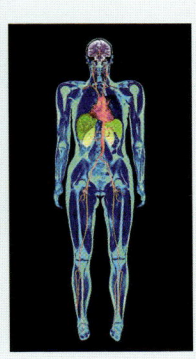

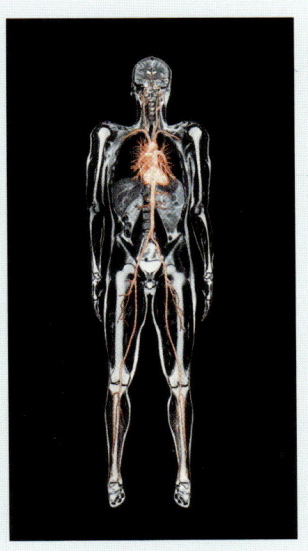

Celebs in the MR scanner. Whole body images of athletes like world champion swimmer Hannah Stockbauer (top) and basketball player Narcisse Ewodo (bottom) have been reprinted in newspapers and magazines, increasing public awareness of the new Magnetom Avanto. The scanner has made it possible for the first time to obtain whole body MR scans with a single pass. The scans require only half as much time, but offer four times the precision, of previous versions.

The Yin and Yang of Innovation

message that is promoted aggressively. "Innovation and communication are the yin and yang of the innovation process," says Montag. The message should be based on the KISS principle, which is familiar to marketing people everywhere: "Keep it simple, stupid."

Total Imaging Matrix, for instance, – "Tim" for short – is a deliberate simplification that's not exactly descriptive of the technology but was chosen intentionally to attract attention. "In our marketing communications we've got to work at a higher level of abstraction," Montag asserts. That means shifting from technical details toward customer benefits, as in: "A whole body scan in 15 minutes!" instead of: "The magnetic field strength has been increased by such-and-such percent." Montag adds: "Just imagine having to explain to a customer in one minute why the new MR scanner is the world's best, and why this and no other model is the one to buy. If you manage to do that, the customer will be enthusiastic enough to lobby the administration to buy this machine."

Montag, who has since been appointed divisional manager of Computed Tomography, recently had to overcome a similar challenge in the market introduction of the Somatom Definition CT scanner (see also "Machines for People"). In this case, Siemens wanted to break through the industry's "arms race" in multi-slice CT and unleash an entirely new concept against the competition's scanners. Until then, different manufacturers had vied to outdo one another with CT scanners that had more and more detector lines capable of imaging ever greater numbers of body slices in a single scan. Montag frowns on that: "In this industry there's something like a law of gravitation that governs technical development." What he means by this are trends that just go on and on, like a law of nature that nobody questions. Just as the clock frequency is being pushed ever higher in microprocessors, so CT scanners have been developed with ever-higher slice capabilities.

What Customers Really Want

But is that what the customers really need? Or could it be that technological advances in a different dimension would be more beneficial? In the view of the Siemens development engineers, the trend to ever greater numbers of slices had reached its limits – not due to technical limitations but because a further increase made no sense as a means of improving medical diagnoses. The real problems – how to "freeze" the motion of the beating heart, or how best to differentiate between bones and soft tissues in a single scan – still remained unsolved. However, there was no pressure yet from the end users – the physicians – to drive innovation in that direction: They hadn't been questioning the industry's trend toward ever more slices. So Bernd Montag and his team could have chosen the easy route and simply persisted in improving the roughly one-year lead of Siemens in multi-slice CT technology.

But they were determined to give the customer something new and unique that would provide real benefits for the diagnostician as well as the patient. Here again, just as in the Tim MR scanner, it all began with a vision. And the message would be "Siemens builds the first CT scanner suitable for round-the-clock emergency duty." This system could even be used in life-threatening situations such as heart attacks to obtain a definitive diagnosis in minimum time – without the need to administer beta blockers, which had previously been required to artificially slow down the patient's heartbeat.

The solution to this problem was found swiftly: The next generation of CT scanners would contain two x-ray tubes and be so fast that it could obtain perfectly sharp cardiac images, even if the patient's heartbeat was fast and irregular. And with this technology it would not only be possible to reduce the x-ray dose by half, but also to separately visualize different body structures in a single exposure, for example vessels outlined with contrast media as well as bones. This would be achieved by operating two x-ray sources at different tube voltages. In Montag's view, it's a matter of intuition to decide when a new technology is sufficiently advanced to overcome the "gravitational pull" of the established technology and to become accepted by customers. There is no way to predict that exactly, but his team was convinced that for the CT scanner this advance was long overdue.

Marketing Definition

Very early in the development process, the team members thought about some names that might clearly differentiate the new scanner. They settled on Somatom Definition, and that's what the new model series is called. "Definition" doesn't stand for a specific technology or functionality, but is compelling and easy to remember. An equally handy name was found for the new dual X-ray tube principle in "Dual Source CT" – deliberately chosen so that it would be accepted into the customers' vernacular without giving them the sense that they were conveying a Siemens promotional message. In the ideal case, says Montag, the marketing brochure with its key messages should be created before the functional specifications – i.e., before any hardware or software is designed. Most important of all is a crystal-clear message for the in-house

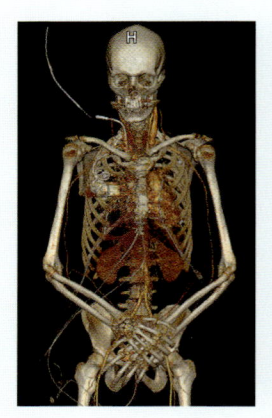

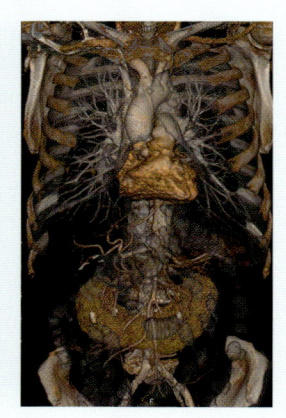

Redefining computed tomography. The Somatom Definition's resolution of better than 0.4 millimeters clearly visualizes even the smallest blood vessels. What's more, the system is twice as fast as any previous CT scanner – and exposes patients to only half as much radiation.

people. "That's important for our own orientation," he emphasizes, "and to make sure we won't lose track of our objective." This in-house vision, he adds, must never be abandoned, even when technical hurdles are encountered during development.

Yet this vision can get lost all too easily under the pressure of everyday work. The CT division has therefore developed a communications culture with regularly scheduled discussions that are nearly always attended not only by the development engineers but also by the people from Marketing and Sales in the shared pursuit of the best solutions. These meetings also serve to "synchronize" people, says Montag, to whom it's important that there is no gap in his division between management and the development engineers but that everyone talks with everyone else.

Montag makes it quite clear that he is opposed to excessive constraints on the innovation process. The process that had been planned down to the last detail for developing the Tim technology in MR scanners was indeed very successful – but, in his view, a clear and compelling vision is just as important as the process. "Every manager has to set an example by clearly identifying with this vision on a daily basis; then the process details will work out too," he says.

Bernd Montag was appointed divisional manager at the age of 35 – of a division responsible for a significant part of Siemen's profits – which

Lessons learned	Bernd Montag's advice for innovators
• The beginning of an innovation is usually defined by a specification of technology and costs. What's often lacking is a vision that appeals to customers and inspires one's own employees. • Marketing communications about innovations have focused on technical details. Instead, they should conceptualize more and highlight customer benefit in compelling slogans. • Until recently, a sales advantage in CT scanners was pursued mostly by increasing the number of detector lines. But the attributes that are most important to physicians and patients (such as a short scan time) can be identified only by talking to those affected by them. • The bold pursuit of unconventional solutions, such as Tim and Dual Source CT, and the use of aggressive communication are swiftly rewarded by an increasing market share. • It's essential to the innovation process that participants talk to each other. Too many constraints tend to stunt the process rather than promote it.	• Innovation and communication must function as a unit – like yin and yang in Chinese philosophy. • One should always strive to use an innovation to start a new trend. • Communications must begin at the very start of the innovation process, and must always be taken into account. • In both communications and innovation, always remember the KISS principle: "Keep it simple, stupid." • Foster good personal relations with customers.

attests to the high level of confidence his superiors have in him. In his view, gauging one's own strengths is always difficult, but he believes that one area in which he probably excels is the ability to keep track of what's essential, along with the drive to simplify and explain what's complicated. In that context Montag views theoretical physics and marketing as being somewhat alike: Natural laws have a certain elegant simplicity – and so do the ground rules of marketing.

The fact that Montag understands the laws of marketing too is evidenced by Siemens' market share in computed tomography, which today is about 30 percent. General Electric, the market leader, is still ahead by a few points. This exactly parallels the situation in MR scanners before Tim technology was introduced. Yet today Siemens is the market leader in that field and is continuing to further widen its lead. Montag is confident that in CT scanners too Siemens will soon overtake GE.

Just as Walter finishes his story, the taxi turns into the freeway exit to the airport. John says: "Thanks, Walter, that was a really good story to finish on, about the way innovation and communications have to function in unison, like yin and yang. I had never heard it put that way before, but it's very true. Internal communications between development engineers, managers, production and sales professionals are just as important as external communications with partners and customers."

"Bernd Montag's notion that the key features in our communications, the main messages, should be defined even before the functional specs also makes sense to me," says Christian. "Because it's really all about the vision, the key customer benefit. And that vision in turn is what unifies and inspires the team – so it really has to be formulated very early in the game."

"I think that in most cases an innovation team already has a pretty good idea of what it wants to develop," responds Stacey. "Maybe not in such crystal-clear detail but a little fuzzier. The really new thought that comes across in the Bernd Montag story is that the core messages shouldn't involve technical detail but be much more straightforward – it shouldn't take longer than a minute to explain to anyone what's so ingenious and different about the innovation. 'Keep it simple, stupid.' How true!"

"Well, that about wraps it up," says Bao Jun and gets ready to exit as soon as the taxi has come to a halt. "Forgive my rush, but I've got to make sure I'll catch my plane. If the line moves fast enough, we might still be able to meet in the lounge to say good-bye."

Space for your own thoughts

How can you strengthen your innovation management and the culture of innovation at your company? Which tools and activities would help in this regard?

Is there a new business model you would like to implement? Beyond technology and process, which offer can generate entirely new value?

Please briefly describe your innovation idea. What is the main benefit for customers, and what is your vision?

From Idea to Business Success

The Commercial Significance of Innovations

*C*haos has broken out at the airport. There's been a bomb scare, and all the flights have been grounded. Security guards are searching the terminal building. Having somehow managed to check in their baggage, the six travelers meet as planned in the departure lounge. Christian is the last to arrive. "It's great to see you all again," he says. "Actually, I don't mind too much that our flight is delayed. There's something I've been meaning to ask you in connection with our stories about innovation – and maybe you can come up with a few good examples. It's a simple question: How can innovations help you to achieve sales of billions of euros?"

"Good question, Mr. Salesman," says John, grinning. "If there were a simple answer, we wouldn't have met so often. We've already talked about lots of factors, but there's another important one that we haven't mentioned yet: ease of use. User-friendly products can result in markets that are worth billions. In the world of IT, for example, structures are complex and the speed of innovation is very high. I've been taking a look at what makes IT products successful, and standardization and ease of use are crucial for the mass markets. Bill Gates made his fortune because Windows allows even complete beginners to use a computer. Not long ago I met an innovator who has been combining innovative ideas with good business sense for many years. Let me tell you about Thomas Schott, who calls himself the 'grandfather of control technology.'"

From "Local Hero" to Number One in Automation

What makes a product successful? In a digital camera, for example, it's lots of megapixels. In a car, it's an engine with impressive horsepower – combined with good fuel economy, of course. Ease of use, on the other hand, still doesn't top the list very often when engineers and marketing professionals define a new product's attributes. But actually, many digital cameras would be more attractive with fewer of the superfluous functions that make their menus so confusing. And many cars would be improved by air-conditioning controls that can be used by drivers who don't have engineering degrees. So it's all the more surprising when a manufacturer of industrial controls cites ease of use as the main requirement in product development – even though its products are used exclusively by engineers and skilled technicians. "Simplicity is our recipe for success," says Thomas Schott, who heads Factory Automation at Siemens Automation and Drives in Nuremberg, Germany.

Schott's recipe has been working very well for more than 20 years. The history of the Simatic product series began back in the 1950s, but sales didn't really soar until the 1979 introduction of the S5 product series, which integrated automation, programming and documentation. Schott, who studied electrical engineering at Schweinfurt Technical University, had joined Siemens a year earlier as project manager for systems engineering. In 1984 he was appointed sales executive for automation products, and Simatic marketing manager in 1989. So, as one of the originators of the Simatic line, Schott – though only 52 – has good reason to joke about being the "grandfather of control technology."

The history of factory automation, which is closely linked with the Simatic product line, is an inspiring Siemens success story. One of its most remarkable chapters is the track record of the Industrial Automation Systems division of Automation and Drives in Nuremberg. The division rose from being a "local hero" to become the world's undisputed number one, with a 36 percent market share. What's more, this market share is steadily growing thanks to a continuous flow of innovations. **Thomas Schott** has been an important contributor to this success for more than two decades – so long that he jokes about being the "grandfather of control technology."

Automation in all Industrial Sectors

Before Simatic – and before personal computers and intuitive mouse operation – machinery and entire production lines were controlled by large, expensive process computers that had to be programmed by specialists. This is why many companies in the process industry were hesitant to automate their production. This changed radically with the advent of Simatic. Simatic controls were designed from the very start for non-specialists. Any engineer or technician should be able to learn to use them with minimal effort. Especially in the United States and Asia, where highly qualified specialists aren't always available, ease of use is still the most important selling point. Another is the ongoing, burgeoning trend toward integrating controls into plant-wide automation processes for different industries, from breweries to chemical plants.

Marketing data clearly shows that this trend toward greater automation is continuing. When Siemens launched the Simatic line, the company was a "local hero" fighting to win customers in the domestic market. Today, Simatic is the undisputed number one worldwide, with a market share of 36 percent. Year after year, its market share has been growing by a percentage point. If this continues, Schott is confident that the market share would eventually reach that of Windows in PC operating systems. That's around 90 percent.

Becoming the "Windows of production control" is a dream that's unlikely to come true, but at least Schott's team is working on it. "Being the next Bill Gates would be really nice," Schott laughs, but he isn't entirely kidding: At least in terms of profits, Simatic is certainly impressively lucrative. With its return on sales, factory automation is one of Siemens' most profitable businesses.

Industry Expertise and Customer Relations

This may all sound quite simple – but success doesn't just arrive out of the blue. It's the result of hard work, continuous innovation and exciting developments in the computer industry, of course, such as miniaturization and rapidly increasing computing power. Staying in the forefront over almost three decades requires an innovation process that's different from those of other Siemens businesses. That's because innovations in factory automation are less a result of brilliant ideas than of close customer relations and in-depth understanding of industry requirements. This is largely due to the fact that production control systems are a "supplied product" that don't acquire their full capabilities until integrated into a customer's machine or production line. The customer buys a Simatic control system and then augments it with custom software for the intended manufacturing process.

In this industry, then, it's the customers who set the pace of innovation. Suppliers, including Siemens, have to keep in step. "Radical innovations aren't very common – our product cycles last five to seven years," says Schott. But he adds that this doesn't make the task any easier. The 170 members of his core team must constantly keep a finger on the pulse of the latest technology, day after day, to ensure that they can promptly use it in new products as soon as customers demand it. They employ a dual strategy to achieve this: They often talk with lead customers in the principal markets to learn what new developments are expected to

Automated factories. With Simatic you can control the most diverse production facilities precisely, flexibly and efficiently – from a chemical plant (top) to a state-of-the-art brewery (below).

emerge in the next few years. They also explore new technology trends in house and in collaboration with leading universities. The trends involved range from Internet connection to completely digital factories with self-organizing production units. The real art nowadays is to reconcile what customers want with what's technically feasible. "That used to be a gut decision," Schott admits. "Today we watch the market much more intensively and systematically."

That's all the more important because different markets have different requirements for innovations. With Simatic, though, Siemens strives to supply a "global product." A Simatic product manager's product should be able to meet at least 80 percent of all customer needs in a given mar-

From "Local Hero" to Number One in Automation

ket, Schott insists. To ensure that no new trend is overlooked, executive management is organized according to product groups and industrial centers of competence. In addition, more than 2,000 sales specialists have daily customer contact and regularly report on market developments. The fact that the little gray cubes containing the intelligence of the Simatic control functions actually meet customer requirements in diverse industries is a remarkable accomplishment – and the basis of Simatic's great success in the marketplace.

Shaping Trends

Though this industry isn't known for radical transformations, Simatic is based on the principle that "Nothing is more constant than change." In the decades since Schott joined Siemens, customer requirements and the possibilities offered by technology have changed repeatedly. The first Simatic controllers had a storage capacity of four kilobytes, which was awe-inspiring at the time. Today that value is expressed in megabytes, or even gigabytes. The increasing use of PC-based architectures during the past decade is another change that demanded a response from the 1,200 engineers and scientists developing Simatic. A more recent trend is integrated safety technology – in other words, the integration of accident prevention functions into a production control system from the outset, instead of subsequently retrofitting them to a production line.

Still another radical shift is now emerging: As the volume of data involved continues to soar, the industry's entire development process is changing. In the product design phase, for instance in automotive development, design programs generate an enormous volume of data that hasn't been used much in the past. But now it will be applied more and more in production planning. For example, as a designer plots the shape of a fender on a computer, the control data for the machines that will make this part are co-generated automatically. This direct transformation of CAD data into production layouts and machine control software is still in its infancy. But it could have a tremendous impact. In fact, such an innovation could reduce costs by as much as 50 to 70 percent.

With the elimination of the trial-and-error phase on the factory floor, another advance will be a much shorter time interval from planning to the start of production. The engineers in Nuremberg are already working on simulations that use appropriate data to run entire production processes on a computer – and to ensure early detection of errors that would otherwise require expensive modifications at a later date. This approach is expected to shorten the start-up time of a new production system by as much as 30 percent.

Schott sees his role as that of an "idea generator." And, like any generator, he must get energy from an external source. That's why Schott loves to talk with customers, who supply him with new food for thought. This inexhaustible wellspring of new insights enables him, time and again, to inspire his employees. The agility to respond swiftly to new trends seems to come naturally to Schott, who is a father of two children and a passionate tennis player and skier. His special talent probably owes something to his wealth of experience, which includes various jobs in sales, development and marketing communications.

Experience: Better than Job Rotation

Schott is convinced that experience is of the utmost importance. Many Siemens Groups follow the practice of rotating employees every few years to give them a boost. Automation and Drives adheres to a different philosophy: Employees are retained in their positions for longer periods, provided they have performed well and enjoy their work. "If you keep putting new people into a job all the time, they'll keep making the same mistakes over and over," Schott believes. And that's not exactly an advantage in a market where continuity and solid customer relations count for so much.

That doesn't mean mistakes are unheard of in Schott's enormous sphere of responsibility, of course, and he doesn't always have all the answers. "Something can always go wrong," he concedes, adding that 70 percent of the ideas originating in his department ultimately prove successful, generating more than enough earnings to compensate for the other 30 percent. "The only way to avoid mistakes is to never change anything, and that's the worst mistake of all."

There are no motivational programs in Schott's workplace, where everyone enjoys what they do. He believes such programs are needed when things are going downhill. Under Schott's leadership, though, things have been continually improving for more than two decades. "Let's not kid ourselves," says Schott. "Success is the greatest motivator of all."

Lessons learned	Thomas Schott's advice for innovators
• Customers love simplicity. That's why engineers develop products with a focus on the customers' needs rather than on technical possibilities. • Continuous innovation is more successful in the long term than an ingenious idea every decade or so – at least in factory automation, where customers set the pace of innovation. • It's impossible to predict exactly what customers will need ten years from now, so you have to keep up with all relevant technologies – either in-house or working with partners, for example at universities. • Business success is most likely to be achieved with products that can be sold anywhere in the world, without the need for adaptations. • In a business that depends above all on good customer relations, experienced employees are vitally important. That's why it's also important to keep employees longer in a division.	• Always listen carefully to customers – especially lead customers. • Adhere to an overall strategy, and don't get lost in details. • Replace your own technology and products before your competitors do. • You've got to be fast: Time-to-market is a key success factor today. • Put a high value on experience, and don't move people around all the time.

"Wow – using innovations to continually gain market shares for decades, that's just amazing!" exclaims Matthias. "Aside from the focus on ease of operation, the real secret of this success is constantly determining customer needs and market trends. And the feedback regularly provided by 2,000 sales specialists in daily contact with customers in many different industries must have been very useful too. Then there was the challenge of coordinating the 1,200 development engineers working on Simatic."

"I especially liked the way Thomas Schott emphasized the value of employees' experience," says Walter. "That's an especially welcome note at a time when everyone else seems to think it's necessary to change jobs often to get ahead. I don't think you can go very far in this industry without people who have a lot of experience and are top experts in their field. Like Schott said: Putting new people in the same job all the time would just result in the same mistakes being made over and over."

Amused by his two colleagues' enthusiasm, John picks up where he left off: "I was talking about the value of simplification, and how certain products become almost a de-facto standard in a given industry, like Simatic in factory automation. Another example that comes to mind is from medical engineering: It's about a universal user interface, a sort of 'Windows for medical systems.'"

The Universal Language for Medical Systems

If you ask Dr. Manfred Wangler about his work, be prepared for a complicated answer containing specialized terms such as "Algol, 8080, SPARC, .NET and JBOSS." Wangler has been working in IT for three decades. Back when he started out, memory cards were as big as a piece of letter-sized paper and could hold 32 kilobytes of data, not much more than the total number of characters in this text. Computers were as big as washing machines, and Bill Gates was completely unknown. Wangler, 59, has witnessed the development of computers all the way down to today's high-performance machines and has come to know many generations of processors, such as the 8080 and SPARC. He has also worked with all of the key programming languages, including Algol, Chill and Fortran. He smiles when he talks about the old days, and sometimes you can see a touch of sentimentality in his eyes when he mentions the tiny capacities the early devices had.

Wangler did not study computer science; instead, he holds a doctorate in particle physics. However, just a few computer lectures at college were enough to turn him into an avid amateur programmer who developed software at home in his garage. Computers have remained the focus of Wangler's work, but his activities in this field are at a much higher level now. Wangler was up until recently head of development for *syngo* at Siemens Medical Solutions (Med). *syngo* is a software program that enables hospital personnel to operate medical devices such as computer tomographs, ultrasound scanners and magnetic resonance tomographs in the same simple manner. Wangler explains *syngo* as follows: "Imagine that you have to use completely different types of medical equipment – well, *syngo* is the standardized, easy-to-use interface for all devices." The system enables routine procedures to be carried out with just a few clicks of the mouse. In other words, *syngo* is like Windows for medical

The *syngo* software platform, which is used with numerous medical devices and processes, has for years been one of the most important distinguishing elements at Siemens Medical Solutions. It is also one of the reasons for the great success enjoyed by this sector. **Dr. Manfred Wangler** has been the brain behind *syngo* and the leader of its global development team.

technology. Its interface can be utilized for more than just operating specialized equipment; it also helps with processing patient data and images and producing doctors' reports, thereby significantly reducing the workload of hospital personnel.

syngo was launched on the market in a computer tomograph (CT) in 1999. "That was really a big bang – the people in the industry were thrilled," Wangler recalls. More than five years of development work had gone into the complex software system that was so easy to use. These days, *syngo* is a well-known brand name. All Med imaging equipment, and many therapeutic devices as well, bear the label "*syngo*-speaking," which has now become something of a pledge of quality. "And it's also a unique selling point," says Wangler. "No other company has so consistently implemented a standardized operating interface for its devices as we have."

Revolution in Clinical Imaging

Today, some 650 people work on the further development of *syngo* at five locations in five countries under Wangler's direction. There are also an additional 1,200 software staff members at other Med Groups who write control and analysis programs based on *syngo*. Every month, Med SW sells approximately 1,500 *syngo* licenses to Med Groups and OEM (original equipment manufacturer) partners. The advantage for doctors and other members of staff who use *syngo* is that all the equipment works with the same interface, so they don't have to undergo long hours of training if they switch from an ultrasound unit to a CT device, for example. Another benefit is offered by the virtual "fold-out card" system, whereby a mouse click is all it takes for the user to switch between different program functions such as the examination mode and the 3D-imaging mode. In the past, one function had to be shut down before another could be launched. In other words, someone typing in patients' data would have had to leave the data entry section of the software in order to call up images of another patient, for example. Once they had finished, they could go back to the data entry section and resume typing. *syngo* made the system "interruptible," which saves a huge amount of time. The ability to switch back and forth between functions had long since become the norm in the world of Macs and PCs when *syngo* was launched, but, as Wangler says: "It amounted to a paradigm shift in clinical imaging."

Wangler had to overcome a lot of opposition to push through the *syngo* idea. Still, he doesn't see himself as the actual innovator. "There were so many other people who played a decisive role in developing the concept," he says. "I was more like a facilitator who helped make everything come together." The development of *syngo* had its ups and downs, and much of its history parallels the evolution of computer technology. Wangler's own biography also runs in anything but a straight line – which was exactly his intention. In many instances, he followed his "gut feeling" when making important decisions. Wangler began studying physics in his home region of Franconia at the University of Erlangen-Nürnberg, where he conducted research in the laboratory for medium-energy physics, ultimately obtaining a doctorate in particle physics. "We did a lot of hands-on physics there," he recalls. "We worked on diffusion pumps and lots of electronic equipment." He started learning about computers on the side – and stuck with it over the years. "I didn't want to stop writing software," he says.

After completing his degree in 1978, Wangler went to work for Siemens in Munich at the company's PBX Technology Group, where he developed communication equipment. Among other things, he and his colleagues built a unique telex device for the Swiss Army. The unit was equipped with an "editing function" in the form of a small monitor for text entry. Wangler and his colleagues also built the heart of the device, which consisted of several 8080 processors. He stayed in Munich for five years, where as an amateur programmer he also learned how a professional software development process works. "The first thing is to understand what the customer wants," says Wangler. "This is still one of the most difficult aspects of software development, because customers express themselves in everyday language, which has to be translated into computer language." Wangler also learned how to conduct projects in English in Munich. Support came from a consulting group from Boston with an office in the city, which used English as its business language. "That was a big innovation for the good old PTT technology at Siemens," he says.

Quality Up, Costs Down

In 1982, a colleague transferred to Medical Solutions in Erlangen, where the Magnetic Resonance Tomography division (MR) was being established. Wangler was asked if he too wanted to be part of it – "back in my home region of Franconia, which is also a great place to live." He was told that he was to become a software developer in the Data Collection and Image Computation working group. "That appealed to me," says Wangler, "because image computation is an area where you can really bring software development and physics together." He took the job, despite the fact that they were ready to make him a departmental director in Munich. He then switched several times between software and hardware development at MR – and eventually became a departmental director as well, responsible for all software used at MR. This was still before *syngo* – but management was already looking for lower software development costs through synergies. "Quality up, costs down" was the motto.

The solution was to develop common middleware for computer and magnetic resonance tomographs – a sort of "software belly" – on the basis of the new, powerful SPARC processors. This cut development costs in half and also triggered a reappraisal that would bring the Groups even closer together. As a result, CT and MR began working together. At the same time, customers were demanding simpler operation for medical equipment. The researchers therefore decided to standardize the user interface for devices from both MR and CT to create a common look-and-feel. "There were, of course, drawn-out arguments because everyone felt that their customers' requirements were the really important ones," Wangler recalls. He and his colleagues then went a step further by developing a graphical user interface that included a mouse. Up until that time, hospital staff had to enter all parameters via keyboard and work through a long menu. In the future, they would be able to slide the cursor across the screen, as was already the case with the Apple Macintosh computers. "This was the big bang for medical technology when it was presented at the Radiological Society of North America's annual conference in Chicago in 1991," says Wangler. "And I think it's one of the reasons why Siemens Med is still considered an innovation driver in the industry today." The system's black-and-white graphics appear quite primitive by today's standards. For example, there was no "fold-out card" system with "interruptability." For its time, however, the software system known as Numaris 3 was tops in the industry.

Customers then started asking for more. For example, they wanted the standardized interface extended to other imaging equipment such as ultrasound units. Wangler got excited about this concept of merged, standardized software. Together with a few developers at MR and with the support of Corporate Technology's Design Lab, he began working on the idea in "a small conspiratorial group of people – many of whom are still good friends today." Thus was born the "fold-out card" system. The idea was that every device generated images, many of the devices required a 3D-imaging feature, and every system needed to manage patient data – so why not create standard functions – tools – for all systems? Such tools would further reduce development costs, since each division was developing its own separate tools at the time. Quality would go up and costs would go down – and Med management was therefore thrilled with the idea. Money was made available and the directors of the divisions all agreed to cooperate. A Common Human Interface Group was formed for the development of the joint functions. "That was the big breakthrough," Wangler recalls. "It's what started us on the path to *syngo*." A group of some 40 employees from various Groups was given the assignment to draw up the concept in Erlangen in 1994; today there are nearly 260 employees working on the system in Erlangen.

Windows on the Future

Wangler was one of the few people who correctly assessed the course that the development of the computer market would take with regard to PCs and imaging possibilities back in the early 1990s. It was clear to him that Microsoft PCs, which used the Windows operating system, had a bright future. Up until then, Unix – which was stable, refined and, above all, expensive – was the operating system of choice for professional programmers. Wangler realized that Windows would create a gigantic mass market and that prices would decrease substantially as a result. The new Windows NT launched back then was also much more reliable and stable than previous Windows systems. Wangler therefore launched what he refers to as a "religious campaign" against Unix. He was rebuffed by management at first, as Unix was the preferred system and served as the basis for all developments. But Wangler saw a glimmer of hope when two members of his staff were allowed to move ahead with his department's software using PCs – "for future scaled-down versions to be used in doctors' offices and in small office operations."

The big breakthrough came a good six months later, in the summer of 1995. It resulted from the fact that while Unix programmers had to work according to a strict regimen, the Windows experts were given a free hand. The creativity of their solutions convinced management, and Wangler began pushing harder for his approach. His argument here was that Windows NT was capable of running on a variety of processors. The decision was then taken to go with PCs – and Prof. Erich Reinhardt, a proponent of synergies who was a new member of the Group's Managing Board at the time and who now heads the Group, asked Wangler if he wanted to take over a development group. Wangler said yes. After that, his campaign really began to get serious, as he now had "to convince fervent supporters of Unix to work with Windows." He took his tightly knit team to Microsoft Deutschland and asked for the company's help. The people at Microsoft agreed and subsequently sent "real experts who could talk to our Unix specialists on their level." Wangler gradually persuaded the Unix experts – "above all, key people like our chief software architects" – to switch systems.

Still, not everyone was thrilled by the ongoing software merger. "There are always skeptics," says Wangler. Indeed, whenever major problems occurred people from various divisions would say things like: "The middleware is good, but I think we'll take care of the applications ourselves." Reinhard continued to protect Wangler and his staff from external pressures, however. "At the same time, he kept driving us forward – and I'm glad he did," says Wangler. That's because development was taking a long time, and the new *syngo* software was far from ready. Developers therefore had to report on their progress every couple of months by present-

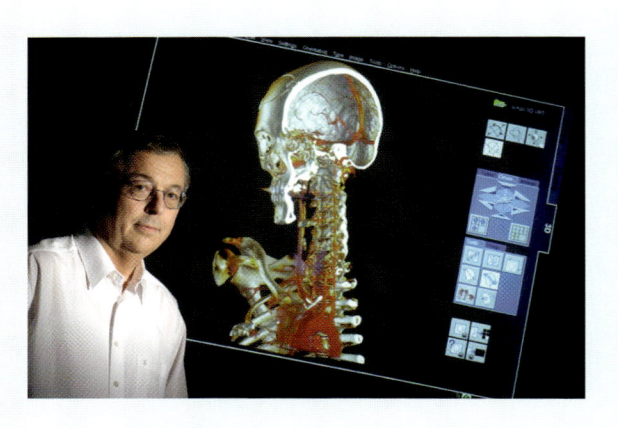

Universal software. *syngo* not only enables the most diverse devices to be operated via standardized menus, but can also be used to process patient data and images, write reports and switch functions with just a click of a mouse.

ing demonstration versions and testing their modules in simulations, all the while attempting to determine whether the software was fast enough and whether it did the things the customers wanted it to do.

Global Development – Vegetarian Solutions

A setback occurred in 1997, when part of the software was being developed in Bangalore, India, to fulfill the "costs down" requirement. Unfortunately, there was also huge personnel turnover in India, where talented people were being quickly lured away from their jobs. Suddenly, two-thirds of Wangler's developers were gone, and it became practically impossible to meet deadlines. Wangler went on the offensive by bringing his 45 Indian employees to Germany, where he set them up in Erlangen for half a year – and kept them there with generous bonuses for working abroad. To keep everyone happy, he also organized bus trips and weekend excursions, and because the Indians – most of whom were vegans – had difficulties with Franconian cuisine, Wangler made arrangements with an Indian restaurant nearby for daily meals. His efforts paid off. After six months, the developers had completely caught up with the schedule.

Wangler likes to get close to his employees so as to be able to understand what they need. These days, his staff includes many developers from Eastern Europe, the U.S. and India. Staff members in Erlangen keep in touch with suppliers from abroad, and an elaborate exchange and visiting program ensures close ties with colleagues in low-cost countries. "Direct contact is crucial and videoconferencing is no substitute for it," says Wangler. The people in Erlangen also have monthly "NICE Meetings" – one-and-a-half-hour conferences in which staff report on new developments from their division, introduce new colleagues and formulate questions to be posed to management. The divisions also regularly report on their experiences with *syngo*, which is "the most exciting part of the agenda," according to Wangler. Then there are the Team Pizza Meetings, which Wangler holds with individual development teams from Erlangen over a two-month period. The conferences take place several times a week during a pizza lunch at the respective development team's office. Wangler holds such events to promote transparency, especially when problems occur. "The first thing we do when there's a problem is to talk about it in detail in a totally open manner," he says. "Then we find the guilty party – not to punish them, but instead to determine the cause of the problem in order to solve it."

Two Birds, One Stone

Not everyone can discuss problems so openly. That's why Wangler has also set up an electronic "Grumble Box" in order to "gauge the mood and find out where the frustration is." "I push my people hard sometimes," says Wangler, looking strict for the first time. "When things heat up, I expect them to work hard – even on Saturday, and Sunday too, if necessary." It's at such times that Wangler questions the strict German rules governing working hours. "I'm definitely a workaholic," he admits.

Still, as the father of four children, Wangler also has insight into the feelings of others. He believes he gets along well with his employees, and the truth is that he does. Once, right before *syngo*'s market launch, the people in Bangalore began to fall behind again. This couldn't have come at a worse time, as this was the era of dot-com hype. New companies were sprouting up everywhere, and many Indian software developers were moving to the U.S. Wangler understood this and came up with the brilliant idea of getting a colleague from the U.S. to quickly open up a *syngo* development office in Iselin, New Jersey, thus killing two birds with one stone. His Indian employees were able to work in the U.S., and he was able to keep his important people. *syngo* was finally launched on the market in 1999, bringing a new look-and-feel (in color) to all the equipment. The new system also caused a big bang at the RSNA conference.

Med has learned to appreciate the value of *syngo*. The results of a conservative study show that standardized software for all devices has saved the company a net total of approximately €150 million in development

Lessons learned	Manfred Wangler's advice for innovators
• Those who wish to implement an idea must have solid arguments for it. • A protective hand makes it easier to ultimately push through ideas even in a difficult phase. • Problems must be precisely identified and discussed openly, as this is the only way to make effective changes. • Success requires a good team. • There will always be skeptics.	• Ensure transparency in cooperation. • Take your employees seriously. • Motivate your employees. • Demand commitment. • Work hard when necessary.

expenditures, and that reduction takes into account the costs of development for *syngo* itself. Nearly all *syngo* software packages are used in Siemens medical devices, although Med also supplies around ten percent of them to two OEM partners. Wangler started out with a small "conspiratorial" team, and up until the fall of 2006 he served as the director of Med's largest development team. He now heads the Software & Engineering department at Corporate Technology – Siemens' central research organization. When asked what he believes to be his most distinguishing trait, he replies: "My tenacity. It's pretty much impossible to stop me from pursuing an idea once I've started."

After John finishes his story, Walter says: "The factors for success here are like those with Thomas Schott: You need to recognize market trends and customer needs early on and put together a great team that displays passion and commitment." Matthias nods: "And don't forget – you must have a charismatic team leader who has the support of top management, goes on a mission to promote his beliefs, and knows how to get the best out of his people."

Bao Jun agrees: "It takes tremendous skill not only to keep your developers in Germany focused on the mission, but also to optimally integrate employees from other cultures. Wangler did an excellent job with that..."

Christian laughs and says: "That's great – weekend trips for Indian staff, a development office in the U.S. to hold on to the Indians in the company who wanted to go there, lunches with Indian food in Erlangen, and the Team Pizza Meetings. Speaking of food: I wouldn't mind getting something to eat. What do you say we go grab something from the buffet before the next story?"

After everyone has returned, Stacey begins talking: "The last two stories taught us about the important role software plays in innovation. I know someone who came up with an incredible simplification that helped to save millions of dollars by cleverly combining software and hardware. This story also started at an airport. It's about postal automation."

The Man Who Helped the U.S. Postal Service to Save Hundreds of Millions of Dollars

The little boy wasn't even five years old when he stood in the hall at Zürich Airport, watching a plane take off to America with his father on board. At that time, the boy, whose name was Gert Seidel, never would have dreamed that nearly four decades later, in the year 2000, his job would require him to begin flying regularly from the very same airport to the U.S. Seidel's life has in fact been marked by many twists and turns, some of which even seem a little puzzling.

Who, for example, would turn down an offer to study at an elite American university? Well, Gert Seidel did. That was before he quit a job working on computer systems for missile propulsion test stands to take a position in the postal automation industry – an area which certainly doesn't look like rocket science. Working with an international team, however, Seidel, 47, eventually established a billion-dollar business in that field.

In the end, he probably made more right decisions than wrong ones, which is why he seems so balanced and relaxed as he looks out from his office window over to Ameriquest Field, home of the Texas Rangers baseball team, where there's a small fireworks display on at the moment. Arlington, Texas, located near Dallas, is home not only to the Rangers but also to the U.S. headquarters of Siemens Postal Automation, the world market leader for postal automation systems. "You should have seen me five years ago," says Seidel, recalling the most intensive phase in the development of the Postal Automated Redirection

The secret of **Gert Seidel's** success is that he gets to know his customers' processes down to the last detail. In the case of the U.S. Postal Service (USPS), Seidel traveled from post office to post office. His journeys enabled him to find out how to optimize postal automation systems to prevent a tremendous amount of misdirected mail – in the U.S. alone, as much as five to six billion pieces were being sent to the wrong addresses every year.

System (PARS). "Back then I was running around like a madman from post office to post office, studying the processes used to forward misdirected mail." As things turned out, before long PARS would begin saving the United States Postal Service (USPS) €188 million per year.

Seidel's innovation came in response to a basic business problem: USPS, which holds a letter-carrying monopoly in America, was trying to cope with an increasing volume of misdirected mail. About 17 percent of the population in the U.S. moves to a new residence each year on average, contributing heavily to the five to six billion pieces of misdirected mail (mostly letters) that in many cases are eventually returned to the sender. Most of this misdirected mail first made the journey to the intended recipient's former address, often covering thousands of kilometers across several time zones, with stops at sorting hubs, regional mail centers, and local post offices. Ultimately, the mail had to be readdressed by hand and shipped – provided, of course, that USPS was able to come up with the right address. Thus would begin the second long journey.

"Arlington-based AEG ElectroCom was already supplying mail-sorting machines to the USPS back in the 1980s," Seidel explains. "At that time, I was working in Konstanz at a sister company, where I developed highly reliable computer systems for critical applications in the industrial automation, defense technology, and space systems sectors."

An Ingenious Idea – and a Patent Dispute

By the early 1990s, the ElectroCom people in Arlington had gained a solid understanding of the complex processes at USPS, many of which were subdivided and formalized. They noticed that there was tremendous potential to improve efficiency in the area of address-change forwarding especially. Americans get very touchy about any increase in the cost of sending a letter. That's why USPS – which employs around 700,000 people, making it one of the world's biggest companies – is always open to suggestions for streamlining its operations. With this in mind, ElectroCom made a proposal in the mid-1990s: Addresses, which were already being scanned by ElectroCom readers at the locations where they were sent from, would also be immediately compared with a database containing all mail forwarding requests in a system that would be continually updated. "An incorrectly addressed letter would then be picked up at the very beginning of the process rather than at the end," Seidel explains, "and could then be automatically sorted out and redirected before being sent out again."

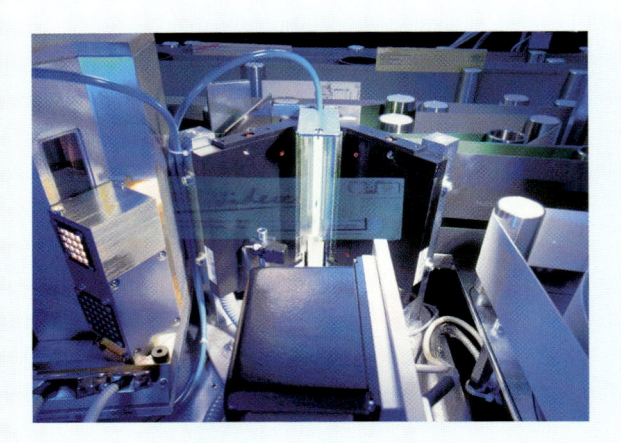

High-tech at the post office. High-performance scanners automatically read up to 60,000 addresses per hour from the letters they process. The PARS system can also search a database for forwarding addresses, and then print these on the letters – even as the mail continues to race through sorting machines.

Seidel's current colleagues in Texas had so much confidence in the new idea that they immediately applied for a patent. Unfortunately, this move marked the start of a prolonged patent dispute with USPS. The problem was that USPS also thought the idea was brilliant – so brilliant, in fact, that it decided it could have come from its own organization. USPS challenged the patent, which ultimately was awarded to ElectroCom anyway. The customer then became disgruntled, and work on the new automated forwarding system dragged on for several years. Siemens, in the meantime, had acquired ElectroCom in 1997, one year after Seidel had been named departmental director for Coding Systems at ElectroCom's Postal Automation unit.

Now a Siemens employee, Seidel accepted an assignment in 1998 to develop an alternative proposal to be submitted to USPS for technical implementation of the mail forwarding system, while at the same time continuing his work in Konstanz. "I was sent to Washington to present my ideas to the customer, together with another Siemens colleague from Arlington, who presented his," Seidel recalls. "The fact that USPS chose my proposal didn't make me a lot of friends in Texas at the time."

In 2000, the decision was made to put Seidel in charge of the project group in Texas, and from that point on he began commuting regularly to Dallas from Zürich, which has the closest international airport to Konstanz. He started out with just a handful of people who followed his lead, even though they were not officially his employees. "I was like a king without any subjects," Seidel says, "and not a very popular king at that. I was the 'German' who had walked in and taken control of the teams in Arlington as technical project manager. And they'd have much rather implemented the system their way."

Living the Post Office Life

Seidel asserted his authority and gained his new colleagues' respect by working hand-in-hand with the customer to become completely acquainted with the enormous systems and processes at USPS, which weren't always logical. To this end, he also visited post offices large and small, and sorting centers around the country. "After a while, I felt like I was living in a post office," he recalls. His colleagues were soon feeling the same way, as the launch of formal development (the patent dispute had since been forgotten) was followed by a period of late working hours for them as well.

Seidel's team was assigned the task of harmonizing all the equipment and software – from the fast-working address scanners, the labeling and sorting machines, and the software platform (for database comparisons of addresses in fractions of a second while letters continue to race through the machines), all the way to the gating out of the letters and their re-labeling with correct addresses. "Sometimes we would get back to the hotel at two in the morning after a 16-hour day, raid the refrigerator, and then try to figure out what we needed to do the next day to avoid getting kicked out by the customer – and putting the entire project in jeopardy, which would have been a very expensive setback," Seidel says. Like every other complex development project, PARS was also plagued by phases in which it seemed that nothing would function properly: Sometimes the software refused to work, while at other times the misdirected mail wasn't gated out correctly – which really got the sorters grumbling. Moreover, the team wasn't always prepared for the fatal consequences of operating errors made by the customer.

Today, the system is operating perfectly in more than 150 mail sorting and forwarding centers in the U.S., and it's also being implemented at additional locations. The revenues generated for Siemens by this mammoth project amount to roughly $1 billion, including the planned follow-up contracts. The savings for the customer are much greater than that, however: According to USPS estimates, at least five to six million working hours are saved annually, time that's now being used to better advantage by mail carriers and letter sorters. This translates into hundreds of millions of dollars in reduced costs.

Confidence in the Face of Adversity

Seidel learned a lot from this experience, especially during those phases in which it seemed the project might fail. "The most important thing I learned is to stay calm," he says. "You can always move forward, and there's always a solution, even when things look grim." Seidel certainly knows a thing or two about setbacks. As he was about to complete

Lessons learned	Gert Seidel's advice for innovators
• Projects designed to produce solutions for customers should give top priority to acquiring a good knowledge of the customer's business model and processes: Otherwise, the project will fail.	• Find out exactly what your customers want, even if they're initially somewhat vague about their needs. That's because, even if all contract details have been addressed, customers will be upset if they don't ultimately get what they had in mind originally, however vague. It's bad for winning follow-up contracts.
• It's alright to "get your hands dirty" to obtain the necessary knowledge – even if you're a top manager.	
• With regard to such projects: A close relationship with the customer's top-level management team must be established from the very beginning. Maintaining contact only at the working level poses a greater risk that problems – which can turn up any time – will become critical situations and threaten the business.	• Major projects are often difficult to manage. This is why it's important to break down complexity by defining and managing small work packages (Earned Value Method), enabling the project management and controlling teams to gain a comprehensive overview. This is also what makes an effective early warning system possible.
• People given management tasks who try to assert themselves solely on the basis of their position will fail. You earn the respect of your team and the customer through your individual performance – your knowledge and your ability to communicate, across cultures as well.	• Balance your life: Becoming ill or burned out from too much work means you're no help to the project or your company.
	• Never give up: Even if things look grim, life goes on. This attitude was a key to the success of the PARS project.
• If you believe in the solution you're offering, it pays to invest at the beginning of a project: Our initial investment in PARS was about $17.5 million, roughly the equivalent of our annual earnings at that time.	• Be honest with the customer. Don't make things up, and don't try to come up with a thousand excuses when something goes wrong; this will damage your credibility and destroy the trust between you and your customer.

his degree in Industrial Engineering in Karlsruhe, his sister suffered an accident. So instead of taking advantage of an attractive opportunity to go on and obtain a Master's Degree in the U.S., he decided to stay near his parents in Konstanz.

Who knows? Had he fulfilled his dream of going to the U.S. at the age of 23 and studying at an elite university, Seidel might today be conducting research somewhere off the beaten path, rather than building up a billion-dollar business with about 150 employees – a business he developed himself. Much of the PARS technology can also be used in other countries. After all, it's not just USPS that benefits when fewer letters and packages are flown or driven to the wrong destinations; logistics companies worldwide can also profit from such a system.

Seidel once again looks out his window at the fireworks, which are shot into the sky before Rangers games. "I always wanted to do something special, really over the top," he says. "When I was a kid, I wanted to climb the highest mountain." So what type of challenge would excite him today? "If you ask me seriously, I'd say I'd either like to fix the run-down power grid in the U.S. or manage a manned mission to Mars," he replies, evidently considering both assignments to be similar in scope and complexity to providing support for the USPS project. These days, Seidel feels almost more American than German, and his wife is also from the U.S. "I probably speak English better than German now," he says.

Still, he enjoys visiting his hometown of Konstanz – not just for business, but also to see his parents. And whenever he's preparing for his next trip to Texas, his mother packs him a German lunch – sometimes airline food just isn't the same as home cooking. Then it's the parents' turn to watch their son fly off to America.

> *"That innovator really took his customer contacts the whole way," says Matthias. "I mean, he got so involved in the postal service's processes and systems that he felt like he was living in a post office!"*
>
> *"Okay, but his extreme focus on the needs of the customer is definitely what made him successful," John says. "Especially when you consider how difficult the situation was when he started out: He had that patent dispute with the customer, a team of employees who initially rejected him, and a completely new environment to deal with. In a situation like that, you really need to be extremely persistent and be able to win people over with your abilities."*
>
> *"On top of that, the whole thing was a financial risk – the initial investment equaled their annual earnings at the time," Christian adds. "That was really a big hairy audacious goal," John says. "What's that?" asks Christian. John explains: "That's a term I got from a book called Built to Last, by James*

Collins and Jerry Porras, two economists from California. Their approach was similar to what Arie de Geus did in his famous book, The Living Company – they tried to find out how companies manage to survive over many decades, or even centuries. For example, like a living organism, a company has to develop its own identity, which takes the form of a stable but flexible company culture. It also needs to have visionary goals that keep it moving forward. That's exactly what happened with the first passenger jet – the Boeing 707 – which was built in 1952, or during the design of the IBM 360 computer in the early 1960s. Failure of these projects would have put the company's continued existence at risk. These types of 'big hairy audacious goals' can also be found at smaller organizational units, of course – and their achievement not only leads to business success; it also gives the team a huge amount of confidence. So that's why I mentioned it."

"Wow, that's an interesting aspect," says Christian. "Up until now, I've only known of the concept of the innovator as the 'creative destroyer' described by Joseph Schumpeter. Risk also plays an important role in that concept." "I don't like the idea of a destroyer at the moment," says Walter. "After all, we're stuck here at the airport because of a terror warning, so I'm not particularly enthused about solutions that involve destroying things."

"OK, so we were talking about major corporations versus small start-ups," says John. "Start-up entrepreneurs have got it relatively easy because they can set up a company on the basis of their innovation, and they don't have to show any consideration for existing structures. But when you've got a major established company that employs a lot of people, you're going to have a dilemma if you're thinking of starting a new business to replace an old one. But you've got to deal with this dilemma if you don't want to endanger your future. Innovation can not only take you from an idea to a billion-dollar market; you can also lose that billion-dollar market if you take too long to implement the idea. And I can tell you about an innovator who experienced both."

Ups and Downs in the Communication Age

Rudolf Bitzinger had two dreams when he was a teenager. Having played on Austria's National Youth Soccer Team, he dreamed of becoming a soccer star. But he was fascinated by math, so he also dreamed of becoming a scientist. Finally, at the age of 18, he reached a decision and began a course of study in mathematics. Now 57, Bitzinger has never regretted his decision.

"I can clearly remember having those two dreams," he says, seeming to gaze back into the past. In an instant, though, he's focused again on the present. It's hot – more than 30 degrees Celsius – but Bitzinger doesn't want anything to drink. It's also close to lunch time, but he doesn't want anything to eat, either. The phone rings, but Bitzinger doesn't get nervous about the time it's taking for the interview. He simply stays focused. And he likes to talk, speaking with a strong Vienna accent. A true Austrian, Bitzinger's conversational style is always relaxed and pleasant, even when he uses technical terms or the occasional English word.

For 32 years, **Rudolf Bitzinger** has been developing innovative communication ideas at Siemens, and doing what it takes to implement them. Persistent and strong-willed, he always has an eye on the business – and the utility of his ideas for customers.

While attending university, Bitzinger minored in "programming and systems theory," which is known today as computer science. That's how he ended up in the field of information technology – and at Siemens. Today, he is Chief Technology Officer at Siemens Enterprise Communications GmbH & Co. KG in Munich, where he is responsible for product strategy and the technology program, as well as for partnerships, investment and patent management. Bitzinger has been implementing innovative ideas at Siemens for 32 years now, and the many innovations that he's pushed through were all designed to enable electronic communication, while making such communication and telephone calls more convenient and less expensive.

Telecommunications Transformation

In the early 1980s, Bitzinger invented a central control computer, known as CP113, for use with Siemens' very first digital telephone switching system, EWSD. "That was my first big assignment," he recalls. Then, in the late 1980s, Bitzinger was the chief designer for the ISDN switching system Hicom. It's systems like Hicom that have made it possible for people to talk on the phone and surf the Web simultaneously. This is taken for granted today, but back then it was a real innovative breakthrough. CP113/EWSD and Hicom ultimately generated billions in sales for Siemens.

HiPath, the successor to Hicom, features Internet technology as a supplement to ISDN. "The HiPath Internet solution transmits voice communications via data lines," Bitzinger explains. In other words, data and voice services are integrated, which means that both can be provided simultaneously via the Internet using the Voice-over-Internet Protocol (VoIP). Bitzinger implemented this innovation in the mid-1990s while serving as vice president for Software Development at Siemens Rolm Communications in Silicon Valley.

Another offshoot of Hicom is HiPath OpenScape, which cleverly manages all communication channels on a given platform, including e-mail, instant messaging, mobile telephony, VoIP, and audio, video and web-conferencing. OpenScape can, for example, show callers in Germany whether or not a colleague in the U.S. is available to talk on the phone. If the person is not available, the system automatically connects with a phone where the colleague can be reached, by dialing their cell phone or a landline number at a hotel, for example. OpenScape also supports audio-conferencing and "collaboration sessions" for working on documents together.

When asked how he stays innovative after 32 years, Bitzinger pauses and then replies: "Some people see a train coming when it's ten kilometers away, while others don't see it until it's a hundred meters in front of them and about to run them over. I see things early on – I guess you could say it's like a special gift." He then laughs and says that he sometimes has good ideas "in the shower and while dreaming."

Pragmatic Solutions

Whether it's a gift, intuition, or inspiration, Bitzinger has always taken a very pragmatic approach to all of his innovations. His solutions aren't developed aimlessly; they're firmly based on the needs of customers. The HiPath 8000 is a good example: In 2002, IBM informed the Siemens Managing Board that it was no longer interested in investing in Hicom technology, which jeopardized a business relationship worth $70 million per year. Naturally, Siemens management got very nervous, and there was a lot of pressure to get IBM back. Bitzinger flew to IBM headquarters in New York and spoke with the company's executives. "I wanted to understand the customer and hear their expectations in terms of a communication system for the future," Bitzinger recalls.

The IBM people told him they wanted all their communication systems to run on a data network using open, manufacturer-independent standards – and they wanted this at a reasonable price. They also wanted all services to be managed by a small number of central computer centers. After speaking with other companies, such as the telecommunications giant AT&T and the Ford Motor Company, Bitzinger discovered that "the requirements of these companies varied but there was a certain pattern of similarities." He then went to work with a 12-member team, and together they figured out in a little less than six months how to meet all the requirements. Their solution was the HiPath 8000, which provides integrated data and voice services via data networks. As a result, instead of expensive and high-maintenance hardware, customers only needed to acquire software. As it turned out, IBM was the first customer for the new technology.

The HiPath 8000 story is typical of Bitzinger's approach to all of his innovations. "You can only implement an idea if it's going to make money – in other words, if a customer or, better yet, several customers, are interested in it," he says. Good products also generally require a high level of development expenditure. However, as Bitzinger points out, it will take longer to achieve a return on your investment if you decide to use a completely new technology. Still, any company that wants to be a leader in technology must be prepared to take that risk.

According to Bitzinger, implementing innovations in Germany is no longer as easy as it used to be. That's because cost pressures are greater now, and managers sometimes focus too much on the short term, which keeps them from making courageous decisions. Moreover, "the basic inventions in the communication sector are already in place. These days, the important thing is to create something new by combining various areas. In this sense, it's much more difficult today to explain a new technology's value to a customer." A fundamental problem here is that new ideas are always met with skepticism in the beginning. "Roughly 90 percent of the people involved will definitely have misgivings," says Bitzinger. That's why he's convinced it's so important to believe in your idea and stand behind it one hundred percent, because if you believe in it, you'll get others to believe in it too.

The Innovator's Dilemma

One of the most widely read books on innovation is *The Innovator's Dilemma* by Harvard professor Clayton M. Christensen, which describes how new technologies can ruin large, established companies. The pattern here is simple: A company is making a lot of money with established products and is therefore unable to recognize that new technologies can help create less expensive solutions. As soon as the new technology attains the level of quality demanded by the market, the established business begins to decline rapidly. Bitzinger experienced this himself: Back in the 1990s, Siemens' Communications Group was making a lot of money selling telephone systems. Bitzinger was working in Silicon Valley at the time, and it was there that he began to realize that telephony would, in the future, increasingly be carried via data networks rather than telephone networks. While this was not necessarily the best idea in a technical sense, it was clearly the cheapest solution from the customers' point of view.

The sector's managing board didn't recognize the potential of the new technology, however, and the mistakes that were subsequently made could fill a chapter of *The Innovator's Dilemma*. Group management failed to invest courageously enough in the future, choosing instead to freeze the development budget for Internet-based voice communication solutions. It relied here completely on the assessments of internal top managers, who admittedly had been very successful up until that point. Basically, no one could imagine that this decades-long success would not continue. Moreover, the new technology didn't seem very attractive; it was inferior to conventional solutions in terms of audio quality and usability features, for example. It also would have generated much lower profits for Siemens. As a result, the technology for making telephone calls via data networks was dismissed as a kind of toy, which is why Siemens rejected an offer from the U.S. company Cisco Systems at the end of the 1990s to establish a joint venture for the development of VoIP systems. Today, Cisco is the market leader in communication via data networks and is currently worth more than the entire Siemens corporation on the stock market. This misreading of the situation led to the loss of many jobs and also sparked several restructuring measures.

Good Communication with Managers and Customers

"We learned our lesson," says Bitzinger – and things are certainly different today in the Group. For example, managers regularly hold discussions on ideas for innovations with managing board members, and there are also interdisciplinary teams that report directly to the managing board. Innovation projects are no longer talked to death; instead, they are launched in various regions with important customers who are in tune with the times. Executives today view cooperation in new technologies with other companies and suppliers as an opportunity.

Lessons learned	Rudolf Bitzinger's advice for innovators
• There will always be skeptics, so it's important to clearly define an innovation's value for the customer. Otherwise, you won't have a chance to implement your idea. • Never give away your idea completely; instead, remain involved in the associated project and ensure you have a say in the direction it moves in. That's because you, as the originator of the idea, will motivate the project team. • Acceptance of top management is a must for securing adequate financing and support in difficult times. • Use everyday language to make your idea accessible to everyone – from managing board members to commercial staff and marketing specialists. This can mean being somewhat vague on technical details – and although technology specialists have problems with this, they should remember that an idea that's not understood will not be supported. • A company can never afford to rest on its laurels; it must always be innovative. This can be achieved if executive management is open to innovation. Innovation projects shouldn't be talked to death at headquarters; they should be launched in various regions with important customers who are in tune with the times. Cooperation in new technologies with other companies and suppliers should be seen as an opportunity.	• In the end, innovations can't be planned. On the contrary, they often arise from chaos. That's why people need freedom in order to be innovative. You can't just integrate someone into a process and say: OK, now be innovative. Ideas aren't generated by pushing a button; they are formed through inspiration – like music. • Innovators have to stay curious, look beyond their immediate horizons and learn about areas other than their own specialist field. • You have to be convinced of the value of your idea – otherwise, you won't be able to persuade others. You have to fight for your ideas in the face of skeptics. • It's great to have an idea, but you also need to have a feeling as to whether or not it will sell itself well. Everyone must be aware of the value the idea represents, and the return on investment shouldn't lie too far in the future. • That's why it's best to have one or more customers already lined up – and then incorporate them into the development project from the start. This makes a good impression with executive management. The higher the development costs, the more customers you should have lined up.

"We examined our mistakes, and this has put us in an excellent position for future success," says Bitzinger, who never lost his courage. His work is his hobby, and stress and frustration are not part of his vocabulary – at least when it comes to research and development. "I did feel stress, however, when I was forced to let some people go," he says. "It's also stressful when you have a boss who's not open to new ideas. But I've never felt stressed by my daily work of developing and implementing ideas, even though I work more than 40 hours a week." Bitzinger firmly believes in "going the extra mile."

The most important thing is that his wife, son and daughter understand the nature of his work and its effect on him. For example, he often thinks about work when he's home, which makes it seem as if he's absent, in a sense. His family has gotten used to him focusing on an idea and "disappearing" for a while. The inquiring scientific spirit runs in the family, however: Bitzinger's son has followed in his father's footsteps, establishing a company for VoIP, ethernet solutions and network applications at the tender age of 20. "I talk to my son a lot, like I talk to many experts from different areas," says Bitzinger. "These conversations are very important for combining ideas."

Bitzinger's enthusiasm for his work doesn't wane, even after a nearly three-hour interview. He is an inexhaustible source of anecdotes and recollections – just as he is a source of innovative ideas in his daily work.

"That's really an innovator's dilemma par excellence, don't you think?" says Matthias. "People in established companies are wary of the risks of creative destruction, so they tend to wait too long when faced with disruptive innovations. All that's left then is to watch the competition cash in. The situation is even more difficult in a field like Bitzinger's, where innovation cycles are very short. With just a few wrong decisions by top management, you can lose an entire market in the blink of an eye. But ultimately there's no alternative to creative destruction, right?"

"Yes, that's definitely true," says John. "That's why personnel development measures should also focus strongly on innovators, especially in business sectors as strongly impacted by innovation as ours. That's because a successful innovator who's promoted to management is more likely in a situation of change to take a chance on the future, rather than simply continuing to ride out the success of the past, leaving others to play the role of trendsetter. I realized that recently when I spoke with Franz-Josef Bierbrauer, who's still a passionate innovator despite the fact that he's responsible for an established business that generates billions in sales. Bierbrauer's innovation involves a subject that we haven't dealt with yet – light."

The Triumph of the Halogen Lamp

A pair of boxing gloves lies on a cabinet in Franz-Josef Bierbrauer's functional office in Munich. Is he a fan of the German heavyweight legend Max Schmeling? "No, not really. A colleague gave them to me to mark my 25th anniversary at the company," says Bierbrauer, head of General Lighting at Osram. It's also pretty much 25 years to the day that Bierbrauer, a 30-year-old product manager at the time, attended a trade fair in Münster, Germany, for disco equipment and special lighting. Unimpressed, his boss back then suggested that he make more effective use of his small travel budget. However, at this show – at the stand of rival General Electric (GE), of all places – Bierbrauer, then a product manager for halogen lamps, had a bright idea. The product he was scrutinizing was a large, heavy spotlight that didn't last very long and didn't produce much light. "I can do that better with a halogen lamp," he thought. "A halogen lamp gives you much more light at much greater brilliancy, it has a longer life, it's much smaller in size and, above all, it weighs much less."

It was a bright idea with big consequences. Bierbrauer went on to invent – and patent – a lightweight super spotlight lamp with a light-emission angle of just three degrees. "The great thing about this lamp is that you can illuminate a single picture from a distance of around five meters without anyone being able to see where the light is coming from," he says. Bierbrauer's second innovation was the cold-light lamp. Here, together with several Osram developers he spent months designing a glass reflector with a special high-grade coating. This lamp is special because the heat generated is dissipated at the rear rather than being directed at the illuminated object itself. At the same time, the lamp shines in iridescent colors, can

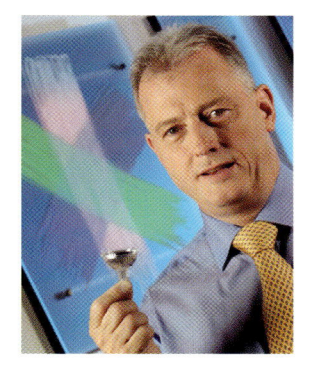

Driven by a characteristic mixture of enthusiasm and tenacity, electrical engineer **Franz-Josef Bierbrauer** took the halogen lamp out of the car and into the home exactly 25 years ago. He first persuaded lamp and socket manufacturers – and then the engineers and managers at Osram. With halogen lamps now available in numerous variations, Bierbrauer laid the foundations of what is today Osram's most profitable line of business.

be used to illuminate rooms evenly and has an exceptionally long life. As early as 1981, Bierbrauer was already predicting a mass market for the halogen lamp, which till then had only been used by Osram as H4 lamps for car headlights or in slide and narrow-gauge film projectors. He asked himself a simple question: "Why not exploit the benefits of being able to generate lots of bright light with a small-sized lamp for other areas of everyday life – for example, homes, salesrooms and store windows?" Bierbrauer had found himself a job.

New Engine of Growth

At Osram's company offices on Munich's Hellabrunner Strasse, the development and sales departments couldn't work up much enthusiasm for Bierbrauer's idea. "Way too expensive, way too complicated to manufacture, nobody'll buy it and we've already got so many other products," were the standard responses. Despite this resistance and the internal inertia, none of his immediate superiors actively prevented him from simply pushing ahead with his plan. "Product marketing played an important role at Osram even then, and it was our job to try and push new things," Bierbrauer recalls. What's more, there was encouraging feedback from his medium-sized business customers. Lighting manufacturers such as Erco, Zumtobel Staff, Hoffmeister and Artemide were all perfectly aware of the superb lighting properties of halogen lamps. "For my customers, being provided with a new light source was like having a new engine of growth," says Bierbrauer. He convinced them of the benefits for their own business: "I told them that they were basically investing in a new tool that would produce new designs. In other words, they could be generating extra sales within a year."

In the event, things took a little longer than that. Bierbrauer wrote his first business plan, which forecast annual sales of 50,000 units by year five – modest by today's standards, but at that time a bold claim. "You can never tell what the future holds," he says in retrospect. "But I just had to have that lamp on the market and I would have arranged the figures any way I had to in order to make it look viable. There was little or no hard analytical evidence there." In fact, Bierbrauer relied almost entirely on what he had seen and heard at many trade shows and what customers were telling him. He also doggedly stuck by his growth forecast during a site meeting at the Osram plant in Eichstätt. At the time, the employees were making similar products for the photographic optics business. They were also working short hours. "My idea for a new product made a huge impression," he recalls.

Long Hours and Big Rewards

Until then, the young product manager had nothing concrete to offer beyond his industry, perseverance and a good education. Industry was something he had learned while growing up in Saarland, where he had seen his father work long hours at the family construction firm. "It was tough when Dad didn't get home till late on Christmas Eve," he recalls. On the other hand, "I've always respected anyone who works long hours, on account of my father." After finishing high school, Bierbrauer studied electrical engineering at the Technical University of Karlsruhe and subsequently became a teaching assistant at the Army College in Munich, where he also studied business administration at the Technical University. The latter course of study did much to strengthen the young engineer's confidence. "If my business plan with the halogen lamp hadn't come off, I'd have just tried something else," he says. "After all, life itself is one big risk!"

But sometimes you need patience as well, as Bierbrauer was to learn when the testing of his cold-light lamp in the Osram basement lab made only slow progress. "All in all, we had to vapor-deposit 21 different layers on the glass reflector," he recalls. That took months, and there were repeated setbacks because "we also had to do a lot of the basic research ourselves." How do you cope when you have to wait a whole year before the first prototype is ready? And another one until the first lamps can be delivered to the customer – not to mention the many years before management and the production department are finally convinced by the sales figures?

"I don't know how I got through it either!" laughs Bierbrauer. Today, as head of General Lighting at Osram, he is responsible for a business that generates annual sales of €1.4 billion. "You definitely need the occasional success, just to keep you going." However, the development engineers were also proud to be the only people in the world working on this type of lamp. Altogether, some 20 man-years went into Bierbrauer's inventions, the super spotlight and the cold-light lamp. "We invested a couple of hundred million euros over the years," he says, although relatively little of that amount went into the actual development. The fully automated production lines at Osram's Eichstätt plant ate up a lot more, with one line alone costing €20 million.

Osram's halogen business now posts annual sales of around €300 million and is highly profitable. Some 1.2 billion halogen lamps are sold every year worldwide, and sales are still growing at an annual rate of seven percent. Osram is the world market leader in this segment. "We can be very pleased with the way business has developed," says Bierbrauer with

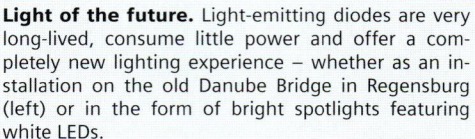

Light of the future. Light-emitting diodes are very long-lived, consume little power and offer a completely new lighting experience – whether as an installation on the old Danube Bridge in Regensburg (left) or in the form of bright spotlights featuring white LEDs.

more than a little understatement. But Bierbrauer is happy about more than just the commercial success. He still gets a big kick out of seeing how his halogen lamp has changed the face of shopping malls and office complexes around the world. "It always gives me great pleasure to see our lamps when I'm away on a business trip."

And there's another reason for his enthusiasm. "Light is hugely important to our well-being," says Bierbrauer, who knows his way around the topics of light therapy and lighting design. "Light greatly influences our moods; that's something I find fascinating." He's also proud of the fact that he has been able to shape an entire market since the 1980s. "Our developments have had an enormous impact on the sector." For example, they provide "work for three-quarters of the 500 employees in Eichstätt," as well as 500 of the 2,500 jobs in China. The entire supplier chain for the reflectors and sockets also benefits, as do the lamp manufacturers and, by extension, electricians, planners and architects.

Educating the Customer

With all its product variants, it took around 15 years for this market to become fully established, from the original idea to the finished articles. Bierbrauer soon realized that there was more to this process than just coming up with an innovative product. It was also crucial to educate consumers, "who dictate the pace of an innovation," the lamp manufacturers and the rest of the players in the market. "I set up Osram Light Consulting in 1985 because there was so little know-how around and lots of our customers initially had technical problems designing halogen lamps," he says. This subsidiary provided workshops for electricians, planners and architects, teaching them the finer points of low-volt electrics and halogen lamps. In this way, it was possible to prepare the market for the new technology. In the early days, Bierbrauer also had the occasional disagreeable meeting with a dissatisfied customer. "In the early 1980s, a bank that had installed 50,000 halogen lamps complained that far too many of them were failing," Bierbrauer says. Given that the lamps weren't all burning out at the same time, it looked very much as if the technology as a whole hadn't been perfected. However, together with the lighting designer who had worked on the building, Bierbrauer was able to convince the customer that Osram had already invested heavily in halogen technology and would continue to do so in order to further improve the longevity of the lamps.

Bierbrauer, who travels a lot for his job, could have rested on his laurels a long time ago, but that's not his style. As a speaker, the charismatic manager is in big demand at a variety of events. In fact, his presentations are legendary. At the Executive Circle Innovation, a Siemens top management seminar, Bierbrauer's audience expressed admiration for his "courage to invest in groundbreaking innovations at a time when the company is still the market leader in the forerunner product," rather than taking things easy and letting others assume the role of trendsetter. "That's the kind of attitude we need in our organization as well," said one participant. As if to confirm this, Bierbrauer proudly shows off his latest pride and joy, which stands on the cabinet in his office: "You won't find an LED lamp as bright as this one on the market yet." The body of the lamp also acts as a cooling unit, while the power supply is based on a solution from the automotive industry. The Osram development team has dedicated the first prototype to Bierbrauer in gratitude for his energetic and very early support during the innovation process.

Beating the Bunker Mentality – and Conquering New Markets

For the past three years, Bierbrauer has been supporting the cause of light-emitting diodes with the same tenacity and enthusiasm he once displayed in promoting the halogen lamp – or later on when, as Managing Director of Osram Korea, he bought a building for the German school and appointed teachers, so that the class containing his two sons could get a good education. "It might be a semiconductor technology, but it's still light and therefore falls under the category of general lighting,"

Lessons learned	Franz-Josef Bierbrauer's advice for innovators
• Trust your gut feelings – these are the result of many conversations conducted with people in the sector and impressions gathered at trade shows. • Merely inventing and developing a new product is often not enough. You have to educate the other market players and let them acclimatize. • A market needs time to mature. An obsession with short-term results is fatal for innovation. • A management style that grants free rein is healthy for innovation. • Competitors often provide the best stimulus for innovation.	• If you believe in an idea, pursue it regardless of the consequences for your career within the company. Creative destruction is what drives the economy – it's therefore better to push ahead with innovations yourself than wait for your competitors to do so. • Hard work, perseverance and enthusiasm are essential when it comes to convincing development engineers, management, sales staff and customers about the benefits of an idea. • Customers are often allies and the real driving force behind innovation. • Small successes in development or sales help you make it through a long hard haul. • When venturing forecasts with regard to your own innovations, be sure to maintain credibility with colleagues, management and customers.

he emphasizes. He's fully aware of what this might mean in the future. Thanks to their high efficiency, their compactness – which creates new scope for lighting designers – and their longevity, LEDs could well end up replacing conventional light sources in a host of applications. Bierbrauer isn't the sort of person to shrink back from what is one of the most difficult of management tasks: replacing existing products while they are still earning a lot of money with better ones that might not turn out to be a financial success. Taking such a step requires courage, but Bierbrauer's motto has always been "It's better to shape the market yourself than to wait for your competitors to do it." He therefore wheedled part of the activities away from a colleague and is now busy turning them into a new lighting segment at Osram. And he didn't even have to put on his boxing gloves. He also has other weapons: enthusiasm, conviction and perseverance.

"Did I understand that right? Franz-Josef Bierbrauer is head of the general lighting business, which must therefore also include classic light bulbs?" Christian asks. "That's right," says John. "And instead of fighting the LED, which of course represents a challenge to traditional light sources, he makes it part of his portfolio in order to develop the technology and push it in the market?" "Exactly. Managing a successful business and at the same time pushing innovations that could well end up replacing that business – that's what I call real leadership."

"Leadership by innovation," says Stacey with a smile. "By the way, do you guys remember our conversation about some customers not being ready for a new product? Franz-Josef Bierbrauer even found an answer to this problem. Following the launch of the low-volt halogen lamp, he simply set up a company to teach electricians and architects how to use the new technology. In other words, he not only put a new product on the shelves but also created the market and a substantial portion of the demand for his innovation."

"That sums it up perfectly." John gets to his feet. "Look, everyone, flights have been resumed. That's what I call perfect timing!" "Well, I must say this unplanned stopover has certainly been very worthwhile," says Christian. "My thanks to everybody. I've learned a lot about what it takes to turn a good idea into a billion-dollar sales success. And I can already see several ways how we might move ahead with a project in my field that is currently on ice because it could supposedly endanger our existing business ..."

Space for your own thoughts

Often, it's the seemingly simple ideas that can revolutionize a whole sector. Take a step back from your everyday business and think for a moment. Are there any simplifications that might change your sector?

Are there developments in your field that don't get the necessary attention because they might endanger an existing business?

Can you identify any solutions for taking these innovations forward nevertheless?

A Final Picture

What Mad Meg and Prometheus Have to Do With Innovation

e-mail from: Matthias
To: Christian, Stacey, John, Walter, Bao Jun
Re: Keeping in the picture

Dear colleagues,
Christian is setting up a new business unit in India and Stacey has a new job in an external start-up in Canada. So I thought it would be good if we brought our discussion on innovation to a close with a final picture. John and I would like to show you a couple of artworks – food for thought, as it were – that encapsulate a lot of the things we talked about in our stories. Let's meet up in Munich's new Gemäldegalerie on Friday, March 2 at 12:00 noon. It would be nice if you could all make it down to Munich on that day.
Regards,
Matthias

A Manager's Most Important Task

Handshakes all round at the main entrance to Munich's new Gemäldegalerie. "If it wasn't for my remark about Werner von Siemens, I'm not sure that I'd be here at all. That's basically what kicked off this whole discussion," says Walter with visible skepticism. "What on earth has innovation got to do with painting?" "Just you wait, Walter!" replies John with a smile. "We're not going to be talking about aesthetics but about what you need to be a good manager." "And what might that be?" "It's the common thread of all our stories: the question of how to create the right culture of innovation as the basis of successful growth."

"The way I see it, the thing that unites all of our innovators is their ability to identify new market trends at a very early stage, to involve customers in the innovation process and to motivate their own teams," says Christian. "Yes, those are all certainly important aspects, but let's just take a look at the first picture I want to show you," says Matthias, leading the group into the next room.

He stops in front of a large, powerful canvas full of detail: "This painting, known as 'Dulle Griet,' is one of the most important works of Pieter Bruegel the Elder. It dates from around 1562 and depicts the outskirts of a city on a river. There's a bridge across the river over there. On this side of it a woman, Dulle Griet, is striding resolutely toward the top of a small hill." "Look at the guy on the house in the middle raking coins out of his backside, and all the people underneath brawling over the money. I bet that's supposed to be a merchant," says Christian with a grin.

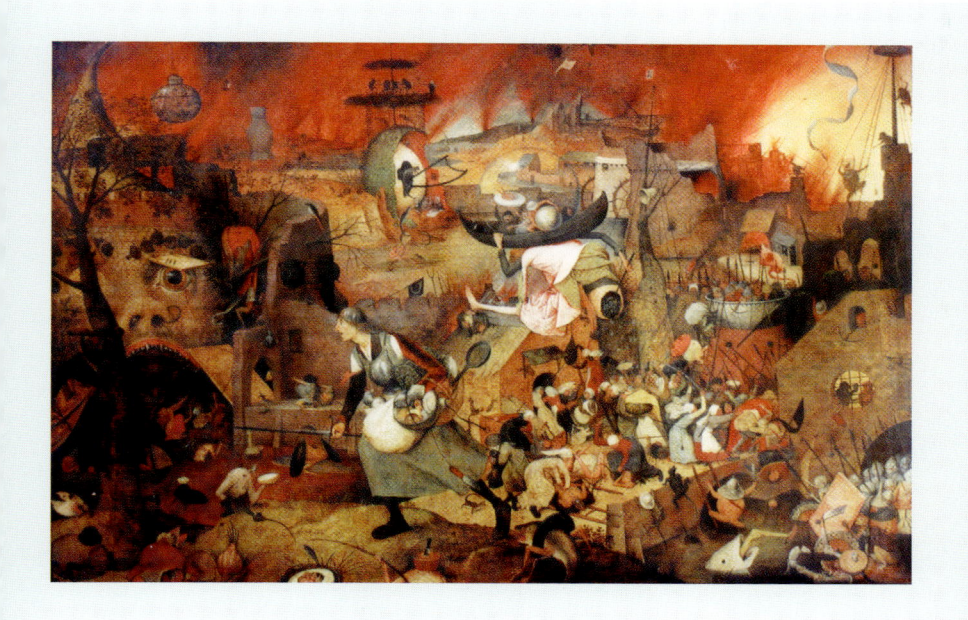

Matthias laughs. "You could be right there, Christian. Bruegel's pictures are full of allegory. At the time, trade was flourishing in the Low Countries. The result was a prolonged rise in prices, which in turn meant that increasingly large numbers of the poor were barely able to afford even the basic essentials. The stark gap between extreme wealth and extreme poverty sparked off unrest, and there were revolts sparked by the high price of bread, coupled with attacks on warehouses. There was general anxiety about change, with many people fearing for their livelihood."

Driving Forward in the Face of Change

"That all sounds very familiar," Stacey interjects. "It's just like today's discussion on globalization!" "That's right – this picture conveys exactly the same mood of doom and gloom that we now see in some of the chat shows and newspapers. On the other hand, such an attitude is to some extent understandable. After all, in times of upheaval, entrenched property is threatened. Even today, you still get riots when whole groups within a society feel they're becoming losers with no future. Just look at the recent unrest in the Paris suburbs. Back in Bruegel's time, there were also revolts in the Low Countries. Some people say that this picture shows the futility and madness of war. However, in my opinion, what's burning here is the old order, which is passing away. Look at Dulle Griet. She's staying well away from the trouble and striding purposefully toward new ground. She's the only person on this side of the river. For me, she's like someone leading an innovation project or an entrepreneur moving into unknown commercial territory."

"Matthias!" says Stacey. "Look at all the stuff she's got with her: a frying pan, a sword, a kitchen knife, a helmet. What's all that about?" "Yes, that's fascinating. According to my interpretation, those would all be management tools required to deal with the unknown. Some of the things she's got with her have already proven their worth, such as the armor, but others look a bit strange in this new environment. But what's so strange about that? At the launch of any innovation project, you often don't know much about the market you aim to conquer or the technologies you'll need to do so. You may well already have reliable management tools at hand, but a lot still has to be invented or adapted to deal with the changed circumstances. You can't plan everything in advance."

"OK, let's take this a little bit further," says Christian. "All the strange creatures dancing on the hill – they look like they've been painted by Hieronymus Bosch – could symbolize unknown territory. And Griet needs all these unconventional tools to deal with them." "Just think back to the story we heard about Manfred Wangler's programmers and Indian food, or the weekend in a castle organized by Robert Krieg, or Jun Kong's intercultural challenges. When you're exploring unknown terrain, you need to be brave as well as open to unconventional methods and ideas."

"Dulle Griet certainly looks as though she's on a difficult mission," observes Christian. "And she doesn't look particularly happy, either – a bit crazy, if anything. Hence the work's nickname – Mad Meg."

The Best Ideas Need Plenty of Support

"That's certainly possible," Matthias replies. "But it's no different for innovators. Just imagine, Christian, you're a project manager looking at a progress report before the big breakthrough, or you're on the supervisory board of a start-up looking at how the money is being practically burned up… Lots of managers in that situation would think it crazy to carry on investing in a new company or to endanger an existing business by supporting an innovation that might never make it. And despite all their courage and methodical approach, lots of innovators sometimes have genuine doubts about whether their project is going to succeed. That's exactly when they need management's support. If we, as management, burden Dulle Griet, our innovator, with all our misgivings, she'll collapse under the weight. It's better to go along with her, give innovators plenty of elbow room, and maybe even to think ahead a little and see where we might be able to help – for example, during the final stage, the market launch, where the talents of management are mostly in demand anyway."

"Well, I can see the sense in that," says Christian, "even though, as a commercial manager, I want to keep innovation projects as plannable as possible and am usually against experiments. But thanks to these stories, I've now got a much better idea of what makes innovators tick and where they need help." "However," he laughs, "my goal is still to make money; that's why I invest in innovation."

"There's another picture I want to show you," says John and leads the others toward the section for contemporary art. A large canvas lights up the room. "This picture is by Manuel Ocampo, an artist who was born in the Philippines in 1965 and now lives in Berkeley, California. He also gets compared to Hieronymus Bosch, on account of the expressive power of his paintings. And although he's still relatively young, his work has

A Final Picture

been shown at major exhibitions in Berlin, Venice and Seville and has fans at art galleries in New York, Los Angeles and Luxembourg."

"It's expressive, all right. That looks like quite a fight. But what's it got to do with innovation?" asks Walter. "Just take another look. Ocampo often has a surprising effect on the observer." The group studies the picture in silence. Bao Jun starts to smile, and soon the others follow suit. "See, it's a completely different picture when you study it a bit longer," says John. "For me, the phrase ´THE STREAM OF TRANSCENDENT OBJECT MAKING CONSCIOUSLY WORKING TOWARDS THE GOAL' is all about innovation: it means deliberately working to achieve your objective by constantly creating things that go beyond the boundaries of the world as we know it."

Walter is still at a loss. "Oh, yeah. And what's that supposed to mean?" John grins and explains: "It means that what looks like a big fight is in fact much more like something out of a comic strip. And the message is that you shouldn't get lost in the cloud but instead work consciously and with all your energy to achieve your goal." "Now I see what you mean. Arguments are all part of the innovation process; and the more radical an innovation, the more intense are the disputes you're going to have. The image of a fight is not so far off the mark. If something gets done differently, it's primarily the defenders of entrenched property and the status quo who are in fear of losing their power, and things can sometimes get quite rough."

"That's exactly what I was getting at, Walter," John replies. "When I think about the stories we've heard, there are certainly quite a few fighters there – 'stubborn,' as Walter Gumbrecht would say – but they don't make the mistake of getting caught up in such fights. Instead, they look for constructive solutions, consciously working toward their goal! Think of Bernd Gombert or Giorgio Cuttica, who came to Siemens not because they needed to earn money but because it offers the best environment for them to be able to realize their goal, their personal vision. This picture shocked me a bit at first, but Ocampo is well known for his ability to transform the horrible into the beautiful and to lead the observer through various emotional states. The longer I look at it, the more energy it gives me – and as far as innovation is concerned, it makes me confident that if genuine innovators consciously work toward their goal, they can avoid getting delayed by petty disagreements."

Innovation: Fire in the Ashes

"OK, I give in, you've convinced me," says Walter, leafing through the exhibition catalogue. "These pictures certainly do express a lot of the essential things involved in innovation. Look, I've also found something worth looking at in the catalogue. As you know, I like to think of the innovator as an inventor, a visionary and an entrepreneur working to realize his or her own idea. And I believe that perseverance will enable you to reach your goal. Look at these pictures. Now, I don't understand much about art, but I know a little about mythology. The first picture is of the phoenix rising out of the ashes to live again in renewed glory. That's exactly what an innovator must do. It's also what a company like Siemens must do in order to endure down the centuries. It must continually reinvent itself and show that it has remained young at heart and has the power to reshape itself. That's what we mean by continuity and change: safeguarding our traditional strengths but also encouraging progress in order to achieve sustainable growth. The second picture is from Greek mythology ... You remember the story of Prometheus?"

"Isn't he the one who made some people out of clay and then proclaimed himself their master?" asks John. "And then Zeus got so mad that he chained him to a rock and let an eagle torture him?"

Walter grins: "Yes, in the end, you always have to pay for what you do – one way or the other. Zeus later had to let him go when Heracles showed up, but that's another story. Prometheus was the first visionary and unconventional thinker – he simply didn't want to accept the rules the gods had made. That's why the translation of Prometheus is 'the one who thinks ahead.' This painting shows how he gives the fire of the gods to the prostrate, weak and despondent person he has created. In my opinion, the discovery of fire and its utilization was one of the most important innovations in human history. For me, this picture therefore means: think ahead, be visionary and develop new inventions that will help advance the human race. Isn't that exactly what innovation is all about? Not only achieving commercial success but also helping make life easier, safer and more comfortable for people all around the world?"

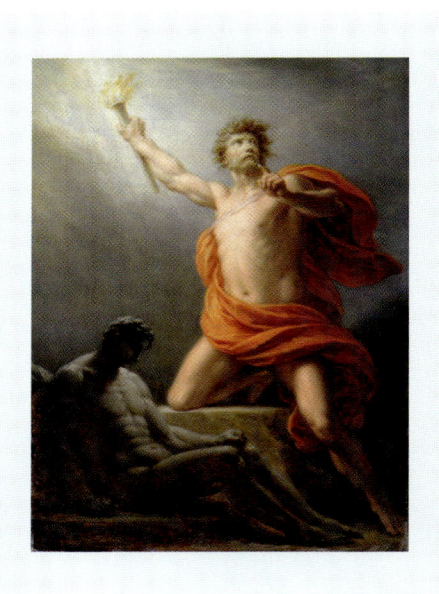

The Authors

Dr. Ulrich Eberl, 44, is head of the Technology and Innovation department of Siemens Corporate Communications in Munich. Eberl studied physics at the Technical University of Munich. His dissertation for his doctorate in biophysics was titled "The First Picoseconds of Photosynthesis." In 1988, he began working as a science and technology correspondent for various newspapers and magazines, including the Sueddeutsche Zeitung, Berliner Zeitung, Tages-Anzeiger (Zurich), Focus, Bild der Wissenschaft, Spektrum der Wissenschaft (German edition of Scientific American) and GEO. The topics he has covered range from nanotechnology to evolution biology and excavations in Troy. After working for DaimlerChrysler technology publications from 1992 to 1995, Eberl joined Siemens in 1996. He is also the founder of SciPress, a communications service for technology, economics and science. Since 2001, Eberl has been publisher and editor-in-chief of the research and innovation magazine *Pictures of the Future* (www.siemens.com/pof), which has been the recipient of several international awards.

Contact: ulrich.eberl@siemens.com

Dr. Joerg Puma, 39, was project manager and trainer at Siemens Learning Campus until 2006. He began his professional career with an apprenticeship at Deutsche Bank's Augsburg branch office, after which he worked in a post-merger integration team in Milan following Deutsche Bank's acquisition of an Italian bank. Puma studied business administration, sociology and psychology, and obtained a doctorate with his dissertation on "Value Based Management." In 1997 he was hired as a consultant and trainer for strategy, organizational development and finance by Siemens in Munich. In this capacity, he supported experts, managers and project teams with the implementation of strategy, change management and innovation projects. Puma has been director of the Krones Academy (www.krones.com) since 2006.

Contact: joerg.puma@krones.com

Andreas Kleinschmidt, 25, currently lives in London, where he is studying at the London School of Economics. Kleinschmidt attended the German School of Journalism in Munich and studied journalism, international political economy and dramatics in Munich, Salzburg and London. While working as a reporter for the Bayerische Rundfunk broadcasting company, Kleinschmidt received the 2005 CNN Journalist Award for a special he did on Russia. He has written for publications such as Spiegel, Financial Times Deutschland and Sueddeutsche Zeitung, and has contributed to *Pictures of the Future*. Kleinschmidt wrote the portraits of Osman Ahmed, Eve Aretakis, Giorgio Cuttica, Raymond Liao, Jun Kong, and Gert Seidel.

Florian Martini, 30, works at Siemens Corporate Communications in Munich, where he writes articles on the natural sciences and technology for Siemens publications. Martini studied American cultural history, new German literature, and intercultural communication at Ludwig Maximilian University in Munich, and worked for Bayerischer Rundfunk, Radio Gong and the Münchner Merkur newspaper. He wrote the portrait of Hans Meixner.

Bernd Müller, 44, lives in Esslingen. He studied physics and journalism, and has worked as an editor for the magazines Bild der Wissenschaft and Wirtschaftswoche. Since 2002 Müller has been director of Media and Public Relations at the Fraunhofer Institute for Systems and Innovation Research in Karlsruhe. He also writes for well-known newspapers and magazines such as Handelsblatt, VDI nachrichten, Focus and Spektrum der Wissenschaft, as well as for publications of major corporations. Müller wrote the portraits of Robert Krieg, Bernd Montag, Josef Röhrle, Klaus Riedle, Thomas Schott, and Henrik Stiesdal.

Arthur F. Pease, 54, is head of Marketing and Communications in the Software & Engineering Division at Siemens Corporate Technology and executive editor of the English edition of Siemens' *Pictures of the Future* magazine. He studied English, philosophy and Italian at Trinity University in San Antonio, Texas and the University of Florence, Italy, and film production and journalism at the University of Texas at Austin. Following completion of his graduate studies, he worked for several university-based medical journals in New York before moving to Munich and Siemens in 1985. In the context of his work as editor and author for *Pictures of the Future* he has received numerous international awards. Pease wrote the portrait of Dorin Comaniciu and was responsible for editing sections of this book.

Gitta Rohling, 31, works in Stuttgart as a freelance writer, editor and PR consultant with a focus on information technology. She specializes in corporate publications for customers and employees, as well as brochures. Rohling studied history, political science and German language and literature in Tübingen and Braunschweig. After completing her studies she worked for several PR agencies before setting out on her own at the beginning of 2003. Rohling wrote the portraits of Rudolf Bitzinger and Ullrich Brickmann.

Tim Schröder, 36, is a freelance science journalist based in Oldenburg. Schröder has a Master's degree in biology and a minor in marine physics. After completing an internship he worked as an editor in the science section of the Berliner Zeitung. Since 2001 Schröder has been working as a freelance author, writing for magazines and newspapers such as Financial Times Deutschland, Neue Zürcher Zeitung, Bild der Wissenschaft, Mare and PM. He also works for companies and research institutes such as the Fraunhofer Gesellschaft and the Max Planck Society. Schröder's writing focuses on the natural sciences, technology, applied research, basic research, energy and the environment. He wrote the portraits of Maximilian Fleischer, Walter Gumbrecht, Thomas von der Haar, Lars Löwenstein and Manfred Wangler.

Rolf Sterbak, 57, lives in the town of Hochdorf near Stuttgart. After initially training as an electrician, Sterbak later studied at a College of Education to become a teacher of German and history. After that he spent several years teaching elementary and high school before deciding to become a journalist. Sterbak first worked as an editor and author for various technical publications and corporate publications for customers. Today he writes for DaimlerChrysler Internal Communications, mainly on topics dealing with automotive research, development and production. Sterbak wrote the portraits of Frank Forster and Bernd Gombert.

Dr. Peter Stuckenberger, 38, is a speech writer for Siemens Transportation Systems. Until the end of 2006 he was communications manager at Siemens Power Transmission and Distribution in Erlangen. After studying art history and library science and obtaining his doctorate, Stuckenberger began working as a freelance journalist for various publications in the field of cultural and economic history. Stuckenberger joined Siemens in 2001. He wrote the portrait of Michael Weinhold.

Dr. Evdoxia Tsakiridou, 41, lives in Munich. She has a Master's degree in biology and a doctorate in neurophysiology from Eberhard-Karls University in Tübingen. After completing her studies she worked as a journalism trainee at the Westdeutsche Allgemeine Zeitung in Essen. Following that, she joined Siemens in Munich as a press officer for Technology/Innovation and was also an editor for the science section of the Sueddeutsche Zeitung. Since 2000, Tsakiridou has worked as a freelance journalist for various newspapers and magazines (including VDI nachrichten and Neue Zürcher Zeitung) and magazines such as Bild der Wissenschaft. She also provides radio reports for Deutschlandfunk and works for internal and external communications at various companies. Tsakiridou wrote the portraits of Tzoanna Ekaterinidi, Gerd Hribernig, and Tilo Messer.

Sebastian Webel, 26, is an intern at Siemens Corporate Communications in Munich, where he specializes in technology and innovation subjects. Webel studied international economics in Göttingen and international technical journalism in Bremen and Cape Town, South Africa. Webel wrote his Master's thesis on the "Mutual Influence of Political Change and the National Print Media in South Africa." Webel wrote the portrait of Torsten Niederdränk.

Nikola Wohllaib, 40, works as a freelance technology and business journalist in Berlin. She studied political science and Latin American studies in Berlin and currently writes primarily for VDI nachrichten and Neue Zürcher Zeitung on telecommunication, IT and business issues. In addition, her work focuses on Asia, in particular China, South Korea and India. Wohllaib wrote the portrait of Franz-Josef Bierbrauer.

Ulrike Zechbauer, 38, studied biology and physics at Frankfurt (Main) University and worked as a research assistant at the Max Planck Institute for Brain Research in Frankfurt. Her work as a science journalist has been published in newspapers and magazines such as Handelsblatt, Focus, Tages-Anzeiger (Zurich), Spektrum der Wissenschaft and VDI nachrichten. She lives in Munich, where she works at Siemens Corporate Communications, specializing in technology and innovation. Zechbauer wrote the portrait of Markus Brehler.

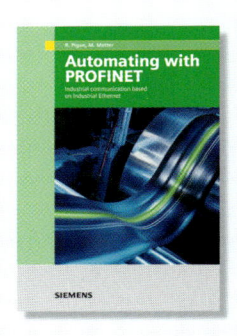

Raimond Pigan, Mark Metter

Automating with PROFINET

Industrial Communication based on Industrial Ethernet

2006, 355 pages,
207 illustrations, hardcover
ISBN 978-3-89578-256-5
€ 54.90 / sFr 88.00

This book serves as an introduction to PROFINET technology with SIMATIC products. Configuring engineers, commissioning engineers and technicians are given an overview of the concept and the fundamentals they need to solve PROFINET-based automation tasks. Technical relationships and practical applications are described using SIMATIC as example, and quickly lead the reader to his goal of autonomous planning and problem-solving. The book gives decision-makers and plant designers, trainees and students a compact overview.

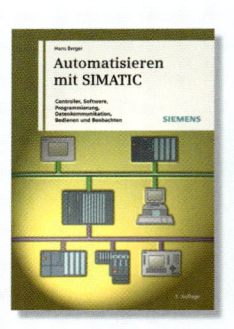

Hans Berger

Automating with SIMATIC

Controllers, Software, Programming, Data Communication, Operator Control and Process Monitoring

3rd revised and enlarged edition, 2006,
230 pages, 105 illustrations, hardcover
ISBN 978-3-89578-276-3
€ 44.90 / sFr 72.00

Through a description of the automation system SIMATIC S7, the reader gains an insight into the structure and operation of a state-of-the-art programmable controller. There is also an introduction to configuration and parameter setting for the hardware by means of STEP 7, along with an explanation of control tasks using various PLC programming languages. For this third edition, the book's entire content was revised and updated.

www.publicis-erlangen.de/books | http://books.erlm.siemens.de

Arnold Zankl
Milestones in Automation
From the Transistor to the Digital Factory

2006, 248 pages, 189 coloured illustrations, hardcover with book jacket
ISBN 978-3-89578-259-6
€ 34.90 / sFr 56.00

The story told in this book extends from the beginning of Simatic, the world's most successful programmable controller family, to today's state-of-the-art technology, enhanced by specific solution examples and a brief look into the future. Easy to read and creatively designed, the "Milestones in Automation" offer technicians, engineers and managers a profound look into the development history and possibilities for use of a technology which left its mark like no other on industrial processes and a huge range of technical systems.

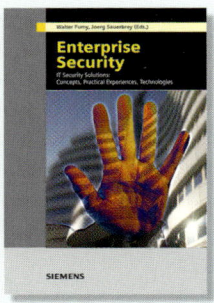

Walter Fumy, Joerg Sauerbrey (Eds.)
Enterprise Security
IT Security Solutions: Concepts, Practical Experiences, Technologies

2006, 264 pages,
65 illustrations, hardcover
ISBN 978-3-89578-267-1
€ 39.90 / sFr 64.00

This book provides a broad knowledge on the major security issues affecting today's corporations and organizations, and presents state-of-the-art concepts and current trends. Areas covered include information security management, network and system security, identity and access management, authentication, and security certification. In-depth discussion of relevant technologies and standards is provided, complemented by information on practical experiences in different sectors.

www.publicis-erlangen.de/books | http://books.erlm.siemens.de

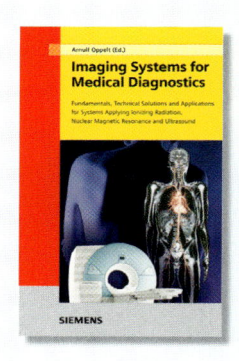

Arnulf Oppelt (Editor)

Imaging Systems for Medical Diagnostics

Fundamentals, Technical Solutions and Applications for Systems Applying Ionization Radiation, Nuclear Magnetic Resonance and Ultrasound

2nd revised and enlarged edition, 2005, 996 pages, 692 illustrations, hardcover
ISBN 978-3-89578-226-8
€ 119.00 / sFr 188.00

The book provides a comprehensive compilation of basics, technical solutions and applications for medical imaging systems. It is intended as a handbook for students in biomedical engineering, for medical physicists, and for engineers working on medical technologies, as well as for lecturers at universities and engineering schools. For qualified personnel at hospitals, and physicians working with these instruments it serves as a basic source of information. The applications comprise the fields of X-ray diagnostics, computed tomography, nuclear medical diagnostics, magnetic resonance imaging, sonography, and molecular imaging. Emphasis is also laid on the imaging software platform and hospital information systems.

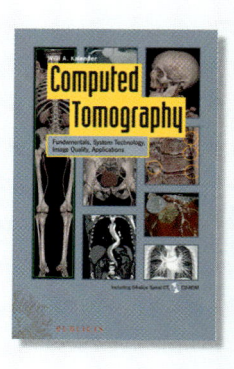

Willi A. Kalender

Computed Tomography

Fundamentals, System Technology, Image Quality, Applications

2nd revised and enlarged edition, 2005, 306 pages, 130 illustrations, hardcover
ISBN 978-3-89578-216-9
€ 49.90 / sFr 80.00

This book gives a comprehensive and user-oriented description of the theoretical and technical system fundamentals of computed tomography (CT) for a wide readership. It covers in detail all characteristic parameters relevant for image quality and all performance features significant for clinical application. Readers will thus be informed how to use a CT system to an optimum depending on the different diagnostic requirements.

www.publicis-erlangen.de/books | http://books.erlm.siemens.de

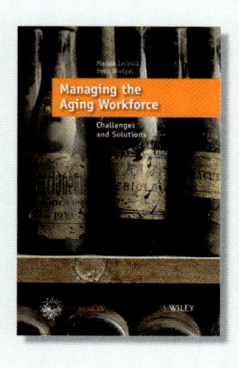

Marius Leibold, Sven Voelpel
Managing the Aging Workforce
Challenges and Solutions

2006, 244 pages,
24 illustrations, hardcover
ISBN 978-3-89578-284-8
€ 32.90 / sFr 53.00

Managing the Aging Workforce is one of the crucial topics for many of the world's enterprises. Where experts are needed, the workforce's age may even increase between 5 and 10 years in only one decade. The challenges arising from this include leadership, health management, knowledge management and learning, as well as to drive ideas for diversity and innovation. For executives and HR managers, this book presents an analysis of the present and upcoming situation, and an introduction into the concepts enterprises will need to survive in aging societies.

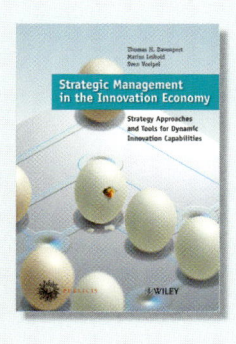

Thomas H. Davenport, Marius Leibold, Sven Voelpel
Strategic Management in the Innovation Economy
Strategy Approaches and Tools for Dynamic Innovation Capabilities

2006, 441 pages,
38 illustrations, hardcover
ISBN 978-3-89578-263-3
€ 32.90 / sFr 53.00

For both advanced students and business managers, this book presents a well-balanced combination of recent theory, published articles by prominent scholars, and case studies, all designed to substantiate a new strategic mindset, innovative tools, and practical applications for significantly increased innovative capabilities.

www.publicis-erlangen.de/books | http://books.erlm.siemens.de

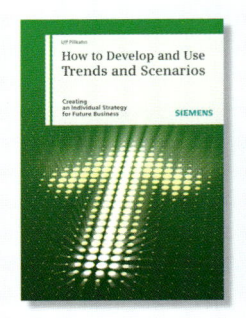

Ulf Pillkahn

How to Develop and Use Trends and Scenarios

Creating an Individual Strategy for Future Business

December 2007, ca. 400 pages, ca. 150 coloured illustrations, hardcover
ISBN 978-3-89578-304-3
ca. € 49.90 / sFr 80.00

The book presents the two most powerful tools for future planning: environmental analysis, based on the use of trends, as well as the development of visions of the future through the use of scenarios. While scenarios are generally regarded as a classical management tool, it is expected that the importance of trends will gain tremendously in the coming years. Pillkahn demonstrates how to build robust strategies by aligning the results of environmental and enterprise scenarios, thereby offering entirely new insights.

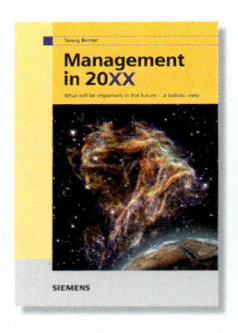

Georg Berner

Management in 20XX

What will be important in the future – a holistic view

2004, 224 pages, 141 coloured illustrations, hardcover
ISBN 978-3-89578-241-1
€ 39.90 / sFr 64.00

The book describes some remarkable future scenarios and ambitious visions. It will help you come up with new ideas for the future of your company, and points out the changes you will have to make in order to meet the challenges of the future.